T0281463

Cybercultures

At the Interface

Probing the Boundaries

Cybercultures
Mediations of Community, Culture, Politics

Edited by
Harris Breslow and Aris Mousoutzanis

Amsterdam - New York, NY 2012

The paper on which this book is printed meets the requirements of "ISO 9706:1994, Information and documentation - Paper for documents - Requirements for permanence".

ISBN: 978-90-420-3578-2
E-Book ISBN: 978-94-012-0853-6
©Editions Rodopi B.V., Amsterdam - New York, NY 2012
Printed in the Netherlands

Table of Contents

Part 4   Mediatisation of Memory

Introduction

Harris Breslow and Aris Mousoutzanis

Since their emergence, discourses, practices and theorisations of cybercultures have been accompanied by questions of surveillance and activism, power and resistance, fixity and flow, a dialectic that was embedded in the connotations surrounding the prefix 'cyber-' since its very first use around the middle of the twentieth century. First used in 'cybernetics' (from the Greek *kubernetes*, meaning 'steersman'), the term was coined by Norbert Wiener in the late 1940s to refer to his newly-founded discipline that would investigate the preservation of consistency, order and control within systems. Cybernetics was described by Wiener as the 'study of messages, and in particular of the effective messages of control,' whose founding premise was that 'control' and 'communication' were concepts tightly intertwined to that of the 'message.'[1] For Wiener, the importance of cybernetics was that it was not just a discipline but what Lily E. Kay has described as 'a metadiscipline, something akin to what Michel Foucault would later term 'episteme.''[2] In his popular textbook on cybernetics, *The Human Use of Human Beings,* Wiener announced that

> society can only be understood through a study of the messages and the communication facilities which belong to it;…in the future development of these messages and communication facilities, messages between man and machines, between machine and man, and between machine and machine, are destined to play an ever-increasing role.[3]

Information, control and communication were thus operating together to bring about a synthesis of the organic and the mechanical in a discipline whose theoretical underpinnings should be seen within the wider political post-war climate. The significance of Wiener's text extended beyond the theoretical level; for Kay, even more important was the fact that his popular textbooks 'spread the cybernetic vision in a culture that was becoming enamoured with the nascent, computer-driven technosciences: systems analysis, operations research, industrial and military automation.'[4] These connotations of the first use of the prefix 'cyber-' point towards the first dominant orientation in cyberculture studies, which concentrated on issues of power, surveillance, and panopticism within online environments and amongst virtual communities. One representative example of such an approach during the period that witnessed the boom of cyberculture studies, the 1990s, is Steven Jones's description of the Internet as 'another in a line of modern technologies that undermine traditional notions of civil society that require unity and shun multiplicity while giving impressions that they in fact re-create such a society.'[5] Among the papers included in this collection, one that follows this approach is Fidele Vlavo's analysis of the nature of political protest in the age of cybercultures in her discussion of 'electronic civil disobedience.' One fundamental problem to cybercultures is, for Vlavo, the lack of physical contiguity. Vlavo contrasts protest actions in cyberspace with those in the physical world, which take place on the street, a distinction that is not inconsequential: acts of civil disobedience in the physical world take place in a public sphere where protestors, those whom they protest against, and those on whose behalf they protest are often, perhaps typically, situated within a single, contiguous space. Within this space the act of protest becomes one that is subject to negotiation and that promotes solidarity amongst those who protest.

In cyberspace, however, this cannot be said to be true. Vlavo's discussion of acts of electronic civil disobedience indicates that civil disobedience in cyberspace may have become rhizomatic in nature. In this respect, then, electronic civil disobedience becomes impossible to predict or locate. Moreover, there are no longer any guarantees that those who protest either evince or engender solidarity on the part of those for whom they protest. In an analysis of the first act of civil disobedience in cyberspace, the Swarm project undertaken by the Electronic Disturbance Theater on behalf of the Zapatistas, Vlavo notes

> At present there is no means of gaining information regarding the location of the thousands of virtual protesters who participated in the Swarm project, however, it can be safely assumed that with the Internet penetration levels of the time, very few participants were located in the conflict area of Chiapas, or indeed, in Mexico... . The point made here is not that socio-political movements need to remain localised and self-contained. Rather, my intent is to draw attention to the idealised possibilities of digital technology and the limiting view of an exclusive form of activism... . In this case, electronic civil disobedience becomes a form of resistance, whereby global participants can select social movements online and "click to protest" from the comfort of their secured environment, unaware of and unaffected by the possible outcomes of their virtual engagement. Ironically, the visions of so-called transnational solidarity and global mobilisation actually seem to deny, or minimise, the importance of local populations and their distinctive struggles.[6]

Vlavo's analysis, in other words, seeks to interrogate the second dominant orientation in cyberculture studies, which investigates online environments, communities and cultures in relation to ideas of subcultural resistance, rhizomatic multiplicity, and flow. According to Vlavo,

> The positioning of cyberspace as a unique location for social protest corresponds to a representation of the virtual environment which can be related to a "cyber-*imaginaire*" .... [A] phenomenon that sees any major technological developments as representative of a collective utopian project. The particularity of this trend is that often, it occurs within disparate social groups... . Digital technology is attributed with a new redeeming function, usually disseminated through distorted narratives that promise new social order, fair economic growth and democratic political structures.[7]

This second orientation may, again, be traced in earliest beginnings of cybercultural formations and communities, which may be located in the creation of the so-called 'Tech Railroad Model Club' at the Massachusetts Institute of Technology (MIT) in 1959, allegedly the first hacker community, who, as Steven Levy has described in his book *Hackers: Heroes of the Computer Revolution* (1984), coined the terms 'hacker' and 'hacking' even as they established major tenets of 'hacker ethics' that were to be influential amongst the hacker cultures of the 1980s and later on. Indeed, since their slow yet gradual emergence from the 1960s onwards, communities that would later crystallise into 'cybercultures' were defining themselves in terms of their opposition or contradistinction to mainstream culture - it would not be before the mid-1990s, when the Internet started becoming increasingly more accessible to a wider audience, that cybercultures would acquire a more central place in 'the mainstream.' The associations of the 'cyber' with resistance and subcultural articulation were imbued in the prefix with the emergence of the science-fiction subgenre of 'cyberpunk' during the 1980s, whose major representatives, such as William Gibson, Bruce Sterling, Rudy Rucker and Pat Cadigan, amongst others, offered visions of a 'not-so-distant future' of post-industrial urban decay and squalor that served as settings for collaborations and conflicts between low-street computer hackers and representatives of the forces of corporate capital. The earliest theorisations of cybercultures were predominantly following this orientation, and what are now considered classic studies, such as Douglas Rushkoff's *Cyberia* (1994), Mark Dery's *Escape Velocity* (1996), or Pierre Lévy's *Cyberculture* (1997) were predominantly utopian in their approach, whereby cybercultures represent either 'computer-age subcultures' or even 'a new form of universality: universality without totality.'[8] One of the most significant contributions that follows this orientation and dates from this specific cultural moment would be the work of Howard Rheingold who, in the text where he established the term 'virtual community,' describes the Internet as

> a tool that could bring conviviality and understanding into our lives and might help revitalize the public sphere... . The vision of a citizen-designed, citizen-controlled worldwide communications network is a version of technological utopianism that could be called the vision of "the electronic agora."[9]

Insofar as perceptions such as the above must be seen as part of the cultural moment in which they were articulated, contributions in this collection, such as Jernej Prodnik's, seek to re-examine them from a contemporary perspective. Prodnik adopts an attitude similar to Vlavo's, in that he is sceptical of either exclusively utopian or dystopian perceptions of online communities. Instead, he suggests a threefold model for the understanding of communities, one that focuses on their subjective, symbolic dimensions, the lived practices and experiences surrounding them, and the objective material structures. However, more importantly, for Prodnik, the foundation of any community is language and communication. 'To talk about community is first and foremost to talk about language and communication. ... Language and social cooperation enable the creation of institutional reality and structures that enable the construction of a social and political environment that achieves the status of objective social fact.'[10] In so reminding us, Prodnik observes that, in cyberspace, language and communication are freed from the so-called traditional spatial confines of the nation-state. This does not invalidate the notion of an imagined community, but rather liberates it from any requirements of legitimation that are claimed by and through the existence of the state's borders and the authority that these borders invoke. This reminds us that what is crucial for an imagined community is neither spatial integrity nor communal homogeneity, but rather the imagination.

> People without direct interpersonal relations imagine themselves as members of a community through the communication of symbols and cultural artefacts of a particular kind, which can arouse deep and strong attachments. All communities are imagined... perhaps even those that are most tightly knit together, and they should be

distinguished by the style in which they are imagined, not
by their authenticity or falsity.[11]

The two opposite and complementary approaches to cybercultures
delineated above are hardly a new phenomenon in the perceptions and
experiences of new technologies. In fact, all new technologies have generated
contradictory responses of enthusiasm and apprehension. What is distinct
about cybercultures is the ways in which this dialectic has emerged not only
in response to the encounter of the human subject with technology, but more
specifically in the relations among the subject, technology, and *space* - in the
above cases, online, virtual space, but also, as the contribution by Breslow
and Allagui underlines, national space, and familial space. Breslow and
Allagui, on the one hand, examine the ways in which the nation-state, the
historical location for the production of the subject and subjective experience,
begins to blur in cyberculture. Using the results from their annual survey for
the Emirates Internet Project in the UAE, they discuss the effect that
cybercultures have upon the imagined community that is constituted within
the nation-state. For Breslow and Allagui the effects upon the UAE are
threefold: There is pressure placed upon the linguistic homogeneity of the
nation-state; the polity and politics of the nation-state begin to break down;
and the space of the nation-state, once constituted through its civil society,
also comes under stress. 'For the majority of residents in the UAE there is a
turning away from the concept of a unified polity within a fixed and
contiguous locale in favour of a series of parallel political circuits whose
existence is enabled by a variety of telecommunications media, but most
importantly those channels found online.'[12] Breslow and Allagui go even
further, however, and argue that cybercultures play a constitutive role in the
reorganisation of social space in the UAE. Here they argue that residents in
the UAE

> do not occupy a single national space, but rather move
> through social circuits that are akin to Moebius strips; two
> dimensional spaces that enable the flow of information,
> participation and structures of feeling that are enabled [and]
> articulated across the Internet, but which have no social
> efficacy or permanency... .[13]

We will not go so far as to argue, here, that this signals the death of
the state, or even an infringement upon its geospatial integrity. Breslow's and
Allagui's work, however, signals that the space of the nation, as something
that is cohesively articulated within a given state's borders, is being subjected
to a rearticulation within cyberspace - and in this sense, their discussion
converges with Prodnik's, who makes a crucial observation concerning the

role that the imagination plays in the articulation of the imagined community that can be said to constitute a nation.

A common denominator that may be said to unite the articles outlined above, as well as others introduced below, is the view of the experience of cybercultures as encapsulated by the concept of the flow. By 'flow' we refer to a global infrastructure, an apparatus, that enables the rapid movement of individuals, goods, finances, images, ideas, and cultures, all of which are either coordinated or move via digital information networks, which function as a meta-structure that enables flow.[14] From this perspective, the phenomenon of flow, enabled by the Internet, has fundamentally changed the nature of our relationships, our economies, our experiences, our sense of self, and our cultures. Cybercultures, in this respect, are cultures that are enabled by, exist within, and articulated across, the Internet. As such, and at root, all cybercultures, regardless of what they are expressive of and of how they are expressed, are cultures that are enabled by the flow of digital information. More importantly for this volume; *cybercultures are cultures of flow.*

This approach suggests that cybercultures know neither boundaries, nor limitations, nor inhibitions. They are the *ne plus ultra* expression of flow, spreading as, when, and how they can. Cybercultures do not follow predetermined paths, nor do they exist in predetermined states. In this respect cybercultures, as flow phenomena, exist according to the localised conditions that they make use of to further extend their existence. In other words, cybercultures flow as rhizomes. At their most elemental unadulterated level, as Scott Sundvall reminds us, cybercultures are rhizomatic in nature. 'It is, to a large degree, the technology (or technic) that has most significantly come to immerse, mediate and inform sub-ject-ification... . [T]he cyber is a technic that functions in the mediation of communication. However, unlike its predecessors, the cyber not only distorts presence as such, it also reconfigures spatio-temporal organisations.'[15] Cybercultures do not articulate themselves according to a specific logic, fixed identity, or set of rules determined by one space or another. They flow from place to place, from node to node, from site to site. In so doing they rewrite the logics, relationships, meanings, behaviours and subjectivities heretofore found within any locale, any node, and any site, on the Internet.

Describing a social phenomenon as rhizomatic does not mean that it does not acknowledge the possibility of stability, nor that it can never articulate itself to a social formation that persists across time or space. Rather it means that this moment of articulation cannot be said to be predetermined, that it does not follow a unitary path, across either time or space. Rhizomes articulate themselves almost purely according to the contingent conditions of any given conjunctural time and space within which they find themselves. In so doing rhizomes exist in a tension with what may be understood as a threshold of stability. One way to understand this threshold is in terms of

Gary Thompson's work on *kairos* and the 'right time,' where rhizomatic entities circulating in cyberspace - images, phrases, narratives, etc. - cross a threshold and become more or less relatively fixed within popular culture. Thompson explores this phenomenon in his discussion of the concept of the rhetorical concept of *kairos*, and its use for understanding cybercultures. 'Ask a rhetorician and the term *kairos* will usually be defined as *the right time or right measure*. We are to speak to children or students or the general public or specialists or authorities in terms and at the length appropriate to each.'[16] There has, however, been a profound shift since the origins of *kairos* in ancient Greece. In particular, notes Thompson, it is the lack of stability found in contemporary cybercultures, resulting in a cultural apparatus whose logics are highly contingent in nature.

> Classically the rhetor's art depended considerably on the ability to invent, organise and polish stylistically the speech, and during the actual delivery, to read the audience so as to sense the right measure and the right moment to move them to action. Context was stable and relatively controlled. Online audiences, however, are not in the same location, usually not accessing discourse at the same time, or through the same media, and are less subject to the rhetor's attempts at control.[17]

Cyberspace not only presents a problem with respect to the conditions of reception by an audience that is no longer unified in time, space, or medium, it also blurs the distinctions between those who create digital information and those who use it, between content providers and those who had heretofore been seen as the audience. Indeed, the introduction of Web 2.0 technologies both acknowledged and intensified something that had long been understood about cybercultures; the Internet not only enables an explosion in the quantity and type of information available, it also enables an explosion of creativity. In the world of Web 2.0 anyone can cheaply and easily produce content. More importantly, in the world of Web 2.0 anyone can reproduce, and reuse the information found online. Riha reminds us that this trend is not exclusive to the Web and Web 2.0 technologies. Rather, all digital information is subject to recycling, existing like found objects waiting to be reconfigured. This is the foundational strength of machinima animation.

> [W]e can think of machinima as "a found technology" (Lowood) ... . Such an object, the readymade, is an everyday object that is placed in a different context, as a form of artistic expression ... neither been designed for or by the artist, nor for the intent of display or artistic

statement. Common objects are assigned a new context. Artist-player designs are the visual products that emerge from their "recontextualisations"... . In machinima, such a recontextualisation is accomplished not by re-designing the game engine, but rather by transforming "found technology" into an animation engine, while exploiting various techniques already learned from other multimedia applications ... . [T]his medium, based on videogames, encourages a sense of "co-ownership" - not in legal terms, but in the sense of the freedom to "replay, reinvent, and redeploy."[18] In particular, the performative use of machinima leads to "high performance play" (Lowood) where the artist-player utilises new applications of multimedia for cultural production.[19]

The processes of media recycling and convergence raise a fundamental problem for those who design the technologies that enable our existence in cyberspace and our involvement in cybercultures is the reception, processing, presentation and management of digital information. This is not merely a problem of the volume of information: As Gundelsweiler and Filk explain, this is a problem inherent to the variety of formats, the diversity of sources, the instantaneity of delivery, and the need to process and organise this information both meaningfully and functionally.

[M]edia convergence takes place in three areas... . The first area is in the formats used for the consumption of media content. This includes devices such as smart phones, notebooks, personal computers, and televisions. Here we see a general trend towards the mobile sector... . The second dimension is time. Time plays an important role when the consumer accesses the content... . The two previous dimensions affect the nature of the processing of media content. Properties of media such as formats, resolution, quality, length, video, audio, text, and others, have to be identified and matched to the particular situation of the consumer. Media content has to be tailored to the user depending on the consumer's situation and the available device.[20]

Fundamentally contingent, cybercultures flow through and rewrite the relationships that exist both between subjects and content, as well as amongst subjects. The devices that Gundelsweiler and Filk describe do not simply process, reformulate, integrate and display information to the subject;

they also enable the rearticulation amongst subjects. Nowhere is this more profoundly experienced then at that site that we call the body. In cybercultures the central place of the body as the site of subjectivity is displaced, and subjective experience is rearticulated away from, the prison of the flesh. The significance of the body with respect to its situation; the spaces that it inhabits, the behaviours that it can engage in, and the experiences that it can be expected to have, is rewritten in and through cybercultures. Indeed, the body has become another network element, another component in a world of flows. This is the lesson that we learn from Judith Guevarra Enriquez's chapter, where she writes that

> The Internet, or cyberspace, interacts with urban space and disrupts and collapses conventional boundaries and enclosures. Places move to other places. Bodies coordinate multiple tasks and conversations, oscillating between [the] highly private and semi-private modes of communication - remaining in one place while connected to the Internet... . Physical co-presence is no longer the only presence possible. There is presence in absence, privacy in public and connectivity, even intimacy, in isolation. The concepts of mobility and spatiality are being deconstructed to say the least.[21]

If the body exists in the twenty-first century as a nodal point whose interiority and exteriority have been rewritten by the body's existence within the apparatus of flows, then memory, which has long been understood to be plastic, must be seen as an entirely contingent product of these flows. We believe, however, that memory's existence can be removed from the domain of time. Instead, we want to argue that memory in the era of flow can be understood as part of the domain of space. However we do not want to claim that this space is grounded in the physicality, for instance, of architectural or urban space, on the one hand, or essentialist conceptions of space as it is said to exist in nature, on the other. Both of these conceptions understand space as something that is immutable. We contend, rather, that the nature of memory in cybercultures is one of contingency, and that it should be understood as the contingent product of the incessantly reconfigured relationships that exist within the apparatus of flow. Zimmerman argues that there is fundamental distinction between memory, on the one hand, and remembrance, on the other. 'Anamnestes embodies the active force that is necessary to find and dig information out of its merely latent presence. Memory becomes an archive from which remembrance selects, updates and takes material.'[22] The memory found in cybercultures is thus impermanent, contingent, and open to endless reconfiguration. 'By depicting memory not merely as a storeroom of the mind but rather connecting it with current events and history ... the boundaries between collective and individual possession are blurred. This blurring also takes place on [Social Networking Sites] on the Web 2.0.'[23]

So, it is not just the memories of the subject that are dynamically prone to blurring, but the memories of the collective, history, that are also subjected to blur once they reside within cyberspace and are subject to the vagaries of flow. Martin Pogačar makes this point quite emphatically, arguing that 'history is increasingly becoming the result of the negotiation of contesting views via the remeshing and remixing of video, image, textual and audio sources.'[24] This, as Pogačar points out, is nothing new; history has always been subject to negotiation, revision, and rewriting. What is new, however, is the nature of this process, and the huge panoply of sources engaged in the rewriting. Although the state does not wither away and die in the era of flow, its ability to occupy an authoritative position with respect to cultural processes such as history does. When coupled with the active rewriting of history within cyberspace, the result is the blooming of a thousand histories, none of which can make an authoritative claim over the others.

> With the role of external referent once assumed by the State severely mitigated, the increasingly predominant user-generated interpretations, representations and mediations of history are, from the perspective of the nation-state, untrustworthy and unreliable. As well, such data are often difficult to keep track of and canonise. Hence, on the one hand, they largely elude control and censorship, and, on the other, they undermine the state-sponsored systems of knowledge dissemination and education.[25]

Rewriting, remixing, blurring, or mitigation is one final theme that runs throughout this volume, and one that we would like to conclude with. Whether it is authorship or subjectivity, text or context, community or polity, memory or *mentalité*, the body or the body politic, cybercultures are cultures where boundaries become blurred. There is no easy point or place of demarcation in contemporary cybercultures. Perhaps there never has been, nor will there ever be. This too, is a phenomenon of flow: As digital networks, come into contact with various terrains - the body, the community, the state, the text, etc. - things that are situated within those terrains - subjectivity, members, subjects, signification - become increasingly fluid at the transversal point of contact. In so doing they become mutable, subject to mixing, and they lose the integrity essential to their identity as singular entities. Perhaps, then, at last, we are truly at the point of witnessing the becoming of the postmodern.

Notes

[1] N. Wiener, *The Human Use of Human Beings: Cybernetics and Society*, Riverside Press, Cambridge, Mass, 1950, p. 8.

[2] L. E. Kay, 'Cybernetics, Information, Life: The Emergence of Scriptural Representations of Heredity', *Configurations*, Vol.5, No. 1, 1997, p. 40.

[3] Wiener, op. cit., p. 9.

[4] Kay, op. cit., p. 46.

[5] S. Jones, 'The Internet and its Social Landscape', in *Virtual Culture: Identity & Communication in Cybersociety*, S. G. Jones (ed), Sage, London, 1997, p. 25.

[6] Ibid., pp. 14-15.

[7] F. Vlavo, 'Click Here to Protest': Electronic Civil Disobedience and the *Imaginaire* of Virtual Activism', in this volume, p. 126.

[8] P. Lévy, *Cyberculture*, University of Minneapolis Press, Minnesota, 2001, p. 105.

[9] H. Rheingold, *The Virtual Community: Homesteading on the Electronic Frontier*, Adison-Wesley, Reading, Mass, 1993, p. 14.

[10] J. Prodnik, 'Post-Fordist Communities and Cyberspace: A Critical Approach', in this volume, p. 78.

[11] Ibid., p. 78.

[12] H. Breslow and I. Allagui, 'The Internet, Fixity, and Flow: Challenges to the Articulation of an Imagined Community', in this volume, p. 117.

[13] Ibid., pp. 117-118.

[14] See M. Castells, *The Rise of the Network Society*, *The Information Age: Economy, Society and Culture, Volume I*, Second Edition, Wiley-Blackwell, Oxford, 2010 (1996), p. 417; M. Castells, 'Toward a Sociology of the Network Society', *Contemporary Sociology*, Vol. 29, No. 5, 2000, pp. 694-696; A. Appadurai, *Modernity at Large: Cultural Dimensions of Globalization*, The University of Minnesota Press, Minneapolis, 1996, pp. 29-37; P. Howard, *Castells and the Media*, Polity Press, Cambridge, 2011, p. 58, and pp. 79-82; J. Urry, *Global Complexity*, Polity Press, Cambridge, 2003, pp. 8-12; J. Urry, 'Small Worlds and the New Social Physics', *Global Networks*, Vol. 4, No. 2, pp. 112-113.

[15] S. Sundvall, 'Post-Human, All Too Non-Human: Implications of the Cyber-Rhizome', in this volume, p. 16.

[16] G. Thompson, 'Electronic Kairos', in this volume, p. 4.

[17] Ibid., pp. 8-9.

[18] H. Lowood, 'Found Technology: Players as Innovators in the Making of Machinima', in *Digital Youth, Innovation, and the Unexpected*, T. McPherson (ed), The John D. and Catherine T. MacArthur Foundation Series

on Digital Media and Learning, The MIT Press, Cambridge, MA, 2008, p. 185.
[19] D. Riha, 'Machinima, Creative Software and Education for Creativity', in this volume, p. 31.
[20] F. Gundelsweiler and C. Filk, 'Future Media Platforms for Convergent Journalisms', in this volume, p. 49.
[21] J. G. Enriquez, 'Bodily Aware in Cyber-Research', in this volume, pp. 59-60.
[22] H. Zimmerman, 'Diverging Strategies of Remembrance in Traditional and Web-2.0 On-Line Projects', in this volume, p. 153.
[23] Ibid., pp. 153-154.
[24] M. Pogačar, 'Music Blogging: Saving Yugoslav Popular Music', in this volume, p. 165.
[25] Ibid., p. 167.

Bibliography

Appadurai, A., *Modernity at Large: Cultural Dimensions of Globalization.* The University of Minnesota Press, Minneapolis, 1996.

Breslow, H. and Allagui, I., 'The Internet, Fixity, and Flow: Challenges to the Articulation of an Imagined Community', in *Cybercultures: Mediations of Community, Culture, Politics.* H. Breslow and A. Mousoutzanis (eds), Rodopi, Amsterdam and New York, NY, 2012, pp. 101-123.

Castells, M., *The Rise of the Network Society, The Information Age: Economy, Society and Culture, Volume I.* Second Edition, Wiley-Blackwell, Oxford, 2010 [1996].

——, 'Toward a Sociology of the Network Society'. *Contemporary Sociology*, Vol. 29, No. 5, 2000, pp. 693-699.

Enriquez, J. G., 'Bodily Aware in Cyber-Research', in *Cybercultures: Mediations of Community, Culture, Politics.* H. Breslow and A. Mousoutzanis (eds), Rodopi, Amsterdam and New York, NY, 2012, pp. 59-71.

Gundelsweiler, F. and Filk, C., 'Future Media Platforms for Convergent Journalisms', in *Cybercultures: Mediations of Community, Culture, Politics.* H. Breslow and A. Mousoutzanis (eds), Rodopi, Amsterdam and New York, NY, 2012, pp. 45-57.

Howard, P., *Castells and the Media*. Polity Press, Cambridge, 2011.

Jones, S., 'The Internet and its Social Landscape', in *Virtual Culture: Identity & Communication in Cybersociety*. S. G. Jones (ed), Sage, London, 1997, pp. 7-35.

Kay, L. E., 'Cybernetics, Information, Life: The Emergence of Scriptural Representations of Heredity'. *Configurations*, Vol.5, No. 1, 1997, pp. 23-91.

Lévy, P., *Cyberculture*. University of Minneapolis Press, Minnesota, 2001.

Levy, S., *Hackers: Heroes of the Computer Revolution*. Doubleday, New York, 1984.

Pogačar, M., 'Music Blogging: Saving Yugoslav Popular Music', in *Cybercultures: Mediations of Community, Culture, Politics*. H. Breslow and A. Mousoutzanis (eds), Rodopi, Amsterdam and New York, NY, 2012, pp. 165-188.

Prodnik, J., 'Post-Fordist Communities and Cyberspace:A Critical Approach', in *Cybercultures: Mediations of Community, Culture, Politics*. H. Breslow and A. Mousoutzanis (eds), Rodopi, Amsterdam and New York, NY, 2012, pp. 75-100.

Riha, D., 'Machinima, Creative Software and Education for Creativity', in *Cybercultures: Mediations of Community, Culture, Politics*. H. Breslow and A. Mousoutzanis (eds), Rodopi, Amsterdam and New York, NY, 2012, pp. 31-43.

Sundvall, S., 'Post-Human, All Too Non-Human: Implications of the Cyber-Rhizome', in *Cybercultures: Mediations of Community, Culture, Politics*. H. Breslow and A. Mousoutzanis (eds), Rodopi, Amsterdam and New York, NY, 2012, pp. 15-28.

Thompson, G., 'Electronic Kairos', in *Cybercultures: Mediations of Community, Culture, Politics*. H. Breslow and A. Mousoutzanis (eds), Rodopi, Amsterdam and New York, NY, 2012, pp. 3-13.

Vlavo, F., '"Click Here to Protest": Electronic Civil Disobedience and the *Imaginaire* of Virtual Activism', in *Cybercultures: Mediations of*

Community, Culture, Politics. H. Breslow and A. Mousoutzanis (eds), Rodopi, Amsterdam and New York, NY, 2012, pp. 125-148.

Wiener, N., *The Human Use of Human Beings: Cybernetics and Society*. Riverside Press, Cambridge, Mass, 1950.

Urry, J., *Global Complexity*. Polity Press, Cambridge, 2003.

——, 'Small Worlds and the New Social Physics'. *Global Networks*, Vol. 4, No. 2, pp. 109-130.

Zimmerman, H., 'Diverging Strategies of Remembrance in Traditional and Web-2.0 On-Line Projects', in *Cybercultures: Mediations of Community, Culture, Politics*. H. Breslow and A. Mousoutzanis (eds), Rodopi, Amsterdam and New York, NY, 2012, pp. 151-163.

Part 1

The Nature of Cyberspace

Electronic Kairos

Gary Thompson

Abstract
The nature and significance of cyberspace are contested. Cyberspace may be analysed using long-established rhetorical concepts. Electronic discourse has vastly multiplied the number of texts competing for attention. Traditional rhetoric accounts for success in persuasion through *kairos,* or the right time or measure. However, because electronic texts are distributed and asynchronous, control over texts has shifted away from rhetor to audience. *Kairos* in electronic discourse may be better accounted for by memetics: memes circulate because of reproducibility, simplicity, ideological relevance, and verbal and conceptual pleasure. *Kairos* can also refer to a time of transcendence, which relates to Benjamin's aura; however, the postmodern nature of electronic discourse disperses such a quasi-religious experience.

Key Words: *Kairos,* cyberspace, aura, meme, electronic discourse, rhetoric, multitasking, drinking the Kool-Aid.

*****

1.   Introduction

'Cyberspace' may be considered a performance space, defined not in terms of what it is but what we do with it.[1] Fundamentally, cyberspace is code, represented for us as zeroes and ones. Other concepts are built up from there, and we experience cyberspace as a visual, verbal, auditory, and interactive medium. We may think of these representations of cyberspace itself as metaphors or fictions, which (adapting an idea from the poet Wallace Stevens), in contrast to myth, we accept conditionally, knowing that they are false; that is, understanding that they are human creations rather than ordering principles of existence.

The version of cyberspace offered here is rhetorical: words, images, movement, etc. are there at least in part to persuade us to adopt an attitude or take an action. Seen in this light, cyberspace does not make us post-human, any more than other media do. While the medium is new, there is much continuity with other forms of communication.

The volume of data available to be conceived of as cyberspace is immense. Len Ball noted at the fifth annual international conference on CyberCultures in Salzburg that there are 34 gigabytes of data transmitted per person per day in North America. Even if our own interactions come to perhaps 1/1000 of that total, how is it that we find and pay attention to those small portions that can affect our lives? How can we reach an understanding of how discourse is changing in the electronic age?

Getting at such an issue is crucial for understanding electronic discourse, while we are immersed in it, is difficult but necessary work. Marshall McLuhan is widely quoted as saying, 'We don't know who discovered water, but we know it wasn't the fish.' To restate: out of all the millions of concepts, phrases, and images perpetually in circulation on the Internet, why do some catch our attention, while others languish in electronic obscurity? Why do some last, while others fade quickly? Why is there sometimes a delay before attaining salience? To attempt an explanation, I will appropriate a term from classical rhetoric, *kairos*, and relate it to two other concepts; the modernist concept of *aura* from Benjamin, and Richard Dawkins's notion of *memes*.[2]

Electronic here refers to any text - verbal, visual, interactive, or whatever - accessed or substantially created using computers or chips. *Kairos* equates to the word *time* in one specific sense: In English time refers either to duration or to the moment. We speak of time as in *time marches on*, or of time as in *this time*, the *next time*, etc. As often happens between languages, there are two different words in classical Greek for the one English word: *chronos* and *kairos*.

Ask a rhetorician and the term *kairos* will usually be defined as *the right time or right measure*. We are to speak to children or students or the general public or specialists or authorities in terms and at the length appropriate to each. For the Greeks, *Kairos* was even a minor deity, the spirit of opportunity. But if you ask a theologian about *kairos* you are likely to find the term given a New Testament context, as the time when God intervenes, as on the day of Pentecost in Acts of the Apostles, or as in the incarnation, or in the mass when the bread becomes flesh, or in Judgment Day. Appropriately, *kairos* (which in modern Greek also means *weather*) is a protean term, itself adapted to new contexts. I propose to insert it into yet another context, that of electronic discourse.

A skilled rhetor can read the audience and judge how slow or how fast to present arguments, judging the proper moment to bring the matter home. But circumstances change with electronic discourse: the audience is not present, but distant in space and even in time; texts as presented may be removed from any carefully prepared context; texts are necessarily a miniscule part of the textual avalanche now available. And in addition to spoken or written words, electronic discourse may incorporate still or moving visual images or music, and may have as part of its essence audience interactivity. Given these alterations in the medium, what can we say about the reasons that some concepts take hold long term, and others flash briefly and then disappear? And is there an equivalent in this time dominated by electronic communication to the sense of *kairos* as epiphany, given

McLuhan's contention that screens are cool media? As a test case, consider the following phrase, which can serve as illustration.

2.   Drinking the Kool-Aid

November 18, 1978: More than 900 people died in a massive murder-suicide at the People's Temple, Jonestown, Guyana, a religious cult under the domination of its leader, Jim Jones. Congressman Leo Ryan, who was investigating the group, was shot and killed at the airport; subsequently, almost all the community was invited or forced to drink a cyanide-laced grape drink (probably not Kool-Aid™ but a knockoff).

Over time, tragedy becomes metaphor or dark humour. It took not quite ten years before the phrase *drinking the Kool-Aid* was used in a 1987 *Washington Post* article about the mayor Marion Barry. The frequency of references increased considerably early in the Bush administration - that is, primarily distributed through electronic media. The *New York Times'* first use was in 1989 about a lawyer suffering penalties for supporting striking air traffic controllers - the sense here is strictly about drinking poison, not about being part of a cult. However, when Arianna Huffington used the term in 2002 about economic planners meeting with George W. Bush in Waco, Texas - 'Pass the Kool-Aid, pardner' - the term had passed to its present dominant meaning, as a common off-hand reference for falling under the baleful influence of a person or organisation or ideology. The phrase has since been applied not only to Bushies, but also to many others outside the political context.

But why the timing? Why was the phrase not adopted immediately, why did it find its way into use in the last decade, and why has it attained the status of rhetorical shorthand or near-cliché now?

We can consider the phrase *drinking the Kool-Aid* as what Dawkins has called a meme. Memes are bits of cultural knowledge - a word, a phrase, a musical bit, an image, a gesture, or a pattern of any sort capable of imitation - passed around from person to person, by analogy with genetic transmission.[3] When something is circulated as a meme, that indicates something like *kairos* - the textual bit catches the attention sufficiently to make us pass it on to others. Electronic media accelerate the process, of course, but they also tend to remove the context, so that most users of *drinking the Kool-Aid* do not think about the grisly aspects of the origin of the phrase. However, its initial use drew on the Jonestown incident for shock value, gaining it wider circulation.

Memes such as *drinking the Kool-Aid* are transmitted on the basis of timeliness and cultural needs. In other words, wide distribution and currency are indications of *kairos*. With respect to this particular phrase, the culture apparently needs a way to describe others who appear to be brainwashed to the point of self-destruction. Assigning this brainwashing to a trivial consumer product, Kool-Aid, calls attention to others' stupidity in falling victim to propaganda.

Other memes may or may not share such a lengthy delay in adoption. The prefix *cyber-* originated with Norbert Wiener, referring to control systems, and *cyber-* was in general use during the era of mainframe computers. The prefix received a considerable boost with William Gibson's coinage of the term *cyberspace* in *Neuromancer*, and the prefix is now widely applied as a means of distinguishing between electronic and material phenomena, as in Aris Mousoutzanis's *cybertrauma* and Scott Sundvall's *cyberrhizome*. Many uses, particularly early on, draw on this distinction to reinforce anxieties about technology which have a long cultural history, going back at least to the Luddites: as with the Luddites, these anxieties are rooted partly in economic displacement, and partly in allegiance to established authority which is undercut by the social uses of new technologies. Resistance to and eventual accommodation with electronic media follows a familiar pattern, as those committed to older media gradually adjust.

A meme with more than verbal qualities is *open source*. Most PCs worldwide use Microsoft's operating system (92.2% as of Jan. 2010), which is based on proprietary software. Slightly more than 5% use Apple's OSX system, with mobile operating systems making up slightly more than one percent. About one percent use Linux, an open source system, based on its users' opposition to monopoly capitalism.[4] Linux had its beginnings as early as 1983, but did not get off the ground until the early 1990s, when an increased density of users made collaboration on the open system a possibility.[5] The concept of open source is now well established in areas such as educational software and e-mail systems.

More than technological development is necessary to make an open source operating system. The ideological roots of open source are in resentment of corporate oligopoly, which may be epitomised by the telephone system in the US in the 20th century. Before the early 1970s, Bell Telephone subsidiaries in the US *owned* everyone's telephone, and the monthly bill was partially rent for the equipment. As a result of the monopoly, the Bell System had no motivation to update and modernise. Once the company was broken up, minor technological improvements rapidly came onto the market. Clay Shirky presents Linux as an instance of 'the wisdom of crowds,' but what he leaves out (perhaps because it is obvious to him and to his readers) is the ideological ground which makes the contagion possible - libertarian-oriented programmers who are opposed to monopoly control of *their* machines. Leaders in the US *talk* about free market capitalism, but corporate oligopoly is the real basis of the system as it exists.

The term *trauma* itself is a meme, deriving most of its initial force (as may be seen in Aris Mousoutzanis' work) from Freud and his early twentieth century work with neurosis.[6] Trauma has at least three categories of use: medical, as in *blunt trauma*, *head trauma*, etc.; psychological, a reaction to a catastrophic emotional event comparable to a medical wound; and a metaphorical extension to apply to a personal or cultural event. As with many such metaphors, this usage tends to dilute the term's literal force, to the point that mere personal embarrassment can be called traumatic (e.g., post-traumatic dress syndrome).

The examples of *drinking the Kool-Aid* and the *cyber* prefix are rather serious examples. Many - perhaps most - memes are circulated because they offer some sort of pleasure. A look at the *Internet Meme Database*, for example, in August 2010 offers the following categories up front: Sad Keanu Reeves; the Lying-Down Game; If You Watch X Backwards, It's About Y; Bros Icing Bros; Paul Yarrow (Photobombing); and many more. Emoticons, ASCII art, LOL-speak, and other linguistic innovations, not to mention image manipulation, are rooted not only in insider jargon but also in play with the capabilities of the technology. These and other memes can be described as circulating rhizomatically, but the metaphor simply gives a new label to a phenomenon as old as culture: we are primates and like to play with our toys.

3.   *Kairos* and Aura

There are of course many thousands of such verbal memes in circulation, of greater or lesser intensity than *drinking the Kool-Aid. Kairos* in the sense of opportunity can account for the prominence and persistence of the phrase; we should examine another sense of *kairos*, found in New Testament usage, that of God's time: 'Behold, now is the accepted time [*kairos euprosdektos*]; behold, now is the time of salvation' (2 Corinthians 6:2).[7] *Kairos* in this passage points to an opportunity that may not come again, an opportunity (so the story goes) for transcendence, for being in GOD's presence.

I want to trace an association between this sense of *kairos* as transcendence and a key term from 'The Work of Art in the Age of Mechanical Reproduction.' The 1930s of course offered no hint of the present rapid conversion to digital representation; however, I would argue that Benjamin's mechanical reproduction has reached its apotheosis in the digital environment.

Benjamin argues that artistic texts possess an aura that is bound up with the work's unique existence in a place and time, its presence. The aura is precisely *that which cannot be reproduced* - in this way of thinking about art, it is not possible to separate the image from its material form. Being in the work's presence creates an ineffable experience; this quasi-religious aura, for Benjamin, is weakened by the work's reproduction as kitsch and in parodic versions, to the point that modern audiences experience the artwork only in diminished form.

When I have presented an abbreviated version of Benjamin's argument to US students, most of whom have not had the experience of seeing artworks *in situ,* they do not buy it. Aura for them is bound up with the notion of celebrity: *Why wouldn't aura be increased by multiple copies?* Celebrity, created in part by repetition across media, points to the postmodern detachment of the artistic image from its material incarnation. Digital copies are the way that contemporary masses experience art, so that simulacra have now successfully redefined aura as the opposite of its meaning for Benjamin.

Benjamin's argument was grounded in the media of his day, radio and cinema, which artfully reinforced the mass hysteria needed for the Nazis' total warfare. Electronic media are more likely to function not as one-to-many or as one-to-one so much as networked communication (cyberrhizomes, if you like). This networking is by now so integrated into culture (as Auslander notes) as to undercut distinctions between live and mediated performance.

The main factor in changes in the nature of *kairos*, I believe, is the increased audience control over time of access, scale of access, and format of access that are involved. The audience at a live event may be resistant to the text being presented, and that resistance would be signified by *sotto voce* comments, shifting in the seat, checking the watch, grumbling, boredom, walking out. But its scale is limited to those nearby, whereas with electronic media the audience has a much more amplified voice.

In Benjamin's terms, aura would be something like the theological notion of *kairos*, to be experienced - if you are lucky - when standing in the actual presence of the artwork, comparable to divine inspiration. But the artwork's presence is now distributed, as contemporary audiences see the image, but not the material work, across computer screens, perhaps with even greater fidelity than the conditions that modern museums would afford. In the case of artistic events rather than graphic texts, not only the presence but the time of the event is distributed and recontextualised to suit the audience's convenience. The implication of this is that *kairos* is now distributed and more open to audience control, or rather, insertion into multiple contexts and the vagaries of audience experience.

4.   Distributed *Kairos*

Discussing reception is always tricky, but we know at least this much: audiences are far more likely to be multitasking now than before the electronic age. *Attention is distributed*: It is not so much short attention span as attention paid to several planes in alternation. And if attention is distributed, necessarily *kairos* must be as well.

Multitasking is however only one factor in the shifting nature of *kairos.* Classically the rhetor's art depended considerably on the ability to invent, organise and polish stylistically the speech, and during the actual delivery, to read the audience so as to sense the right measure and the right moment to move them to action. Context was stable and relatively controlled. Online audiences, however, are not in the same location, usually not accessing discourse at the same time, or through the same media, and are less subject to the rhetor's attempts at control. As with other aspects of present-day communication, the multiplication of texts has meant that the audience can do more to manage what Baron calls 'volume control,' giving different media and texts within those media higher or lower priority.[8]

Digital media, which are capable of endlessly reproducing identical copies, seem to be the ultimate form of Benjamin's mechanical reproduction. However, there is more to it than that: the essential form of digital texts is code, which must be read mechanically - code which we represent as zeroes and ones. The analogue colour spectrum blends smoothly, while digital spectra proceed by very small quantum jumps. A digitised image is therefore an approximation to the analogue image. It might not have, say, the precise reds and oranges of a Cézanne painting, but they are so close that only a colour savant could see any distinction. What happens to the aura when you approach it as a limit? When you perform calculus upon the aura and approach divinity?

Historically, art was available only to the elite, privileged to be in the performer's or the artwork's presence. The aura available in live performance is based at least in part on the fact that everyone who is not there cannot share in the experience. And before museums, only those invited by the artwork's owner were privileged to see it. But if we can have rough approximations to Fine Art easily and in quantity, then we care less about the transcendent aura of the Real Thing. In a postmodern context, the aura is no longer dependent upon the image's physical embodiment in, say, oil paint on canvas, but is instead freed from its material rendering and made available to all, albeit in approximated form. There has been a cultural shift over the long twentieth century, redefining the artwork as the image or even the concept rather than its material instantiation. Audiences are now accustomed to such transferrals, and value them to a greater or lesser extent depending on context. It may be argued that, as with celebrity, these reproductions in fact multiply the effect of the work by building its reputation and popularity.

Accompanying this shift from material artwork to image or concept is a change in what we mean by community. Ordinarily a community would be a group of people in the same location and sharing the same language and cultural traditions. An early use of the Internet was to form on-line communities self-selected for highly specific interests (Usenet groups), and this use has been extended into what Bauman, according to Jernej Prodnik's chapter, calls 'cloakroom communities,' called into existence by an intense response to some event or crisis - in other words, by *kairos*. These commonly disappear as the crisis passes. Perhaps they should be regarded as distributed communities, with their members being part of many such, and this shift an important aspect of postmodern life online.

But of course we should avoid romanticising this notion of community, since something similar happens on a smaller scale even without the Internet. Similarly, from a postmodern perspective, Benjamin romanticises art. While one must be present before the artwork to experience its aura, simply being there might not lead to a transcendent experience. Art is not so much what is on the canvas, but an event - what happens in dialogue between the work and the audience. In digital transmission, that dialogue occurs across a wide expanse of times as well as locations, in a wide range of contexts. Contra Phelan, it is live for each audience when they see it. This formulation leads to a statistical version of *kairos*, bringing a sort of graph of right moments, like a wave which builds and then crashes into random movement. This dispersion - electronic liminality - may be seen as a repurposing of Derrida's famous observation that *il n'y a pas de hors-texte.*

5.   Conclusion

So to return to our original questions: what changes if we emphasise the rhetorical dimensions of cyberspace? And how can something like *kairos* exist in the postmodern digital context?

Our discourse has changed due to the cultural penetration of electronic media, in a distributed, decentred, postmodern manner. Electronic texts are recontextualised in ways controlled by neither the author nor audiences, but rather subject to a combination of factors (hardware, operating system, browser software, as well as our own environments). This way of describing *kairos* as affected by the democratisation of electronic discourse tends to remove human agency and economics from the picture, collapsing the aesthetic and the commercial. But given the volume of data, how can we see electronic communication as liberatory? It's not just the volume per se, but the triviality of much of electronic communication. The question, however, supports an essential continuity between media: if we could gather transcripts of ordinary conversations, most of what we say to each other is also trivial (sports, weather, details about our day, and other things focused on desires of the moment). Since human beings are primates, we are accustomed to selecting the valuable bits from the background, whether it be ripe berries from a tangle of vines or key parts of a live or on-line conversation. That ability to detect what matters is *kairos*, and the principles of timeliness, relevance, and appropriate measure apply across media.

Circulation of memes and therefore *kairos* depends on the ease of reproduction. Memes must possess some quality of memorability, which may be helped by concision, sonority, assonance / alliteration, and other verbal qualities. Second, a successful meme needs a balance between novelty and repetition: the meme needs to strike its audience as a new insight or reformulation, capable of being appropriated for repeating and developing concepts; and it needs to be repeated enough to capture general notice. Perhaps most important is the quality of ideological suitability. The Jonestown tragedy takes on particular resonance as a meme given Americans' commitment to individualism: ideologically each citizen is supposed to decide on his / her best interests, while in practice herd behaviour is easily demonstrated. *Drinking the Kool-Aid* is an affront to the official pieties of individualism. Most current uses take the phrase as useful for describing others who seem to have been brainwashed into (rhetorically) self-destructive behaviour. But those new to the phrase see its origins as shocking, while more habitual readers of political discourse are already objecting to the phrase as a cliché.

This brings us to Jernej Prodnik's suggestion that we junk the distinction between *virtual* and *real* that underscores our discussion of cyberdiscourse. As computer-based means of communication have become general, the separation between cyberculture and culture outside the digital is blurred, or rather, shown to be as false a distinction as that between conversation in person and by telephone. If we grant that a telephone call is part of ordinary discourse rather than cyberculture, what changes between using a cell phone to dial up someone, and its use to text, or to check Google maps, or initiate a flash mob, which would make the latter part of cyberculture? The *cyber* prefix serves merely to designate that something is relatively unfamiliar to a mass audience. The same can be said of cybertrauma: those who are traumatised are part of a cohort that is being replaced by others for whom electronic communications are natural, the same group that accepts digital versions of artworks as equivalent to their material rendering in museums.

Another false dichotomy plays with the notion of community: *real* communities share a location, language, and cultural traditions, in opposition to *virtual* communities, or as Bauman terms them, cloakroom communities. These are marked by intense focus on a single issue or crisis, and their number has multiplied greatly in the age of electronic discourse. But such communities antedate the cyber world, as we may see in thinking about the temporary communities present in performance. In a successful live presentation, the audience elects to become a 'cloakroom community,' being in attendance at an event which is more prized because it is temporary. At the close of *Love's Labours Lost*, Don Armado speaks to this sad intensity at the close of the play-within-a-play and the close of the play proper when he tells his and the play's audience, 'You that way, we this way. *Exeunt omnes.*'

Kairos creates cloakroom communities. Such communities are performed, but this is the case with supposedly more permanent communities. Our notion of a tight, unified, centred community is a nostalgic myth. Trauma is produced by the erosion of this myth. To turn a bit of

Baudrillard's famous observation about Disneyland, virtual communities are there to obscure the unreality - or, better, fictive nature - of what we consider to be our real communities.

Notes

[1] Jernej Prodnik makes this point in his paper, referring to Mark Nunes, *Cyberspaces of Everyday Life*, University of Minnesota Press, Minnesota-London, 2006, p. xiii.

[2] S. Blackmore, *The Meme Machine*, Oxford University Press, New York, 1999, pp. 4-9.

[3] The concept of memes is notoriously slippery, ranging in scale from a few musical notes or a single letter (e- as in e-mail, e-business, etc.) to much longer texts. The definition is circular: it is a meme if it successfully reproduces itself. And treating memes by analogy with genes understates the role of culture, particularly of ideology, in their reproduction.

[4] See C. Shirky, *Here Comes Everybody: How Change Happens When People Come Together*, Penguin Books, New York, 2008, pp. 241-43, on the spread of Linux as system.

[5] Ibid., pp. 241-43.

[6] An interesting sidelight is the similarity between *trauma*, deriving from the Greek word for *wound*, and the German *traum* or dream.

[7] P. Sipiora, '*Kairos*: The Rhetoric of Time and Timing in the New Testament', in *Rhetoric and* Kairos: *Essays in History, Theory, and Praxis*, P. Sipiora and J. S. Baumlin (eds), State University of New York Press, Albany, 2002, p. 123.

[8] N. Baron, *Always On: Language in an Online and Mobile World*, Oxford University Press, New York, 2008, pp. 31-36.

Bibliography

Auslander, P., *Liveness: Performance in a Mediatized Culture*. Routledge, New York, 1999.

Baron, N., *Always On: Language in an Online and Mobile World*. Oxford University Press, New York, 2008.

Benjamin, W., 'The Work of Art in the Age of Mechanical Reproduction', in *Illuminations*. H. Arendt (ed), Schocken Books, New York, 1968, pp. 217-252.

Blackmore, S., *The Meme Machine*. Oxford University Press, New York, 1999.

Gralla, P., 'Windows Market Share Dips Again: World and Microsoft Survive'. *Computerworld*, January 4, 2010, viewed 21 August 2010, <http://blogs.computerworld.com/15344/windows_market_share_dips_again _world_and_microsoft_survive>.

Kermode, F., *The Sense of an Ending: Studies in the Theory of Fiction*. Oxford University Press, New York, 1967.

Kinneavy, J. L., '*Kairos* in Classical and Modern Rhetorical Theory', in *Rhetoric and* Kairos*: Essays in History, Theory, and Praxis*. P. Sipiora and J. S. Baumlin (eds), State University of New York Press, Albany, 2002, pp. 58-76.

Lessig, L., *Code 2*. Basic Books, New York, 2006.

Moore, R., 'Drinking the Kool-Aid: The Cultural Transformation of a Tragedy'. *Nova Religio: The Journal of Alternative and Emerging Religions*, Vol. 7, No. 2, 2003, pp. 92-100.

Mousoutzanis, A., 'Cybertrauma and Technocultural Shock in Contemporary Media Culture', in *New Media and the Politics of Online Communities*. A. Mousoutzanis and D. Riha (eds), Inter-Disciplinary Press, Oxford, 2010, pp. 173-182.

Nunes, M., *Cyberspaces of Everyday Life*. Minnesota, Minneapolis, 2006.

Phelan, P., *Unmarked: The Politics of Performance*. Routledge, New York, 1993.

Shirky, C., *Here Comes Everybody: How Change Happens When People Come Together*. Penguin Books, New York, 2008.

Sipiora, P. and Baumlin, J. S. (eds), *Rhetoric and* Kairos*: Essays in History, Theory, and Praxis*. State University of New York, Albany, 2002.

Gary Thompson holds a Ph.D. from Rice University in Houston, Texas, and is Professor of English at Saginaw Valley State University near Saginaw, Michigan. He is the author of *Rhetoric through Media*.

Post-Human, All too Non-Human: Implications of the Cyber-Rhizome

Scott Sundvall

Abstract
Never necessarily in this order, and always recursively: This serves as an attempt to recover Gilles Deleuze's and Felix Guattari's schizoanalysis and their concept of the rhizome as methodologies through which to better understand cyber-relations; to identify the spatial and temporal configurations of cyber-space which facilitate such relations; and to map the manner in which the cyber-subject is constituted in this manner. To this end, it would be productive to map (spatialise) and recall (temporalise) the rhizomatic performance of cyber-space: a mapping of folds and multiplicities, always-already a shifting middle term; and, contingently, a recollection of an always-becoming, a becoming-n-1 system. Likewise, and reflexively, schizoanalysis demonstrates how such a rhizomatic body de-codes the cyber-subject (by its very endless virtuality), liberating it into 'nothing but bands of intensity, potentials, thresholds, and gradients.'[1] Such a paper would aim to further map how such cyber-subjects come to form relations within the larger rhizome schematic, and the potential this carries. All this being said, it would be imperative to contrast the methodologies of Deleuze and Guattari against other theories and methods related to cyber-space and cyber-relations - as the rhizome seed invites. The concept of the 'cyber' cannot be properly treated within the parameters of tree-like, binary logic. By its very performance, cyber-space and cyber-relations are rhizome seeds, spreading, mutating, shifting. Never necessarily in this order, and always recursively.

Key Words: Rhizome, new media, Deleuze and Guattari, posthuman, digitality, subjectivity, Internet.

*****

The cyber is a rhizome seed, planted - the cyber-rhizome.

To write of the cyber-rhizome is difficult: though admittedly enshrouded in seeming ambiguity, one hesitates to code, trace, or signify - enclose a concept whose function is to break down such practice. Safely, then, it can be said that the cyber-rhizome is *différance*, which is also to say that it is not: the germination of the rhizome seed is what explodes *différance*, emptying out the entrapment of reversibility for the opening up of recursivity, moving from (infinite) linear possibility to the always already multiplicative movement from and towards every - and any - where. The endless interpretive branches that stem from post-structural and/or deconstructive trees assume a base, a trunk, an originating moment, even if the originating moment is destabilised and decentred. Rhizomes are subterranean, moving horizontally; their movement is spontaneously multiplicative, as is their moment of conception. As Gilles Deleuze and Félix Guattari wrote: 'any point of a rhizome can be connected to anything other, and must be;' and the same could be said of the cyber: cyber-rhizome.[2] The cyber-rhizome is a becoming-everything, an *n*-1 system, endlessly producing multiples, a-signifying and uncoding its apprehensions along its course of flight, along smooth, flat lines. The cyber-rhizome is *both/and*, not *(n)either/(n)or*.

The project, then, is not to trace the cyber-rhizome (as such a tracing would lead us to everywhere at once), but to map it. Of central importance to this mapping: the spatial and temporal configurations of the cyber-rhizome, as well as the manner in which the cyber-rhizome sub-*ject*-ifies, the former; implying, informing and guiding the latter.[3] That said, the sub-ject-ivity, or sub-ject-ification, referred to here is not that of a fixed position, a situating. Instead, it is a constant and virtual 'becoming-other.'

> Deleuze teach[es] us that the multiple ways in which the virtual can actualise itself ("what man is depends on what becomes of him") differ profoundly from the teleological striving of the possible that wants to realise itself in a certain predetermined manner "the seed and the tree".... .[4]

That is, the sub-ject is not thrown under that which eventually and inevitably stems upward, though diffusion into nodes and knots that form branches (which form nodes and knots, and other branches). Rather, the sub-ject remains thrown under (subterranean) according to a network that horizontally moves in all possible directions at all possible moments. In other words: the cyber-rhizome-sub-ject.

There are many designations that extend from the cyber: cyberspace, the World Wide Web, virtual reality, the Internet, digitality, etc. It is, to a large degree, the technology (or technic) that has most significantly come to immerse, mediate and inform sub-ject-ification. Like orthography, Morse code, the telephone, radio, and television that all preceded it, the cyber is a technic that functions in the mediation of communication. However, unlike its predecessors, the cyber not only distorts presence as such, it also reconfigures spatio-temporal organisations and facilitates formations of what one could call e-being.[5] And this e-being - as being-under-erasure - is the infinitely multiplicative potential of its technical, (and) systemic 'value:' always (and) everywhere. As Louis Armand articulates it, echoing Derrida

> Mankind - humanity - is thus neither transcended nor contradicted by the machine, but instead, as Derrida

contends, is "produced by the very possibility of the machine." That is, by "the machine-like expropriation" by which the so-called essence of man's Being is encountered by way of "technicity, programming, repetition, or iterability."[6]

In short, '(hu)man' is always already technical, a product of technē, as such. The very iteration of '(hu)man' is an employment of a (linguistic) technic, and it is, in the middle term(s), a programming and a repetition. That is, the technical apparatus that renders us '(hu)man' to begin with is what alienates us (bound to (de)program and (un)repeat. We are always already self-removed (by the inherent technicity that, recursively, makes such a 'self' possible). The spatio-temporal conditions of the cyber-rhizome-sub-ject merely reveal this and make it hyper-visible.

The spatio-temporal configurations of e-~~being~~ are that of a web: it branches out in all directions at once, connecting, reconnecting, and splitting; and these very same lines and branches are lines and branches of temporal difference - acts, utterances, moments that occur both simultaneously and yet in different moments from that which we would dubiously call real-time. Jay David Bolster and Richard Grusin make this clear when they note that '[t]he hypermediated self is a network of affiliations, which are constantly shifting. It is the self of newsgroups and email, which may sometimes threaten to overwhelm the user by their sheer numbers but do not exactly immerse her.'[7] These spatio-temporal configurations are rhizomatic; and these rhizomatic conditions sub-ject-ify e-~~beings~~ that are of endless, uncoded, multiples. The e-~~being~~ in the then cyber-rhizome arena lacks a signifying referent, except unto its self, which are always already multiple selves. In short, 'this networked self is constantly making and breaking connections, declaring allegiances and interests and then renouncing them.'[8] This uncoding multiplicity of e-~~being~~ is, then, what Katherine Hayles considers, 'the construction of the "body" as an absent signifier.'[9]

The e-~~being~~ extends from otherwise ~~being~~; and both being the same and different in their inherent multiplicity (with e-~~being~~ serving only as a placeholder), the e-~~being~~ realizes the naked desire of ~~being~~ to be, as Deleuze and Guattari write, 'nothing but bands of intensity, potentials, thresholds, and gradients.'[10] Essential to this reading is, as Slavoj Zizek states, 'the very basic duality of Deleuze's [and Guattari's] thought, that of Becoming versus Being, which appears in different versions (the Nomadic versus the State, the molecular versus the molar, the schizo versus the paranoiac, etc.).'[11] In this version, the cyber-rhizome makes possible a certain schizoid liberation that the ~~being~~ cries out for, exercised and exorcised in e-~~being~~. Answering to the call, 'Find your body without organs. Find out how to make it....,'[12] ~~being~~ schizo-sub-ject-ifies itself through e-~~being~~ every time it enters the cyber-rhizome: Facebook account, MySpace account, various avatars and screen names, Second Life fantasy. The e-being that constitutes a Facebook persona, for example, is not merely an extension of a primary being, but its own being, extended and folded, as always already, into other (e)beings. Katherine Hayles is correct in identifying cyber-modality as being an "'I'" transformed into the "we" of autonomous agents operating together to make a self,'[13] because of the spatio-temporal organisation and movement of the cyber-rhizome - coupled with the multiplicative nature of e-being.

Nonetheless, the 'we' should never be taken as a totalitarian - or otherwise fascist - erotic lure to incite desire in the being to form and mandate collectivity (extinguishing or eliminating those outside of the Order). Though the cyber-rhizome extends endlessly from multiples upon multiples, Guattari makes clear that 'making yourself machinic ... can become a crucial instrument for subjective resingularisation and can generate other ways of perceiving the world, a new face on things, and even a different turn of events.'[14] The multiplicity of e-being - or being for that matter - should not be viewed as an analogue for fascism; rather, quite the opposite. It is the supreme Order of signification, structural narratives and complacent desiring-production that construct senses of 'self' that render anxiety (fear and trembling) at the very possibility of self-as-such being lost. The self-as-such is as much, then, the ego as anything; and, as Deleuze and Guattari remark on the schizo-potential of the self-as-such, 'the ego ... is like daddy-mommy: the schizo has long since ceased to believe in it.'[15] Likewise (and it should be duly noted), schizophrenia is not to be championed as a necessary liberating force. Schizophrenia, to use Deleuze's and Guattari's clever subversion, is merely an example of how, if trapped within the structural framework of the Oedipal-triad narrative, one has an out - schizophrenia. However, it is the rejection of this structure at large that is accomplished through the multiplicity of being (resembling schizophrenia when forced into Freudian structuralism, but never such when outside of it).

Less provocatively and more specifically; there are more practical, political concerns regarding Deleuze's and Guattari's work, especially those concerning the body. Similar to the manner in which many feminists feel marginalised or alienated by psychoanalysis, many feminists maintain an equal degree of reservation regarding Deleuze and Guattari, even though the two are, in many ways, conducting a radical reformulation of psychoanalysis, if not a total uprooting of it. Elizabeth Grosz neatly outlines some of the more resounding concerns and salient points levelled by feminists in response to Deleuze's and Guattari's project:

> First, the metaphor of "becoming woman" is a male appropriation of women's politics, struggles, theories [and] knowledges ... . Second, these metaphors not only

neutralise woman's specificity, but, more insidiously, they also neutralise and thereby mask men's specificities, interests, and perspectives. Third ... Deleuze and Guattari confirm a long historical association between femininity and madness which ignores the sexually specific forms that madness takes. Fourth ... Deleuze and Guattari, like other masculinist philosophers, utilise tropes and terms made possible only through women's exclusion and denigration.[16]

In addition, it should be added that there is an anxiety towards projects such as this, that seemingly neglect the material, corporeal body - the culturally marked body that, regardless of a growing immersion in digital networking, in- and circum-scribes women (as well as all marginalised, minority groups) every day. As Aris Mousoutzanis reminds us in his work, 'Cybertrauma and Technocultural Shock in Contemporary Media Culture,' the cyber-rhizome does not displace ideology, nor does it displace the all too real problematic of trauma.[17] This seeming neglect of the everyday ideologies and historical traumas that situate the material body (even in its cyber-mediation) appears, at first glance, to be an avoidance of the hegemonic constructions that haunt the physical self. To this end, it could be said that not only is the cyber-rhizome, in theory, incapable of liberating the self (or being), but that it falls into the very trap which it attempts to destabilise: the insidious forms of everyday fascism.

However, both Deleuze's and Guattari's project, and this project, are not attempts to negate the corporeality of the material body any more than projects concerning the corporeality of the material body are attempts to negate the complications and potentials of digital immersion. The cyber-rhizome-sub-ject, as has been implied above, is capable of a rearticulation of the self rather than its mere reproduction. Immersion in the cyber-rhizome opens up the possibility and potential for sub-ject-ivity, rethinks the hitherto understood significance of the corporeal body, and presents a spatio-temporal reconfiguration that makes available a radicalisation of identity politics. As David Wills notes,

> Phillipe Lacoue-Labarthe defined fascism precisely as "the mobilisation of the identificatory emotions of the masses," and for Deleuze and Guattari, "certain assemblages of power require the production of a face...The face is a politics" that requires another politics of dismantling the face.[18]

Thus, and as already mentioned, the cyber-rhizome is capable of producing the paranoiac symptomology - the insidious everyday fascism - that already frames the sub-ject-ivity of what could be considered everyday life. However, the opening up of possibility and potential, the deterritorialisation inherent in the cyber-rhizome, makes the converse equally possible for the e-being, the cyber-rhizome-sub-ject.

And what a dis-appointment, then, it is to have posthumanism - especially that which is concerned with techno-centric conceptions - be the qualifier that discursively overarches projects that investigate cyber-sub-ject-ification. The betrayal of Freudian psychoanalysis and the Oedipal narrative is not far from posthumanism. The fundamental betrayal of posthumanism is located in the enclosure of its very language: post-*humanism*. To presuppose that there ever was anything of a univocal or even loosely grounded understanding of what it is to-be-human (or to even legitimate such a notion); to mark this in the sense of a temporal progression, to situate such an 'event' necessarily within a digital space - these bring the entire discourse back to the compulsion for knowledge-entrapment. Order, signification, univocality, structure: in the race to extend beyond all of this, posthumanism granted immediate concessions to these concepts. The multiplicative potentials of being, especially in e-being, always-already exceed conceptions of the human. The (false) human-animal distinction serving as case in point, Deleuze and Guattari note that '[t]he becoming-animal of the human is real, even if the animal the human being becomes is not; and the becoming-other of the animal is real, even if that something other it becomes is not' - a point that will be returned to shortly.[19]

By extension, it is important here to distinguish the 'real.' Much criticism of e-being is directed at its supposed inauthenticity - its being hyper-real at best and, as such, nothing more than the product of a technic that further alienates the material self (the human, the ego, the hoarding of a false possession). The Enlightenment concept of the human self stands firm, even in the wake of the growing understanding that such a historical moment was one of calculated knowledge-masturbation and self-legitimation. But 'if desire produces, its product is real;' and this is why our fundamental assumptions of reality (or lack thereof) need to be called into serious question.[20] To understand the e-being as simulation or simulacra is to presuppose an originary or authentic real. Jean Baudrillard argues that simulation and simulacra 'no longer [present] a question of a false representation of reality (ideology) but of concealing the fact that the real is no longer real, and thus of saving the reality principle.'[21] What characterises e-being as unreal in contradistinction to (the supposed primacy of) being? E-being is but part and parcel of a larger, sweeping indictment of that which is considered simulation and simulacra: 'The impossibility of rediscovering an absolute level of the real is of the same order as the impossibility of staging illusion.'[22] E-being, to be taken by many as a function of the simulacrum, is charged with producing a real that is not - a concept whose premise lies in Baudrillard's concession that there never was a 'discovered' absolute real that is an always already real fiction at best, and a clever ideology at worst. Or, as has already been discussed, and which is poignantly expressed by Nusselder, 'the frequently heard objection that "life on screen" is unreal or alienated cannot hold, for we are always already alienated.'[23]

E-being and the spatio-temporal constructions of the cyber-rhizome are often charged as being alienating technics, systems of self-surveillance and self-removal. Such theoretical movements and accusations largely stem from the Heideggerian question of technology, which, as neatly stated by Bernard Stiegler, 'finally conflates technicity and inauthenticity.'[24] Eventually, there occurs a struggle, or a 'negotiation: the one, bio-anthropo-logical, the other, techno-logical,' and any unassuming reader can assume to what pole the Heideggerian camp falls into.[25] E-being being directly linked to (post)modern or contemporary technology, and such technology being marked by its spatial and (more importantly) temporal configurations and implications, there occurs an anxiety over potential alienation, loss (the anxiety of potential mourning), disorientation.

> Contemporary disorientation is the experience of an incapacity to achieve epochal redoubling. It is linked to speed, to the industrialisation of memory resulting from the struggle for speed, and to the specifics of the technologies employed in that struggle.[26]

The 'disorientation' that Stiegler describes is envisioned as a potential nightmare by Paul Virilio, and coined as a '"critical transition" of which we are now the powerless witness.'[27] Virilio understands this 'disorientation' as a fundamental transition of accident (and a critical one at that), whereby temporal movement takes the shape of light to such an extent that we can only speak of time as speed (dromology), as such is increasingly 'kept afar, or beyond our grasp.'[28]

One must wonder why temporality is something that *should* or *must* be grasped, that our sense of seeming ownership and spatio-temporal-knowledge-domination ought to be maintained? The deterritorialisation and a-temporal movement of the cyber-rhizome merely exaggerates the already observed temporal technicity and mediation that circumscribe our being: as Nusselder notes, 'the supervention of a "now" ... is, as Jean-Francois Lyotard suggests, 'precisely what *does not* maintain itself.'[29] In fact, even some of the most recent, compelling work on e-being and the spatio-temporal relations of the cyber maintains this. 'The Cartesian I that we use to refer to ourselves is fundamentally mediated, and is remediated by the extensions of ourselves in new media.'[30] But Descartes and the Cartesian assumption *died* quite some time ago, and with him our once-privileged powers of spatial inscription and cogito-being have been dismantled. We are now the powerless witness of nothing more than our own mourning of this loss. Indeed, then, Bolster and Grusin's analysis is correct in that

> now, in the late twentieth century, no one in the virtual reality community can share Descarte's distrust of the senses. The virtual traveller sees and interacts with bodies, not minds, and she must be inclined to deny the traditional hierarchy in which we *are* minds and merely have bodies.[31]

Gregory Ulmer details this sense of 'loss' when he makes clear that 'we are preparing to give up the ghost, the essence of Man and all that goes with it. But this may require a funeral period of mourning.'[32] In the epoch of the cyber-rhizome, we must bury our dead; we must construct the technic of a dirge and sing with our digital voices.

Fredric Jameson laments this loss when regarding the new media and their introduction of a temporality that cannot be seized when he writes that 'nothing can change any longer.'[33] But everything changes - *everything*! - as the cyber-rhizome functions on just such a plane. When considering this over and against Hegel, Jameson makes a startling temporal revelation. 'It ends, in other words, not by becoming nothing, but by becoming everything: the path not taken by History.'[34] To this end, there is a death of History as such; but where History ends, the cyber-rhizome begins. To log on to the Internet, the World Wide Web, cyberspace; to be multiples and to inter-act at multiple 'moments,' at multiple 'places,' as multiple 'selves;' to be entangled in that postmodern baroque where 'the multiple is not only what has many parts but also what is folded in many ways' - this is the wake of a death that is very much alive, buzzing and as organic as anything.[35]

If anything, we are becoming a-temporal, and there is, in effect, a deterritorialisation. The postmodern aesthetic, as espoused by Jameson, is not so much a recycling and pastiche of past forms as it is a result of the re(singularisation) of temporality (per the increase in speed and movement) and, likewise, a new concept(ion) of territory and space - the cyber-rhizome. This is Stiegler's concept of *today's* epochal re-doubling: a cyber-rhizome that engenders new modes and methods for ~~being~~, which is always-already bound up in the already-past, the sense of being-here(-there) in difference to that which is understood as past.[36] In this case the concept and significance of the past, present and future, as such, lose their fundamental meaning if they cease to operate in such a demarcated semiosis.

Moreover, there are some very practical consequences regarding the a-temporalisation of the cyber-rhizome, particularly considering everyday rhetoric. The accelerated multiplicity of e-being within the becoming-a-temporal construct of the cyber-rhizome implies, as Gary Thompson notes in his work concerning electronic kairos, that 'kairos is now distributed and more open to audience control, or rather, insert[ed] into multiple contexts and the vagaries of audience experience.'[37] Thus, the unfolding of the linguistic process in the cyber-rhizome maintains a reflexive motion with the cyber-rhizome-sub-ject. That is, meaning does not precede the cyber-rhizome-sub-ject only to be received by it, but rather is propelled by and through cyber-sub-ject-ification. This, indeed, reverses a totalising semiotic process; it even abandons the tree-like methodology of post-structural and deconstructive interpretation for the fluid, subterranean and networked gesture of the rhizome - the cyber-rhizome.

This is why there needs to be a move past and beyond the Heideggerian question of technology (which was never so much a question as an indictment disguised as an interrogative), towards new lines of interrogation. It is important to remember that the cyber-rhizome does not escape the ethical imperative, as the fascist-Order always searches and seeks (such is its very function). But such an ethical imperative should not fall into the dated ideological conquests of Luddite fandom. Guattari makes this clear when noting that

> There exists an anti-modernist attitude, which involves a massive rejection of technological innovation, particularly as it concerns the information revolution. It's impossible to judge such a machinic evolution either positively or negatively; everything depends on its articulation within collective assemblages of enunciation. At best there is the creation, or invention, of new Universes of reference; at the worst there is the deadening influence of the mass media to which millions of individuals are currently condemned.[38]

Nothing could point more directly to the correct ethical trajectory. The rhizome is the polar opposite of fascist-Order, and while the cyber-rhizome carries the potential of inventive possibility, it also carries the possibility of total surveillance and control (nothing short of what is found in science fiction novels or seen in science fiction films).[39] To this end, while we may consider that the Hegelian notion of History as such as dead, the Hegelian lesson of the master-slave bi-polarity is still of the utmost importance in the ongoing dialectic of being.

Surprisingly enough, perhaps it is Slavoj Žižek who asks the most poignant question (rather than professing digital prophecy) concerning the future of the cyber-rhizome and e-being:

What would the digital virtualisation of our lives, the shift of our identity from hardware to software, our change from finite mortals to "undead" virtual entities able to persist indefinitely, migrating from one material support to another - in short: the passage from human to posthuman - mean in Nietzschean terms? Is this posthumanity a version of the eternal return? Is the digital posthuman subject a version (a historical actualisation) of the Nietzschean "overman"? Or is this digital version of posthumanity a version of what Nietzsche called the Last Man? What if it is, rather, the point of indistinction of the two, and, as such, a signal of the limitation of Nietzsche's thought?[40]

Important here is Žižek's closing remark on the dubiously dubbed 'posthuman' - the unthinkable possibility of there being no distinction between what is firmly held fast to as 'human' and what is approaching synthetically as posthuman. However, this lack of distinction predates the concept of not only the posthuman, but of the human itself. The lack of distinguishing features that mark something as human have always been fictive, invented, and in no way tied to any necessary or fundamental real-ness or Truth. It is no coincidence that, in the same manner in which techno-centric 'post-' and 'trans-humanists' are looking for-ward to relationships between the body and technology (tek-niks), others are looking back-ward at already assumed distinctions between human and animal. It is, and always has been, a certain human exceptionalism, stemming from Western Enlightenment thought that has produced far too many myths that, in turn, have legitimated far too many practices and are now, in consequence, producing far too many anxieties and mournings. Though Haraway disagrees with Deleuze's and Guattari's rhizomatic function, as it is demonstrated in *A Thousand Plateaus*, she commends the text in that 'it works so hard to get beyond the Great Divide between humans and other critters to find the rich multiplicities and topologies of a heterogeneously and nonteleologically connected world.'[41] And in this way we reach not only the limits of Nietzsche's thought, but perhaps our own: the loss of our much-coveted concept of human-ness is a loss whose impact cannot be fully predicted or measured. And yet it has always been lost in the rhizome - the rhizome that is part and parcel of the cyber-rhizome - which is where it will continue to be lost, and lost again.

Notes

[1] G. Deleuze and F. Guattari, *Anti-Oedipus*, University of Minnesota Press, Minneapolis, 1983, p. 19.

[2] G. Deleuze and F. Guattari, *A Thousand Plateaus*, University of Minnesota Press, Minneapolis, 1987, p. 7.

[3] Emphasis is added on the *ject* to emphasise the etymology of the word (*thrown* [*ject*] under [sub]), and to better clarify the extent of its semiosis.

[4] A. Nusselder, *Interface Fantasy*, MIT Press, Cambridge, 2009, p. 34.

[5] 'Being-under-erasure' is being used here to reinforce the notion that not only does being detached from the cyber lack singular stability, but it (perhaps further) lacks it when attached to the cyber.

[6] L. Armand, *Event States*, Litteraria Pragensia, Prague, 2007, p. 261.

[7] J. Bolter and D. Grusin, *Remediation: Understanding New Media*, MIT Press, Cambridge, MA, 2002, p. 232.

[8] Ibid., p. 232.

[9] K. Hayles, 'The Seductions of Cyberspace', in *Rethinking Technologies*, V. A. Conley (ed), University of Minnesota Press, Minneapolis, 1993, p. 180. (Enclosed quotations are mine.)

[10] Deleuze and Guattari, *Anti-Oedipus*, p. 19.

[11] S. Žižek, *Bodies Without Organs*, Routledge, New York, 2004, p. 28.

[12] Deleuze and Guattari, *A Thousand Plateaus*, p. 151.

[13] K. Hayles, *How We Became Posthuman*, University of Chicago Press, Chicago, 1999, p. 6.

[14] F. Guattari, *Chaosmosis,* Indiana University Press, Bloomington, 1995, p. 97.

[15] Deleuze and Guattari, *Anti-Oedipus* as it is demonstrated in *A Thousand Plateaus* , p. 23.

[16] E. Grosz, *Volatile Bodies*, Indiana University Press, Bloomington, 1994, p. 163.

[17] See A. Mousoutzanis, 'Cybertrauma and Technocultural Shock in Contemporary Media Culture', in *New Media and the Politics of Online Communities*, A. Mousoutzanis and D. Riha (eds), Inter-Disciplinary Press, Oxford, 2010, pp. 173-182.

[18] D. Wills, *Dorsality*, University of Minnesota Press, Minnesota, 2008, p. 164

[19] Deleuze and Guattari, *A Thousand Plateaus*, p. 239.

[20] Deleuze and Guattari, *Anti-Oedipus*, p. 26.

[21] J. Baudrillard, *Simulation and Simulacra*, University of Michigan Press, Ann Arbor, 1994, p. 13.

[22] Ibid., 19.

[23] A. Nusselder, op. cit., p. 92. Even potential advocates of the cyber-rhizome fall into the same trappings of *real*-assumption. For example, Katherine Hayles, in 'Seductions of Cyberspace', p. 177, notes that, 'One advantage of cyberspace over ordinary reality is its flexibility To think cyberspace as outside of "ordinary reality" is a perpetuation of technic myth: cyberspace is no more real - or really mystifying - than the very technic that allows us to think human, and to communicate such - language.'

[24] B. Stiegler, *Technics and Time, Vol. 2*, Stanford University Press, Stanford, 2008, p. 6.

[25] Ibid., p. 7.

[26] Ibid.

[27] P. Virilio, 'The Third Interval: A Critical Transition', in V. A. Conley (ed), University of Minnesota Press, Minneapolis, 1993, op. cit., p. 5.

[28] Ibid., p. 7.

[29] Armand, op. cit., p. 6.

[30] Nusselder, op. cit., p. 8.

[31] Bolter and Grusin, op. cit., p. 249.

[32] G. Ulmer, *Teletheory: Grammatology in the Age of Video*, Routledge, New York, 1989, p. 28.

[33] F. Jameson, *The Cultural Turn*, Verso, New York, 1998, p. 59.

[34] Ibid., p. 82.

[35] G. Deleuze, *The Fold*, University of Minnesota Press, Minneapolis, 1992, p. 3.

[36] Stiegler, op. cit, pp. 68-81.

[37] G. Thompson, 'Electronic Kairos', in this volume, pp. 3-13.

[38] Guattari, op. cit, p. 5.

[39] Counter-concepts of fascism and liberation aside, the issue splits in a less severe manner, as noted by Donna Haraway in *When Species Meet,* University of Minnesota Press, Minneapolis, 2008, p. 10: 'Technophilias and technophobias vie with organophilias and organophobias, and taking sides is not left to chance. If one loves organic nature, to express a love of technology makes on suspect. If one finds cyborgs to be promising sorts of monsters, then one is an unreliable ally in the fight against the destruction of all things organic.' Haraway, who shares an alliance and affinity for both eco-preservation and cyborg potential, is nonetheless often simultaneously coded as an (ethical) opponent to both of these very self-proclaimed camps.

[40] S. Žižek, *The Parallax View*, MIT Press, Cambridge, 2006, p. 193.

[41] D. Haraway, op. cit, p. 27.

Bibliography

Armand, L., *Event States*. Litteraria Pragensia, Prague, 2007.

Baudrillard, J., *Simulation and Simulacra*. University of Michigan Press, Ann Arbor, 1994.

Bolter, J. and Grusin, D., *Remediation: Understanding New Media*. MIT Press, Cambridge, MA, 2002.

Deleuze, G., *The Fold*. University of Minnesota Press, Minneapolis, 1992.

Deleuze, G. and Guattari, F., *Anti-Oedipus*. University of Minnesota Press, Minneapolis, 1983.

——, *A Thousand Plateaus*. University of Minnesota Press, Minneapolis, 1987.

Grosz, E., *Volatile Bodies*. Indiana University Press, Bloomington, 1994.

Guattari, F., *Chaosmosis*. Indiana University Press, Bloomington, 1995.

Haraway, D., *When Species Meet*. University of Minnesota Press, Minneapolis, 2008.

Hayles, K., *How We Became Posthuman*. University of Chicago Press, Chicago, 1999.

——, 'The Seductions of Cyberspace', in *Rethinking Technologies*. Verena Andermatt Conley (ed), University of Minnesota Press, Minneapolis, 1993.

Jameson, F., *The Cultural Turn*. Verso, New York, 1998.

Mousoutzanis, A., 'Cybertrauma and Technocultural Shock in Contemporary Media Culture', in *New Media and the Politics of Online Communities*. A. Mousoutzanis and D. Riha (eds), Inter-Disciplinary Press, Oxford, 2010, pp. 173-182.

Nusselder, A., *Interface Fantasy*. MIT Press, Cambridge, 2009.

Stiegler, B., *Technics and Time, Vol. II*. Stanford University Press, Stanford, 2008.

Thompson, G., 'Electronic Kairos', in *Cybercultures: Mediations of Community, Culture, Politics*. H. Breslow and A. Mousoutzanis (eds), Rodopi, Amsterdam and New York, NY, 2012, pp. 3-13.

Ulmer, G., *Teletheory: Grammatology in the Age of Video*. Routledge, New York, 1989.

Virilio, P., 'The Third Interval: A Critical Transition', in *Rethinking Technologies*. V. A. Conley (ed), University of Minnesota Press, Minneapolis, 1993.

Wills, D., *Dorsality*. University of Minnesota Press, Minnesota, 2008.

Žižek, S., *Bodies Without Organs*. Routledge, New York, 2004.

——, *The Parallax View*. MIT Press, Cambridge, 2006.

Scott Sundvall, Graduate Student, Literary and Textual Studies, Bowling Green State University, Ohio, USA.

Part 2

Prosthetic Subjectivity

Machinima, Creative Software and Education for Creativity

Daniel Riha

Abstract
Machinima as user-created content has gained an increasing amount of attention from videogame developers over the past few years. Many videogames include machinimation modules or some form of support for amateur machinima productions. This chapter explores three selected tools for machinima authoring in the context of creativity. Building on Bardzell's methodology for the semiotic analysis of multimedia authoring platforms and the identified principles of digital creativity, this chapter analyses how the features of machinima platforms influence creativity and user community building. The focus here is on a machinima tool based on the videogame platform *Half Life 2*, its modification *Garry's Mod* (2004), and two dedicated machinima production applications: *Moviestorm* (2008) and *Antics3D* (2008).

Key Words: Machinima, creativity, semiotics, multimedia, *Garry's Mod*, *Moviestorm*, *Antics3D*, reconfiguration of videogames.

*****

1.   Introduction

According to Lowood, we can think of machinima as 'a found technology.'[1] He adopts Duchamp's concept of the 'found object' from the visual arts. Such an object, the readymade, is an everyday object that is placed in a different context, as a form of artistic expression. Lowood emphasises that this sort of artefact has neither been designed for or by the artist, nor for the intent of display or artistic statement. Common objects are assigned a new context. Artist-player designs are the visual products that emerge from their 'recontextualisations.' Lowood characterises machinima as a found technology, describing some of its characteristics as the 'player-created use of computer games, such as the availability of game technology as "readymade" for a purpose other than making movies.'[2] In machinima, such a recontextualisation is accomplished not by re-designing the game engine, but rather by transforming 'found technology' into an animation engine, while exploiting various techniques already learned from other multimedia applications. Lowood notes that this medium, based on videogames, encourages a sense of 'co-ownership' - not in legal terms, but in the sense of the freedom to 'replay, reinvent, and redeploy.' In particular, the performative use of machinima leads to 'high performance play' where the artist-player utilises new applications of multimedia for cultural production.

Mitchell and Clarke suggest a classification of videogame art under the following categories:

> *Remixing* - the use of videogame iconography in other media.

> *Reference* - the creation of original games that make known reference to previous games.

> *Reworking* - the modification of existing games, often to create new interactive environments or "machinima."

> *Reaction* - performance (often disruptive or ritualistic) within a multiplayer game.[3]

The category of reworking is equivalent to the characteristic of recontextualisation attributed to machinima by Lowell.

Machinima production, as a type of game-modifying activity, can also be understood as an instance of 'participatory culture,' a concept introduced by Jenkins. Jenkins has differentiated participatory activities into four categories: affiliations (online communities); expressions (production of artefacts); collaborative problem-solving; and circulations (dissemination in the media).[4]

Successful machinima production requires, in the same measure, different levels of artist-player knowledge on various multimedia platforms and membership in the proper machinimistic online communities.

2.   Creativity in Amateur Art Productions

Bardzell attempts to critique the idea of creativity in multimedia authoring software. He compares human computer interaction (HCI) to cultural studies discourses and identifies some common characteristics that cultural studies, HCI, and semiotics share. All theorise creativity in the context of professional knowledge production. These disciplines understand creativity as situated within 'systems-networks of software-supported experts, discursive sign systems, and frameworks of production.'[5]

Bardzell's critique is based on the initial assumption that each software application differs in the way that it promotes authoring. Industry-level image- and video-editing software offers editorial advantages to users who prefer to work with layers when compared to hobbyist software. This, to Bardzell, makes certain content more easily rendered by professional software.

While researching on creativity projected by authoring software, Bardzell lays out a common descriptive language to analyse the different platforms by applying concepts derived from semiotics: paradigms and syntagms, developed by Saussure, and previously used in new media theory by Manovich. A syntagm is a 'grammatical' sequence of signs and a paradigm is a class of unit within a syntagm. These semiotic concepts imply that elements of sign systems are combined to create meaning beyond the aggregated meaning of the single components. To study the use of multimedia authoring interfaces, Bardzell adopted these concepts to explore 'the legal sequences of actions designers could follow, and to explore the paradigmatic classes of options within those sequences.'[6] He found that in all various genres and data-types, the similarities among these software applications were remarkable.

This chapter presents a comparative analysis of selected machinima platforms based on Bardzell's sample syntagmatic analysis of multimedia authoring software. Such a system recognises the syntagms common to most multimedia authoring platforms. A syntagm has to be 'a more or less stable sequence of actions required to accomplish a particular design task.'[7] This common syntagm is the creation of an art element. In multimedia applications, this syntagm comprises the following sequence:

1. Identify a location in space and time in which to work;

2. Create the element;

3. Specify the element's relationship to the remainder of the composition.[8]

A paradigm is, then, a 'set of possible actions that constitute one step in that task.'[9] Bardzell identified three different paradigmatic options of the syntagm for designing a simple art element: set up of the element - from scratch, from primitives, and from components.

One significant method in the production of machinima is the use of computer automation when creating art. Using this method the artist-player designs art from primitives/components. Most software applications can import various data-types to be used as primitives/components.

The syntagm composition includes usage of timelines, canvases, virtual cameras or viewpoints. These are, in Bardzell's terms, 'nearly universal interfaces for handling this step. Object nesting (building complex objects out of grouped simple objects) is another way of specifying relations.'[10]

The paradigmatic options call for different interfaces and user behaviours that 'shape the nature of the art created, and hence its meanings.'[11] The implementation of primitives often offers customisation tools and art design elements with components supported by various wizards and palettes.

When comparing interface and artistic outputs of select software applications, Bardzell notes that each paradigm requires different art production skills on the user side:

> Individual amateur Flash works tend to privilege one art creation paradigm option over others, not because users rationally match their paradigmatic choices to the materiality of their art and their message, but rather because users choose the tools with which they are the most competent.[12]

Bardzell defines the primary syntagms of multimedia authoring, by identifying some of the common paradigms that might be traced in many of multimedia applications (Figure 1).[13]

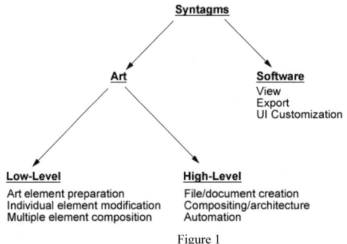

Figure 1

He demonstrates that these applications have 'a similar language of creative expression and correspondingly project a similar notion of creativity.'[14]

In light of of usability research in the context of amateur multimedia, Bardzell suggests that 'the easier or more visible a feature or tool is in the interface, the more likely it is to be used.'[15]

We may trace the convergence of methods of art production in multimedia art that unites the elements of text, photo, video, music, and others into a single product. Bardzell also recognises the function of transformed media to contribute 'to the elaboration of new aesthetics in the parent medium.'[16]

A natural candidate in such a case is machinima, seen by Bardzell as the conflict between cinematic and videogame logic. Similarly, we may identify two forms of production of machinima: cinematic and ludic machinima.

> *Cinematic machinima* feature narratives shot in the world of a particular video game. Many of these films continue with the aesthetic of the game. ... Many cinematic machinima films use the logic of cinema to expose and parody the absurdity of games.

> *Ludic machinima* feature the logic of video games, which includes game rules, physics, and, above all, play (Aarseth, 2004). In this type of film, the found art is the physics engine of the video game, is used in ludic machinima to create commentary through its juxtaposition with other media.[17]

Lowood emphasises the importance of the videogame medium for machinima: 'we can imagine a real-time animation engine without them, but not the same historical culture of modification and experimentation.'[18]

To conclude the review of methodologies for analysing the enabling of creativity in amateur multimedia, we might agree with Bardzell that the smallest meaningful unit is the art element in the form of the primitive or video shot in software applications. Digital creativity then arises from 'the composition of such elements in a process in which these elements are created discretely separate from one another but, more importantly, remain discretely separated, no matter how organic the final composition appears.'[19]

Finally, Bardzell argues that amateur multimedia should be seen as creative only if they meet the criteria here proposed as 'innovation in the rebalancing of production quality and expense on the one hand and meaning-making on the other.'[20] While applying the creative principle of remixing, even very amateur or dated graphical quality digital art production might create culturally valid statements.

3.   Impact of *Garry's Mod*, *Moviestorm* and *Antics3D* Software Applications on Creativity

According to Sihvonen, online game modding including machinima might be understood as 'an important part of what are currently known as "social software" or Web 2.0 technologies, based on user-led content and knowledge production.'[21] O'Neill, Riedl and Nitsche argue that the trend in user activities towards user-created content brings a need for 'tools [that] have been developed to aide in the creative process for several forms of digital media, including machinima.'[22] To proceed with such a design activity amateur artists need advanced IT literacy skills. O'Neill, Riedl and Nitsche identify the current lack of tools needed to 'assist novices in both technical realisation and optimisation of content.'[23] According to these authors, amateur artists need tools that 'focus on the process of authoring content, rather than simply its feasibility.'[24]

Bardzell et al. identify four main methods for constructing virtual environments that are suitable for producing machinima:

> 1. 'Pure games' can be used to create machinima even though they do not include any 'built-in mechanisms' for production. Similar to film and animation, video games incorporate dramatic narratives. Any game environment has the potential to be used for machinima, although the visual quality of the work depends on the sophistication and versatility of the game.

> 2. 'Modded games' involve modifications to the source code of a game to produce a customised environment beyond what a 'pure game' allows. Machinima evolved out of modifications to games like Doom and Quake, leading to achievements with digital environments that are more impressive.

> 3. 'Hybrid games' are suited for machinima because the game's interface has built-in mechanisms for production. For example, some games like The Movies allow players to film the characters' actions as part of game play. These types of games capitalise on the concept that allowing users to make movies within video games offers players a new form of interactivity and customisation.

> 4. 'Pure machinima platforms' are created for the purpose of producing machinima and do not contain 'game related content.' They are examples of tools that are developed specifically for machinimists.[25]

Gundelsweiler and Filk, in this volume, argue from the perspective of human-computer interaction that users must be involved early in the development of interactive applications.[26] They discuss the requirements of new media systems and present a case, where they solve a problem to make users understand the concept of media convergence and its far-reaching consequences:

> This would enable them to give meaningful input in the process of requirements analysis and design. The problem here is that the understanding for this complex subject is not given. A test for whether this knowledge is available fails because the transformation process of media in the society is not yet complete.[27]

Machinima production has, by principle, been affected by media convergence. Ludic machinima designers are mostly digital natives and computer technology enthusiasts, and their feedback is quite often taken into consideration by videogame designers when producing sequels to popular videogames. Furthermore, the attitude of videogame companies to this issue is the opposite of their traditional media rivals: While many fan production activities in the film and other media industries are restricted or banned (such as amateur YouTube videos), amateur fan machinima production is for the most part welcomed and actively supported by videogame developers and companies.

While in the area of ludic machinima production we might expect a relatively higher than average level of computer literacy, in the field of cinematic machinima users or amateur filmmakers require a higher level of support at the interface during machinima production.

In the following paragraphs, building on Bardzell's methodology for the semiotic analysis of multimedia authoring platforms and identified principles of digital creativity, I will analyse how the features of select machinima platforms influence creativity and user community building.

Garry's Mod represents the ludic machinima, the type of machinima that, in short movies, features various experiments with game engine physics.[28] *Moviestorm* and *Antics3D* feature cinematic machinima types of applications that focus on the development of traditional film storytelling. While the cyber-community of machinima producers around videogames recruits mostly from the active players engaged in the historical culture of gameplay and the modification of a selected videogame title, the dedicated machinima production platform is often more popular among amateur animation film enthusiasts.

In ludic machinima, movie production is often realised as a form of 'acting' in 3-D space rendered and saved in real time; as a result this production activity is freed from some of the traditional video-editing chores. But when the artist-player wants to customise the available 3-D content in full, the production line in ludic machinima then requires more advanced game editing or modding skills. The adaptation of models, characters and animation does not usually allow for rapid prototyping.

This is the case in the example of machinima production in the *Half-Life 2* videogame modification *Garry's Mod* (GMod). GMod is a physics sandbox extended with scripted behaviours developed by numerous fan-user communities. As a result, even in scripting, an unskilled user might play with advanced effects included in building blocks not available in the cinematic machinima platforms. The production of machinima in GMod is primarily based on live action puppeteering combined with recording in an external frame-recorder, like Fraps or GameCam. The low-level syntagms of art manipulation present in GMod include individual element modification in position, scale, textures, lightning, and sound. The higher-level syntagms present include imported 3-D game elements and design blocks of assets. Syntagms related to GMod as an authoring platform are then built-in game functions and game view interfaces. A syntagm (the sequence of steps in creation of basic art element in the case of machinima) is understood here to be the creation of a single movie shot. GMod offers two of the three paradigmatic options available for designing a machinima scene - primitives and components. In GMod, unskilled artist-players have an extensive set of game assets available to them, but with a significant limitation in available genres: only sci-fi, detective and World War II themes are included. The tradition of machinima production in GMod includes equally narrative movies and physics scripting experiments. The character modification and animation is a time-consuming and skill-demanding process and finalisation of machinima requires knowledge of external video-editing software. This platform might be recommended for expert game-users instead of machinima novices. In the context of my annual machinima production course, this platform was selected more often by students skilled in advanced ICT operation.

Antics3D is a pre-visualisation tool popular among cinematic machinimists.[29] This platform offers a simple interface with drag and drop functionality for importing assets. It offers an advantageous import prop directly from Google Warehouse. Recording is based on character staging and allocation of animation sequences such as pathfinding and interaction with props from assets. The built-in video-recorder allows for direct output from this application.

The low-level syntagms of art manipulation present in *Antics3D* include individual element modification in position, scale, texture, lightning, and sound. The higher-level syntagms present compositing from imported 3-D game elements in .3ds and Google SketchUp formats, built-in animated characters from assets, the ability to design a scene/room from primitives, and easy import of standard animation files in .bvh format. Syntagms related to *Antics3D* as an authoring platform relate to the semi-interactive 3-D view

---

interface. *Antics3D* therefore illustrates two of the three paradigmatic options of the syntagm for designing a machinima scene: primitives and components. The path-finding system works with a limited number of asset-animated characters. External video-editing software is needed for the finalisation of machinima.

Moviestorm[30] features the first attempt to deliver an all-in-one solution for the cinematic machinima production pipeline, from importing assets, built-in interactive recording, video-editing and exporting in various video formats and functionalities. The low-level syntagms of art manipulation present in *Moviestorm* include individual element modification in position, scale, texture, lighting and sound. The higher-level syntagms present include imported 3-D game elements and design blocks of assets. Syntagms related to *Moviestorm* as an authoring platform are the fully interactive 3-D view interface combined with simplified built-in video-editing software. *Moviestorm* has, therefore, two of the three paradigmatic options of the syntagm for designing a machinima scene: primitives and components. Its main disadvantages are a complicated asset import model, almost an impossibility to adapt a designer's own characters and a standard animation format import into the environment. Similar to *Second Life*, *Moviestorm* offers dedicated *Moviestorm* users a marketplace for the exchange and sale of the Moviestorm Workshop (Plug-In Object Editor) signed objects.

The simplistic interface makes *Moviestorm* the ideal choice for machinima novices, which is confirmed by the statistics of software preference in my machinima production courses.[31] Although *Antics3D* development was discontinued in 2009, this platform still has some advantages over *Moviestorm*, including easier and extended import of props (.3ds format) and import of user preferred animations in .bvh. Since August 2008, I have witnessed *Moviestorm*'s rapid development, so I am optimistic about its role in becoming the primary tool for cinematic machinima production in the near future.

The results of this comparative analysis of machinima platform and their impact on creativity reveal that interface features significantly influence the user-type involvement with a particular platform, which is in line with Bardzell's conclusions.

4.   Conclusion

The Creative Arts Department at Faculty of Humanities, Charles University, in Prague, aims at the utilisation of specific techniques for expression and the communication of creativity. The lessons and workshops such as Creativity as a shift, Gnoseological aspects of visual media, Inter-medial art production, Multimedia project in 3-D, or the above-mentioned multimedia course, Machinima production, applies systemic knowledge of creativity development on both theoretical and practical levels. We may characterise practically oriented education on creativity in the studies of the humanities as 'art production for non-artists ... where ... creative processes have been here deconstructed to emphasise the part of artistic process, when the creator works "for himself" and with all sincerity tries to capture his or hers perceptions and experiences.'[32] The software implemented for the realisation of creative processes includes a range of applications from pre-visualisation engines, to game engines, to popular videogames. Such an approach leads to an understanding of the creative process as 'an innovative tool for identification of the new interactions and experiences, generated during these interactions, both on personal and social levels.'[33]

Notes

[1] H. Lowood, 'Found Technology: Players as Innovators in the Making of Machinima', in *Digital Youth, Innovation, and the Unexpected*, T. McPherson (ed), The John D. and Catherine T. MacArthur Foundation Series on Digital Media and Learning, The MIT Press, Cambridge, MA, 2008, p. 185.
[2] Ibid.
[3] G. Mitchell and A. Clarke, 'Videogame Art: Remixing, Reworking and other Interventions', in *Level Up: Conference Proceedings*, University of Utrecht, Utrecht, The Netherlands, 2003, p. 340.
[4] H. Jenkins, cited in T. Sihvonen, *Players Unleashed! Modding* The Sims *and the Culture of Gaming*, Annales Universitas Tukuenis, University of Turku, Finland, 2009, p. 58.
[5] J. Bardzell, 'Creativity in Amateur Multimedia: Popular Culture, Critical Theory, and HCI', *Human Technology: An Interdisciplinary Journal of Humans in ICT Environments*, Vol. 3, February 2007, University of Jyväskylä, Finland, p. 19.
[6] Bardzell, op. cit, p. 20.
[7] Ibid., p. 21.
[8] Ibid.
[9] Ibid.
[10] Ibid., p. 22.
[11] Ibid., p. 23.
[12] Ibid., p. 24.
[13] Ibid., p. 24. Figure 3. A sketch of Syntagms common to most multimedia platforms.
[14] Ibid., p. 25.
[15] Ibid., p. 26.
[16] Ibid., p. 28.

[17] Ibid.
[18] H. Lowood, *High-Performance Play: The Making of Machinima*, P. 25, <http://www.stanford.edu/~lowood/Texts/highperformanceplay_finaldraft.pD f>.
[19] Bardzell, op. cit, p. 28.
[20] Ibid., p. 29.
[21] T. Sihvonen, op. cit., p. 171.
[22] B. O'Neill, M. O. Riedl and M. Nitsche, *Towards Intelligent Authoring Tools for Machinima Creation*, p. 1, available online, viewed on 10 August 2010, <http://www.cc.gatech.edu/~riedl/pubs/chi-wip09.pdf>.
[23] O'Neill, O Riedl and Nitsche, op. cit, p. 1.
[24] Ibid., p. 2.
[25] J. Bardzell, S. Bardzell, C. Briggs, M. Makice, W. Ryan and M. Weldon, 'Machinima Prototyping: An Approach to Evaluation', in *Nordic Conference on Human-Computer Interaction*, Vol. 189, Proceedings of the 4th Nordic Conference on Human-Computer Interaction: Changing Roles, 2006, p. 434.
[26] F. Gundelsweiler and C. Filk, 'Future Media Platforms for Convergence Journalisms', in this volume.
[27] F. Gundelsweiler, C. Filk and B. Studer, 'Media Convergence and the Future of Online Platforms', in *New Media and the Politics of Online Communities*, A. Mousoutzanis and D. Riha (eds), Inter-Disciplinary Press, Oxford, 2010, p. 139.
[28] *Garry's Mod* for *Half Life 2*, more information at: <http://www.garrysmod.com/news/>.
[29] *Antics3D*, more information at: <http://antics3d.blogspot.com/>.
[30] *Moviestorm*, more information at: <http://www.moviestorm.co.uk/>.
[31] In 2008 14 out of 14 students designed Machinima using a game engine, in 2009 4 out of 14 students designed with *Moviestorm*, currently 12 of 14 signed students prefer to work with *Moviestorm* (preliminary results).
[32] J. Vancat and D. Riha, 'The Development of Visual Literacy in Art Education', in *Visual Literacies*, Inter-Disciplinary Press, Oxford, 2012, p. 8.
[33] Vancat and Riha, 'The Development of Visual Literacy in Art Education', in *Visual Literacies*, Inter-Disciplinary Press, Oxford, 2012, p. 8.

Bibliography

Bardzell, J., 'Creativity in Amateur Multimedia: Popular Culture, Critical Theory, and HCI', in *Human Technology: An Interdisciplinary Journal of Humans in ICT Environments*. Vol. 3, February 2007, University of Jyväskylä, Finland, pp. 12-33.

Bardzell J., Bardzell, S., Briggs, Ch., Makice, M., Ryan, W., Weldon, M., 'Machinima Prototyping: An Approach to Evaluation', in *Nordic Conference on Human-Computer Interaction*. Vol. 189, Proceedings of the 4th Nordic Conference on Human-Computer Interaction: Changing Roles, 2006, pp. 433-436.

Gundelsweiler, F. and Filk, C., 'Future Media Platforms for Convergence Journalisms', in *Cybercultures: Mediations of Community, Culture, Politics*. H. Breslow and A. Mousoutzanis (eds), 2012, pp. 45-57.

Gundelsweiler, F., Filk, C., Studer, B., 'Media Convergence and the Future of Online Platforms', in *New Media and the Politics of Online Communities*. A. Mousoutzanis and D. Riha (eds), Inter-Disciplinary Press, Oxford, 2010, 137-144.

Lowood, H., 'Found Technology: Players as Innovators in the Making of Machinima', in *Digital Youth, Innovation, and the Unexpected*. T. McPherson (ed), The John D. and Catherine T. MacArthur Foundation Series on Digital Media and Learning, The MIT Press, Cambridge, MA, 2008, pp. 165-196.

Mitchell, G. and Clarke, A., 'Videogame Art: Remixing, Reworking and other Interventions', in *Level Up: Digra Conference Proceedings*. University of Utrecht, Utrecht, The Netherlands, 2003, pp. 338-349.

——, *High-Performance Play: The Making of Machinima*, viewed on 10 August 2010, <http://www.stanford.edu/~lowood/Texts/highperformanceplay_finaldraft.pdf>.

O'Neill, B., Riedl, M. O., Nitsche, M., *Towards Intelligent Authoring Tools for Machinima Creation*, p. 6, available online, viewed on 10 August 2010, http://www.cc.gatech.edu/~riedl/pubs/chi-wip09.pdf

Sihvonen, T., *Players Unleashed! Modding The Sims and the Culture of Gaming*. Annales Universitas Tukuenis, University of Turku, Finland, 2009.

Vancat, J. and Riha, D., 'The Development of Visual Literacy in Art Education', in *Visual Literacies*. Inter-Disciplinary Press, Oxford, 2012.

Daniel Riha, Ph.D., is an Assistant Professor in the Faculty of Humanities, at Charles University in Prague, Czech Republic. His research includes issues on Serious Games and Multi-user Virtual Environments Design. He is as well an award-winning artist - *Kunst am Bau* (Art on Construction) International Art Competition, Constance, Germany.

Future Media Platforms for Convergence Journalisms

Fredrik Gundelsweiler and Christian Filk

Abstract

In this chapter we present our discussion of media convergence, in which we explain the evolving requirements and design possibilities for novel online platforms. We also discuss the key ideas on how to design and realise a multimedia online platform for the future. In so doing we explain our theoretical assumptions which are based on our practical experiences. We present our findings, which we obtained during a requirements analysis and show how we came to both our theory and conclusion by evaluating and interpreting our results. In the conclusion we present current research trends of media convergence and human-computer interaction.

Key Words: Media convergence, crossmedia, multimedia, Web 2.0, online community, interaction, Multimedia Production.

*****

1.   Introduction

We are in the process of designing a new course of studies called Multimedia Production (MMP), which educates students in producing and publishing new media content for crossmedia online platforms. Media agencies, news and multimedia companies are all in need of people with these abilities because they have to respond to changes in the traditional media landscape caused by the new media. During the course of their studies MMP students produce multimedia content (print, audio, video) based on new media convergence production processes in cooperation with research institutes and companies. We are also working on a multimedia online platform on which this content will be available in the future. Therefore the produced material has to be edited, pre-processed and archived, which, however, is not the most challenging part. The difficult part is to find a concept that integrates novel interaction and interface design in a usable way with existing web services and the delivery of content to various (mobile) devices.

Web 2.0 online platforms are not standard components in public education institutions like universities of applied sciences. Most institutions use basic websites that show the most important information to their visitors. The reason for this is the limited resources of staff, budget, and time. Although the trends show that institutions that use content management systems are increasing, most of them refrain from using novel web principles and techniques. Older web platforms are far from exploiting up-to-date trends like Web 2.0 and the possibilities of interacting with and searching for information enabled by new platforms. The majority of older web platforms continue to use primitive search functions and result in visualisations that are outdated and static in terms of the interface design for search, interaction and navigation of interactive web applications. An additional issue is how to manage the diversity of content in different print, audio and video formats.

Even well-known media portals like YouTube and Flickr use far less of the novel techniques than those available. Other examples are the webpages of high-circulated journals and newspapers like *Spiegel Online*, *FAZ* or the *Zeit*. The new media formats found on smartphones and the iPad demonstrate the first applications that use interactive multimedia content. These new media formats produce (or reuse) similar multimedia content, like our MMP students, and publish it online. However, they do not make use of trendsetting interaction, exploration, and search techniques.

We can reveal interesting research questions in relation to topics such as user access to information and user interface design. Machinima as user-created content has gained an increasing amount of attention from videogame developers over the past few years. As argued by Riha, in his chapter in this volume, many videogames include machinimation modules or other elements of machinima productions.[1] In the future these plug-ins may work for both computer games and web portals, and thus merge these two media forms. This user-generated machinima authoring for content brings new possibilities to multimedia portals by developing online and real-life communities that exchange information across social and technical gulfs. This is closely related to augmented reality, which is used to process huge amounts of data associated with real-world environments. One additional idea for future web platforms is the possible creation of alternative online environments, as those already available in games such as *World of Warcraft*. With these new web platforms one could easily render these environments more productive by enriching the productivity and information flow between online communities and external users. An important issue that is closely related to augmented reality is managing the movement of both virtual objects and information back to reality by involving people who are neither able nor interested in virtual environments. The cyberworld must be aware of this and try to bridge the gap between the real world and the cyber world.

One area of research concerns the access to information through searching and exploring the information space. This concerns the interface design of search, interaction, and navigation for interactive web applications. An additional issue is how to manage the diversity of content amongst different print, audio, and video formats. Further issues that we address are the techniques to explore and find content that are developed in current research projects. We conclude with a discussion of the open question of how the integration of external web services with Web 2.0 techniques and principles may be realised in the future.

2.   Transformation Processes and Converging Media

In the last two decades the quaternary economic sector and the media industry have witnessed fundamental transformations. In particular, the processes of digitalisation and convergence have triggered enormous consequences for media products, services, business models and respective media-based user roles and transactions. When we examine the traditional media of mass communication, such as newspapers, radio and television, we recognise that they are faced with a hard challenge created by new content standards. These standards are characterised by rapid technological growth, information and communication technology (e.g. mobile communications), and Web 2.0 principles and practices such as user-generated content, 'network effect' and remixability. All these developing new standards show the enormous structural changes of both the media and society.

Above all, the concepts of cross-media and media convergence are of great importance in current theoretical and practical discussions. Both terms describe variants of media economics' added-value, particularly for media companies. The 'value-added step' is meant in the sense of product differentiation:

1. produce content (first value-added step)
2. combine content (second value-added step)
3. distribute content (third value-added step)

The use of media-convergent concepts and strategies in the communications industry points to the increased relevance of visual, communal, and participatory media. The term 'cross-media' was originally used in the context of desktop publishing and served as a description of cross-linked and media-convergent use of content.[2] During the development and implementation of Web 2.0's social media and semantic technologies the expression 'crossmedia' was used as an umbrella term for coordinated communication and distribution channels that can address media users according to target groups: starting with streaming media, branded entertainment and viral marketing through scientific visualisation, micro-blogging and YouTube, to Google News, Ricardo and Facebook.[3] New web services, such as Twitter, Google Wave and Google Buzz, are growing rapidly.

The term 'media convergence' first referred primarily to the technical convergence of print media to electronic media and telecommunications. In this context, established communication, journalism, and content-recovery processes in the media industry dissolved.[4] The prevailing specialisation in traditional production, distribution and reception contexts became obsolete because of the digitalisation and convergence of the (mass) media.[5] As a result, it was necessary to create, bundle and distribute new content. This had consequences for the relevant converging media and communication markets in conjunction with technological, political, economic, legal, and sociocultural aspects.[6] With this market transformation there was significant potential growth, especially of content distribution, the third value-added step within the media economy.[7] The use of mass media was due to the dual contexts of diversifying crossmedia and media market convergence - a highly complex structure of relationships.[8]

3.   Media Convergence and Society

In interdisciplinary research on media convergence a system of business and revenue forms that can be adapted modularly was designed. The 'value chain' concept, discussed by Porter, turns out to be particularly useful since it opens up various options for connections with economic concepts that have been unrelated until now.[9] New forms of usage (digital video disc, Internet) for the traditional media sector result in an extension of the conventional 'profit window' concept.

At this point new cross-media and media convergent products, services and their models are established. The Internet as a global network becomes the promoter for telecommunications through the successive integration of more and more networks, services and applications.[10]

In contrast to neoclassical microeconomics, the markets of the Internet economy can be understood as process dynamics.[11] Uncertainties in market transactions may be avoided by the theoretical implementation of econometrically relevant information on goods, services and transaction partners. We have to reconsider traditional functions and attributions of economic theories because of the direct and indirect network effects of online media: In the Internet economy negative feedbacks change to positive feedbacks. Mass displaces scarcity as a source of value.[12] The Web 2.0 is a 'participative economy.'[13] Sustainable Web 2.0 technologies and related applications (social media, knowledge management, microblogging etc.) support businesses in the development of their products by receiving feedback on products and in making business decisions through customer involvement.[14] It is necessary to find out how companies are connected with customers and how customer involvement can increase to effectively operate the customer relationship management. At this point Web 2.0 solutions are applied: corporate blogs, podcasting, video blogs, web-based applications, mashups, and online games.

Converging media environments and cross-media usage models provide many opportunities to produce, combine, and distribute content. The adaptation of media convergent conceptualisations and strategies in the context of media, economies, societies and cultures requires that society has established a predominant communication pragmatism based on visual, participatory and self-organised forms of media.[15] Cross media formations constitute a participative, convergent, network culture only due to a strong understanding of the importance of visualisation, participation and networks in the society.[16]

4.   Requirements of New Media Systems

From the perspective of human-computer interaction, users must be involved early in the development of interactive applications.[17] In our case, users must have understood the concept of media convergence and its far-reaching consequences. This will enable them to give meaningful input in the process of requirements analysis and design. The problem here is that the understanding of this complex subject has not yet been determined. A test for whether this knowledge is available fails because the transformation of the media in society is not yet complete.

Following our assumptions, media convergence takes place in three areas of this transformation. The first area is in the formats used for the consumption of media content. This includes devices such as smart phones, notebooks, personal computers, and televisions. Here we see a general trend towards the mobile sector, even though fixed TVs are preferred at home by consumers because of their better picture quality and larger screens. The second dimension is time. Time plays an important role when the consumer accesses the content. In general, one can establish the following proposition: In the morning users listen to the radio. On the way to work they use their mobile devices to receive media content. At lunch they use their personal computers to consume media content. In the evening, during their leisure time, they primarily use both mobile devices and devices with large screens for the playback of movies and the organisation of leisure. The two previous dimensions affect the nature of the processing of media content. Properties of media such as formats, resolution, quality, length, video, audio, text, and others, have to be identified and matched to the particular situation of the consumer. Media content has to be tailored to the user depending on the consumer's situation and the available device.

5.   Multimedia Platform of the Future

Our research objectives are subject to different platforms. We want to adjust these in accordance with the process of media convergence and integrate them into one viable multimedia platform of the future. Several projects that were implemented either by us, or our commercial partners, already exist. A platform for transmitting movies, graubuendentv.com, currently distributes video and audio content via different channels (own streaming, YouTube, etc.) from Switzerland's Graubünden to consumers. The next step will be the integration and transmission of digital content via IPTV.

Another project that is currently in the process of implementation deals with digital radio. The project is called Swiss Mountain Holiday Radio (SMHR), and it integrates the content of different radio stations into one channel that is enriched and distributed to consumers. In addition, the backchannel will be used to give the opportunity for producing self-made radio to consumers.

Future multimedia platforms must be able to tailor the format to the situation and the type of user-desired consumption. Within this concept, however, the generation of content by many users is a basic principle that follows the Web 2.0 principle of 'user-generated content.' One example here is news messages that are generated locally: Consumers who are on site where an event happens are becoming journalists or editors, and starting to report live, on site. This is the way new information is produced; by consumers, for consumers. In the future amateurs will become journalists and this will affect the quality of reporting, and thus the quality of the news.

Information flow of convergent media content

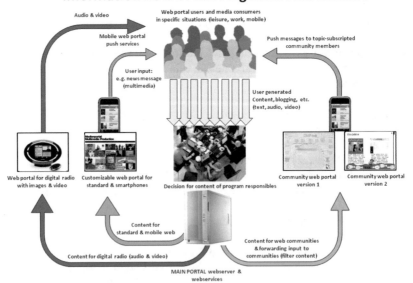

Figure 1: Information flow of convergent media content

As shown in Figure 1, a multimedia platform for the future needs a kind of central, or steering, board. This board decides if the content is distributed directly or if it has to be processed further. In addition, the board defines which content is distributed to different channels.

The technical implementation of such a multimedia platform for the distribution of media content is meaningful only if it is in accordance with the above criteria. Such a media platform requires the following basic functions: The first step is to create a web platform that has a connection to as many widely used web services as possible. Furthermore, it has to have its own database and sufficient storage space for a media archiving system for user-delivered content. Especially important is the integrity and reliability of web services that are provided to users: these services must be reliable and well adapted to each other. At the same time, the entire multimedia platform must be configurable as a kind of learning system that attempts to coordinate situations, devices, content, consumers and producers at all times. In a first pilot project, we try to implement a prototype in practice with these requirements in mind.

The future will bring the convergence of print, radio and television. Devices such as personal computers and TVs will merge and develop an incredibly powerful functionality. Media content and applications will appear on interactive displays with different properties (e.g. screen size, interactive possibilities).

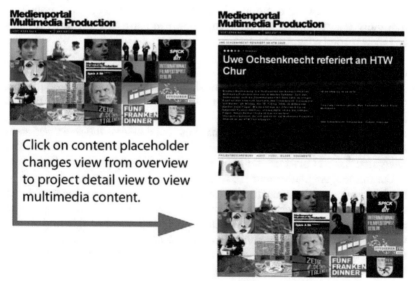

Figure 2: Convergence Multimedia Portal (first interactive version)

Figure 2 shows the actual implementation of our convergent media portal, which will be online soon under http://www.multimediaproduction.ch. The basic idea to bring this platform, depending on the information distributed by the editorial staff and users, to reality, is to use augmented reality. With this technique new devices and materials will be produced that retrieve the necessary information from the web. One actual example is the iPad, but there must be more forward-looking technologies, such as interactive light and flexible paper, which can display multimedia content. One way for these devices to do so would be to display the user-relevant data by placing it directly over the real world. As discussed in 'Gaming Potential of Augmented Reality' we as 'human beings (we) are used to interpret and process the world around us with astounding speed, faster and better than any computer.'[18]

The applications themselves, along with some image processing functions and the calculation of these interactions, will no longer take place on the device, but on an external high-performance computer. Complex operations are much better computed on servers, with the media content (video, image, print, audio) displayed on the screen of the portable device. The devices of the future should, therefore, feature slim, interactive displays. These are, however, new interface types and thus new interaction and visualisation techniques will be necessary. One fundamental reason for this is the usability and user experience for consumers. Market positioning, design, interaction, and the preparation of the content are other important issues. In the future this will make the difference between hardware/software products and their market acceptance.

6.   Conclusion

We argued that the media world is in a process of transition where the convergence of the media is progressing in the areas of technique, content and social aspects. Many companies are missing this transformation process. In order to be better accepted by humans as social beings, the socialisation of multimedia systems in the future will be a unique selling point. The integrated Internet platform for controlling the necessary processes is the core of our multimedia platform of the future. New tools and technologies, such as machinimation and augmented reality, can be used to support and build communities and bridge the gap between digital and non-digital aspects of our society. At the moment we are in the planning phase of this project and we will soon be able to combine interactive and static multimedia content through the use of convergent processes. In our planning process the interaction techniques, such as zooming, panning, and drag and drop, in particular, in combination with visualisation techniques, are of great importance. On the one hand, the user interface needs to be intuitive, while on the other, it has to guide users to navigate and extract relevant information from relatively complex data spaces.

Notes

[1] See D. Riha, 'Machinima, Creative Software and Education for Creativity', in this volume.

[2] A. Müller, *Erfolgsfaktoren für Crossmedia-Publishing-Anbieter*, Logos, Berlin, 2009.

[3] M. Schumann and T. Hess, *Grundfragen der Medienwirtschaft Eine betriebswirtschaftliche Einführung*, Springer, Berlin and Heidelberg, 2009; S. Droschl and Kunstverein Medienturm (eds), *Crossmedia Neue Medien in der Gegenwartskunst*, Folio, Wien and Bozen, 2006; C. Jakubetz, *Crossmedia*, Uvk, Konstanz, 2008; U. Gleich, 'Multimediale Kommunikationsstrategien', in *Media Perspektiven*, Vol. 2009, No. 1, pp. 40-45; S. Münker, *Emergenz Digitaler Öffentlichkeiten. Die Sozialen Medien im Web 2.0*, Surhkamp Verlag Gmbh, Frankfurt am Main, 2009.

[4] T. Holzinger and M. Sturmer, *Die Online-Redaktion Praxisbuch für den Internetjournalismus*, Springer, Berlin, 2009.

[5] U. Grüner, *Crossmedia für Lokalzeitungen. Zeitungen, Internet und Handy Geschickt Verknüpfen*, LZSB Lokalzeitungen Service, Berlin, 2007.

[6] K. Dimitrakopoulou, *Medienkonvergenz und der Relevante Produktmarkt in der Europäischen Fusionskontrolle. Eine Untersuchung im Bereich der Konvergierenden Telekommunikationsmärkte im Hinblick auf die Innovationsförderung*, Stämpfli, Baden-Baden, 2007; A. Fiebig, *Gerätebezogene Rundfunkgebührenpflicht und Medienkonvergenz Rundfunkgebührenpflicht für Internet-PC und Rechtsnatur der Rundfunkgebühr*, Duncker & Humblot, Berlin, 2008; C. Filk, *Episteme der Medienwissenschaft - Systemtheoretische Studien zur Wissenschaftsforschung eines Transdisziplinären Feldes*, Transcript, Bielefeld, 2009; C. Filk, *Rezeption privater Schweizer Radio- und Fernsehangebote unter Crossmedialen und Medienkonvergenten Marktbedingungen - Eine Empirische Studie am Beispiel der Randregion Oberwallis*, Universi, Siegen, 2010; M. Kempf, *Die internationale Computer- und Videospielindustrie. Structure, Conduct und Performance vor dem Hintergrund Zunehmender Medienkonvergenz*, Igel Verlag Fachbuch, Hamburg, 2010.

[7] Schumann and Hess, op. cit.

[8] H. Theunert (ed), *Medienkonvergenz: Angebot und Nutzung. Eine Fach-Diskussion Veranstaltet von BLM und ZDF*, Fischer, München, 2002.

[9] M. E. Porter, *Competitive Strategy Techniques for Analyzing Industries and Competitors*, Free Press, New York, 1980; M. E. Porter, *Competitive Advantage*, Free Press, New York, 1985; A. Zerdick, A. Picot and K. Schrape, *Die Internet-Ökonomie Strategien für die Digitale Wirtschaft*, Springer, Berlin and Heidelberg, 2001.

[10] Schumann and Hess, op. cit.; Filk, op. cit., 2010; B. W. Wirtz, *Medien-und Internetmanagement*, Gabler, Wiesbaden, 2009.
[11] W. Grassl and B. Smith (eds), *Austrian Economics: Historical and Philosophical Background*, Routledge, New York, 1986; N. Leser, *Die Wiener Schule der Nationalökonomie*, Boehlau Verlag, Wien, 1986.
[12] Zerdick, op. cit..
[13] S. Singh, 'A Web 2.0 Tour for the Enterprise', *Boxes and Arrows*, viewed on 1 August 2006, <http://www.boxesandarrows.com/view/a_web_2_0_tour_>.
[14] Singh, op. cit.; T. O'Reilly, 'What Is Web 2.0? Design Patterns and Business Models for the Next Generation of Software', viewed on 16 April 2010, <http://oreilly.com/web2/archive/what-is-web-20.html>; A. McAfee, 'Enterprise 2.0 The Dawn of Emergent Collaboration', *MIT Sloan Management Review*, Spring 2006, pp. 21-28.
[15] M. Giesecke, *Von den Mythen der Buchkultur zu den Visionen der Informationsgesellschaft. Trendforschungen zur Kulturellen Medienökologie*, Suhrkamp Verlag, Frankfurt am Main, 2002; M. Giesecke, *Die Entdeckung der Kommunikativen Welt. Studien zur Kulturvergleichenden Mediengeschichte*, Suhrkamp Verlag, Frankfurt am Main, 2007.
[16] Holzinger, Sturmer, op. cit.; O'Reilly, op. cit.
[17] D. Mayhew, *The Usability Engineering Lifecycle: A Practitioner's Handbook for User Interface Design*, Morgan Kaufmann, San Francisco, 1999.
[18] G. P. Nicolau, 'Gaming Potential of Augmented Reality', in *New Media and the Politics of Online Communities*, D. Riha and A. Mousoutzanis (eds), Oxford, Inter-Disciplinary Press, 2010, pp. 145-154.

Bibliography

Alby, T., *Web 2.0: Konzepte, Anwendungen, Technologien*. Hanser Verlag, München, 3rd Edition, 2008.

Dimitrakopoulou, K., *Medienkonvergenz und der Relevante Produktmarkt in der Europäischen Fusionskontrolle. Eine Untersuchung im Bereich der Konvergierenden Telekommunikationsmärkte im Hinblick auf die Innovationsförderung*. Stämpfli, Baden-Baden, 2007.

Droschl, S. and Kunstverein Medienturm (eds), *Crossmedia. Neue Medien in der Gegenwartskunst*. Folio, Wien and Bozen, 2006.

Fiebig, A., *Gerätebezogene Rundfunkgebührenpflicht und Medienkonvergenz. Rundfunkgebührenpflicht für Internet-PC und Rechtsnatur der Rundfunkgebühr.* Duncker & Humblot, Berlin, 2008.

Filk, C., *Episteme der Medienwissenschaft - Systemtheoretische Studien zur Wissenschaftsforschung eines Transdisziplinären Feldes.* Transcript, Bielefeld, 2009.

——, *Rezeption Privater Schweizer Radio- und Fernsehangebote unter Crossmedialen und Medienkonvergenten Marktbedingungen - Eine Empirische Studie am Beispiel der Randregion Oberwallis.* Universi, Siegen, 2010.

Giesecke, M., *Von den Mythen der Buchkultur zu den Visionen der Informationsgesellschaft. Trendforschungen zur Kulturellen Medienökologie.* Suhrkamp Verlag, Frankfurt am Main, 2002.

——, *Die Entdeckung der Kommunikativen Welt. Studien zur Kulturvergleichenden Mediengeschichte.* Suhrkamp Verlag, Frankfurt am Main, 2007.

Gleich, U., 'Multimediale Kommunikationsstrategien'. *Media Perspektiven*, Vol. 2009, No. 1, pp. 40-45.

Grassl W. and Smith, B. (eds), *Austrian Economics: Historical and Philosophical Background.* Routledge, New York, 1986.

Grüner, U., *Crossmedia für Lokalzeitungen. Zeitungen, Internet und Handy Geschickt Verknüpfen.* LZSB Lokalzeitungen Service, Berlin, 2007.

Harrison, Steve, Tatar, D., Sengers, P., *The Three Paradigms of HCI*, <http://people.cs.vt.edu/~srh/Downloads/HCIJournalTheThreeParadigmsofHCI.pdf>.

Holzinger, T. and Sturmer, M., *Die Online-Redaktion. Praxisbuch für den Internetjournalismus.* Springer, Berlin, 2009.

Jakubetz, C., *Crossmedia.* Uvk, Konstanz, 2008.

Kempf, M., *Die Internationale Computer- und Videospielindustrie. Structure, Conduct und Performance vor dem Hintergrund Zunehmender Medienkonvergenz.* Igel Verlag Fachbuch, Hamburg, 2010.

Leser, N., *Die Wiener Schule der Nationalökonomie.* Boehlau Verlag, Wien, 1986.

Mayhew, D. J., *The Usability Engineering Lifecycle: A Practitioner's Handbook for User Interface Design.* Morgan Kaufmann, San Francisco, 1999.

McAfee, A. P., 'Enterprise 2.0. The Dawn of Emergent Collaboration'. *MIT Sloan Management Review*, Spring 2006, pp. 21-28.

Müller, A., *Erfolgsfaktoren für Crossmedia-Publishing-Anbieter.* Logos, Berlin, 2009.

Müller, H., Squire, D. McG., Müller, W., Pun, T., 'Efficient Access Methods for Content-Based Image Retrieval with Inverted Files'. *Proceedings of Multimedia Storage and Archiving Systems IV (VV02)*, Boston, MA, 1999.

Münker, S., *Emergenz Digitaler Öffentlichkeiten. Die Sozialen Medien im Web 2.0.* Surhkamp Verlag Gmbh, Frankfurt am Main, 2009.

Nicolau, G. P., 'Gaming Potential of Augmented Reality', in *New Media and the Politics of Online Communities.* D. Riha and A. Mousoutzanis (eds), Inter-Disciplinary Press, Oxford, 2010, pp. 145-154.

Norman, Donald A., *The Design of Future Things.* Basic Books, New York, 2007.

O'Reilly, T., 'What is Web 2.0? Design Patterns and Business Models for the Next Generation of Software', viewed on 16 April 2010, <http://oreilly.com/web2/archive/what-is-web-20.html>.

Perlin, K. and Meyer, J., 'Nested User Interface Components', in *Proceedings of the 12th Annual ACM Symposium on User interface Software and Technology.* ACM, New York, 1999, pp. 11-18.

Porter, M. E., *Competitive Strategy. Techniques for Analyzing Industries and Competitors.* Free Press, New York, 1980.

———, *Competitive Advantage*. Free Press, New York, 1985.

Preece, J., Rogers, Y., Sharp, H., *Interaction Design*. Wiley, New York, 2002.

Schumann, M. and Hess, T., *Grundfragen der Medienwirtschaft. Eine Betriebswirtschaftliche Einführung*. Springer, Berlin/Heidelberg, 2009.

Shneiderman, B., 'The Eyes Have It: A Task by Data Type Taxonomy for Information Visualizations', in *Proceedings of the IEEE Symposium on Visual Languages*. IEEE Computer Society Press, Washington, 1996, pp. 336-343.

Singh, S., 'A Web 2.0 Tour for the Enterprise', in: *Boxes and Arrows*, viewed on 1 August 2006, <http://www.boxesandarrows.com/view/a_web_2_0_tour_>.

Theunert, H. (ed), *Medienkonvergenz: Angebot und Nutzung. Eine Fach-Diskussion Veranstaltet von BLM und ZDF*. Fischer, München, 2002.

Wirtz, B. W., *Medien- und Internetmanagement*. Gabler, Wiesbaden, 2009.

Zerdick, A., Picot, A., Schrape K., *Die Internet-Ökonomie. Strategien für die Digitale Wirtschaft*. Springer, Berlin and Heidelberg, 2001.

Fredrik Gundelsweiler is lecturer at the University of Applied Science in Chur, Switzerland and leading the web specialisation of the course of studies called Multimedia Production. He is interested in the convergence of media, usability, software engineering, and his current research and writing is devoted to the usability of online platforms and web portals.

Christian Filk, Ph.D., is Professor of Communication Science and Media Studies and Head of Research & Development at the Institute of Media and Communication, University of Applied Sciences, Chur, Switzerland. His main interests lie in the field of interdisciplinary research on media - culture - technology.

Bodily Aware in Cyber-Research

Judith Guevarra Enriquez

Abstract
This chapter extends the interest in the embodied nature of human experience to cyber-research by exploring 'bodily issues' that have been left to the natural sciences while the social sciences concentrated on cultural and social matters. In education and technology studies, in particular, there is a need to move learning and knowledge production away from the body/mind dichotomy. Discussions concerning situatedness and embodiment in learning in cyberspace must include bodily acts. The body is increasingly recognised in the 'mobility turn' of understanding society and the effects of the new media and ubiquitous computing. There are two interrelated developments that have become significant to the rise of the technologised body: 1. The widespread production and consumption of virtual spaces through the Internet and portable devices. 2. The incorporation of non-human material into the body, not only in the literal sense but also in a more prosaic sense wherein there is a merging of humans and computers (e.g., the 'cyborgisation' of society). The 'corporeal turn' focuses on the mobile practices that reflect the enhancements and mobilities that technologies have introduced into our everyday lives. These include the transformation of human (bodily) encounters and the re-configuration of spaces. This corporeal turn implores researchers to be 'bodily aware' of the embodied performances implied by repeated production and consumption of knowledges and the development of cyber-literacies in terms of what used to be known as oxymorons: absent presence, public privacy, and isolated connectivity.

Key Words: Cyberspace, embodiment, body, mobility, absent presence, public privacy, distant proximity, isolated connectivity, mobile learning, networked individualism.

*****

1. Moving Bodies, Spaces and Technologies

Mobile technologies have reached the point where they converge in identical spatial and embodied practices. Strictly segregated spaces and social organisations of everyday life are increasingly undermined and re-ordered by the permeability and fluid modalities of emerging network and mobile technologies. The Internet, or cyberspace, interacts with urban space and disrupts and collapses conventional boundaries and enclosures.[1] Places move to other places.[2] Bodies coordinate multiple tasks and conversations, oscillating between highly private and semi-private modes of communication

- remaining in one place while connected to the Internet.[3] This kind of situation is a fertile ground for the emergence and multiplication of modes of ordering. Physical co-presence is no longer the only presence possible. There is presence in absence, privacy in public and connectivity, even intimacy, in isolation.[4] The concepts of mobility and spatiality are being deconstructed to say the least. Our senses of place, home, self, identity and of our own bodies are being re-negotiated, shifted and at times suspended. Mobile technologies including the Internet give individuals an 'exit option.' For instance, with a mobile phone one can 'exit' the immediate space and avoid encounters with 'present others' while being elsewhere with 'absent others.' In the physical world, human actors are true 'individuals' for exogenous reasons because they have one body, which provides a stabilising anchor and cannot be separated from their capacity as reflecting subjects or as social actors.[5] Online, individuals become 'dividuals' - in this case, as bits of scattered information distributed across various 'systems.'[6] A number of retrievals are possible from various locations.[7] The individual with a unified sense of identity, who is anchored in a particular physical location, is 'divided' and distributed in hardware and software.

There have already been studies conducted on embodied cognition.[8] However, the relationship between body and technology has been given meagre attention in research that has much enthusiasm in investigating e-learning, distance education, and all the other variants of learning with technologies, mobile or otherwise. This chapter provides a possible framework to explore bodily relations with technologies and spaces. After all, the mind is not dissociated from the body and thought is only possible through actual bodily involvement and movements.

2.   Bodies and Places

With the widespread use of both mobile devices and the Internet, notions of space and place have become increasingly complex. Mobile phones and iPods, for example, invade and transform the physical space of our embodied location in ways that allow presence and absence, distance and proximity, individualism and community to 'occupy' the same temporal and spatial reality. The boundaries between real and virtual spaces have become, to some extent, both irrelevant and ambivalent as a result of new understandings and conceptions of 'mobility' - not just in terms of bodily movements, but also in terms of cognition. Oxymorons like absence and presence, proximity and distance, alone and together, co-exist in mediated spaces. Now, we can talk about 'absent presence,' 'alone together,' in isolated connectivity or in what Wellman refers to as 'networked individualism.'[9] We have also attained rights to 'public privacy.'

Places are performed by bodies. Yet, the human body has for far too long been subordinated to the mind in the social sciences.[10] If we are going to focus cyber-research on the way we perform activities, then we will have to focus on bodies - their positions and positionings. It is rather obvious that we need a body in order to experience places and the world. Moreover, its role in learning is quintessential. To put bodies in place we have to reconceptualise learning differently. We have to make an 'ontological turn' from an epistemological position - placing and attending - to the 'lived body' in the practices of learning, in education (e.g. teacher preparation) and other professions (e.g. medicine).[11] Human practice does not only involve the spatial body, it is also constitutive of emotions, narratives, memories and histories.[12] This discussion is focused on the spatial body.

3.　　'Placing' Bodies, 'Em-body-ing' Places

Our bodily positions and movements configure places. Katz describes the general posture and positioning of people when they are using their mobile phone in public spaces - public pacing, a cricked neck, bent over whilst walking.[13] To make bodies matter and to discuss mobility in corporeal terms as well, I frame the body in four ways. This 'procedure' is not intended to quarter the body or divide it into neat sections. Instead it is a strategy, a heuristic device to initiate a way of seeing the body in educational research partially and temporarily. I draw from Don Ihde's book, *Bodies in Technology*, to begin to understand the body-technology relations from a phenomenological standpoint.[14] Ihde's account makes a distinction between a 'sensory body' and a 'cultural body.' 'Sensory body' refers to relational abilities such as spatial orientation and movement, as well as emotions. 'Cultural body' refers to embodied experiences that are culturally constructed, and that vary from culture to culture. According to Andrew Feenberg, Ihde's book has only focused on 'active' bodies.[15] Feenberg instead suggests that we also have to focus on passive bodies. To this end, he added the types of the 'dependent body' and the 'extended body.' These articulate the passive dimension of 'em-body-ing.' In short, there is a duality of body in practice - the body both acts and is acted upon by others.[16] These body types are introduced here not as 'essences' but as effects of em-body-ing.

The most obvious example of dependent embodiment would perhaps be in places of health services and medicine (e.g. hospitals, clinics). In surgery, or inside the operating room, the body becomes the object of technology. However, we do not have to wait for such an occasion or trouble ourselves with a medical visit; how we become objects of the technologies we use can be experienced with our mobile devices, such as mobile phones, which are considered to be prosthetics of the body.[17] To be without them, or to forget them somewhere, can cause a lot of frustration and discomfort.[18]

Unlike a technologically-dependent body, the 'extended body' is in control of technology. The focus is not on usage though, but on the consequences of its use to the body and on the subject's awareness of those consequences. To explain this fourth body type, Feenberg revisits Merleau-Ponty's discussion of a blind man whose bodily extension is the cane. He agrees that the cane extends the blind man's ability to sense the world. However, Feenberg suggests that this view is rather incomplete as the cane does more than sense the world; it also reveals the blind man as blind. His body is extended not only in the active dimension on which Ihde and Merleau-Ponty focus but also in the passive dimension of its own objectivity. In short, '[t]he extended body, then, is not only the body that acts through a technical mediation, but also a body that signifies itself through that mediation.'[19]

Based on ethnographic data, Al-Mahmood illustrates dependent and extended bodies, thus constructing an alternative narrative, an otherness embedded within the text.[20] The focus of the paper was spatialities, or spatial imaginings. In light of what Clifford calls 'ethnographic allegory,' this 'other' meaning is not an interpretation layered over the original account or transcribed interview data.[21] Rather, Al-Mahmood illustrates a condition of the account's meaningfulness. 'Ethnographic texts are inescapably allegorical, and a serious acceptance of this fact changes the ways they can be written and read.'[22] With the increasing convergence of spatiality and mobility, my discussion foregrounds the mobilities with the body behind the spatial imaginings that Al-Mahmood has described. Al-Mahmood's interest in at least two related papers lies in the interaction of spatiality, identity and online learning.[23] She cites Paechter, et al., in her introduction to both papers, where she captures the significance of examining 'embodied individuals' - bodies in spaces.[24] Not only do we need to pay attention to the spac-ings and plac-ings of classrooms, labs and lecture halls and how these affect the ways we learn, 'but also how we as embodied individuals are changed by our experiences in these spaces.'[25] In her more recent paper, Al-Mahmood discusses two lecturers, Barrie and Sam, as vibrant and experienced face-to-face lecturers.[26] And yet the affective effect of 'being online' affected each of them differently. For Barrie, it was enabling, whereas for Sam, it was disabling.

Barrie has difficulties hearing and wears a hearing aid. However, the online chatroom allowed Barrie to communicate clearly with his students without his hearing aid. The extended body in the physical space was enabled without extensions or hearing aids online.

> I have a lot of trouble hearing the students in class and that might be one of the reasons why I am so wildly enthusiastic about the chat room because I can hear them ... and I say to them ..."I can hear what you're saying!"[27]

Barrie has the option to use either his hearing aids or his computer to hear his students depending on where he is, in the classroom or in the chat room. Either way, the important thing is that he could 'hear' his students. However, the mobilities that emerge in Barrie's embodied practices do not quite end there. There is more difference in mobility that is subtly revealed to us. The signification of the passive, extended body with a hearing aid, the awareness that the technology signifies to others that Barrie has a hearing difficulty, is lost and perhaps rendered insignificant online. In the virtual space, his inability to hear does not matter. In this instance, the passive (disabled) dimension of the body in a physical place is rendered active (enabled) online. Therefore, the trajectories of our mobilities are clearly placed through and with our bodies.

Barrie's hearing difficulty became absent, invisible, online, together with the rest of his body. His presence could be read by distant and absent others, a presence 'written' in one place and embodied elsewhere - an absent presence which will be discussed in the next section. However, his positive experience online was not shared by another lecturer, Sam.

> It can't convey me very well! …Yes well actually I think, online, I'm fairly boring. I respond, I try to raise it a bit, but it's nothing like my face-to-face where you can have a joke and where I do a lot more, you can see I talk a lot but as I don't write a lot, I feel I can't convey me very well, down in writing …
>
> …Well I find it tiring to type, it still doesn't, although I am not a bad typist, but it still doesn't come terribly easily….[28]

For Barrie, his inability to hear clearly was made invisible online. He could hear and was more present and augmented by his physical absence. Sam had a different experience. She was disabled, her ability to communicate by the act of talking was muted by keyboard strokes and text on screen. She felt less present online. She wanted to move 'completely' and occupy the online space corporeally. This is not a matter of right or wrong. It is a matter of meaning and experience, which defines the limits of our skin. Consequently, there is a tendency to measure the mediated space and bodily presence against a full bodily co-presence.[29] Hence the feeling of loss or partiality online as described by Sam above. But as already discussed, our bodies are plastic, we can extend our presence linguistically and imagine ourselves differently.[30]

4.   Absent Presence

A sense of 'absent presence' is made possible and sustained by technologies of separation from the immediate, physical space, such as mobile phones and iPods. Mobile technologies have progressively empowered individuals precisely by removing them from the physicality of immediate relations. What happens if presence and absence, or proximity and distance, are not opposed to one another? Subjects are compelled or orientated towards interiority - a public retreat. Consequently, public spaces are no longer made up of chance encounters. Instead, subjects are 'alone together.'[31] Gergen has identified four challenges posed by the integration or combination of absence and presence as follows:

1. erosion of co-presence or flat community
2. erosion of a coherent and centered sense of self and moral bearings
3. devaluation of the depth of relationships
4. uprooting of meaning from its material context.[32]

The convergence of spatiality and mobility leads to the convergence of the cognitive and the physical, alienating co-presence in public spaces. The immediate and the direct are no longer necessarily the priority, in fact relationships with 'absent others' are sustained more within mediated spaces. Mobile users consume space and appropriate it according to their needs.[33] Besides, there is evidence that tasks are increasingly synchronised to music using iPods.[34]

The above challenges are discussed further by focusing on the combined presence and absence of people in subtle ways in terms of: (a) public privacy - that of being physically (bodily) present and cognitively absent; and (b) isolated connectivity - that of being present with 'absent others' (absent bodies). Such are the norms of the inherent person-to-person system that has emerged in the convergence of communication and spatial mobility.

All social life - work, family, education, and politics - presume relationships of intermittent presence and modes of absence depending in part upon the multiple technologies of travel and communication that move objects, people, ideas, and images across varying distances. 'Presence is thus intermittent, achieved, performed and always interdependent with other processes of connection and communication.'[35] Presence has become body-less.

5.   Public Privacy

In educational institutions, the 'silence rule' in libraries allows for public privacy. 'Silence please' signs are mounted on walls to remind each visitor that one should not disturb others by making noise. With iPods and headphones, such noise may be contained and silence maintained not only in libraries but also in other public spaces. Privatising public spaces is not a new phenomenon. Such a strategy has been practiced long before the invention of mobile phones, radios, computers and other portable gadgets. Reading a book in buses, trains and planes is commonly practiced in order to free ourselves from the immediate social surroundings and to filter out the noise of public spaces. Reading in public spaces signifies that one is unavailable, absorbed psychologically or cognitively with the text at hand.

With the proliferation of mobile phones and other devices, individuals can easily evade any interaction with surrounding 'present others' by making a call or listening to music using a walkman, an MP3 player, or an iPod. These are 'gating' or 'filtering strategies,' or even 'symbolic bodyguards,'[36] particularly for women who do not want to appear alone in public. This is a form of emancipation from the public - to protect oneself from the public gaze and to enjoy civil inattention within crowded or densely populated places.

Furthermore, our mobilities are also mediated by sound. Listening through earphones is another example of the personalisation of public space. An iPod user claims a mobile and auditory territory through a specific form of 'sensory filtering,' tuning out unwanted sounds through his or her own 'soundscape.'[37] Mobile phone or iPod users are 'physically present here,' but 'cognitively absent.' 'Their awareness and behaviour is totally in private cyberspace even though their bodies are in public space.'[38] Absent presence is reinforced by iPods as the headphones makes one 'invisible.' With the white cable dangling in between one's ears, one earns the right to be left alone.[39]

The role of the media in privatising public spaces is not confined to mobile technologies but increasingly also involves the placing of fixed media technologies such as TV screens in an array of public spaces such as airports, shops, planes, and buses[40] - not to mention that the availability of WIFI connections in such places engages subjects with 'absent others.' Inevitably, public privacy re-orders social spaces. Intimacy with absent others is possible through media-generated forms of privacy. This renders 'present others' absent, thus distancing their proximity.

6.   Isolated Connectivity

Media technologies simultaneously isolate and connect.[41] The more we privatise our spaces of communication, the more isolated we become in public spaces. Phone space is prioritised over local space. Geographical space becomes recessed as the speaker occupies or moves to 'another' space. The desire for mediated withdrawal is evident in physical segregation (e.g. different rooms in a household), which is associated with media segregation.[42] In effect, we may be in the same physical space, but with different experiences. This is easily illustrated in the classroom when students bring their own laptops and 'move' to other, virtual, spaces and connect with absent others. Mobile media enable us to 'ctrl-alt-del' our surroundings to filter experience and attend to other things. To maintain immediate, physical presence, students are usually asked not to bring their laptops to class, whereas we are asked to switch off our phones in conferences and meetings. In short, our physical contact and bodies do not guarantee or afford our presence. Furthermore, public spaces are being increasingly designed for minimal or no contact at all - self-check-in counters in airports, purchase of train and bus tickets, even coffee dispensed from a machine. Consequently, community becomes an accumulation of privatised, isolated connectivities.

7.   Conclusion
This chapter focused on those who have been placed 'elsewhere' spatially and bodily. The starting point of cyber-research given our mobilities is *(t)here* - meaning that it is no longer confined within the identification of a physical place to perform ethnography or phenomenology. Instead, the starting point of place implies being elsewhere, mostly in seemingly body-less situations, whilst remaining 'here.' The question that is then asked brings us to an ontological and corporeal turn; how we learn is not just an encounter of intellects mediated by tools, but an encounter of bodies in spaces as part of the ways of knowing in motion.[43] The contingent and distant relations of individual bodies with 'absent others' (both human and non-human, both near and far) assemble cyber-research differently.

Acknowledgement

The arguments and position of this chapter within its main headings were firstly contributed and published in the Taylor and Francis Group's journal, Learning, Media and Technology in the following articles:

Enriquez, J. G. 'Being *(T)here*: Mobilising "Mediaspaces" of Learning'. *Learning Media and Technology*, 2012, <http://www.tandfonline.com/doi/abs/10.1080/17439884.2012.685744>.

——, 'Tug-o-where: Situating Mobilities of Learning (T)here'. *Learning, Media & Technology*, Vol. 36, No. 1, 2011, pp. 39-53.

Notes

¹ M. Crang, 'Public Space, Urban Space and Electronic Space: Would the Real City Please Stand Up?', *Urban Studies*, Vol. 37, No. 2, 2000, pp. 301-317.

[2] M. Callon and J. Law, 'Absent Presence: Localities, Globalities and Methods', *Environment and Planning D: Society and Space*, Vol. 22, No. 1, 2004, pp. 3-11.

[3] H. Geser, 'Towards a (Meta-)Sociology of the Digital Sphere', Zurich, December 2002, <http://socio.ch/intcom/t_hgeser13.htm>.

[4] M. Bull, *Sound Moves: iPod Culture and Urban Experience*, Routledge, London, 2007; Callon and Law, op. cit.; Geser, op. cit; H. Geser, 'Towards a Sociological Theory of the Mobile Phone', Zurich, March 2004 (Release 3.0), <http://socio.ch/mobile/t_geser1.htm>.

[5] J. S. Donath, 'Identity and Deception in the Virtual Community', in *Communities in Cyberspace*, M. A. Smith and P. Kollock (eds), Routledge, London, 1999, pp. 29-59.

[6] M. Strathern, *Partial Connections*, Rowman & Littlefield, Savage, MD, 1991.

[7] Geser, 'Digital Sphere'; J. Urry, *Mobilities*, Polity, Cambridge, 2007.

[8] For examples see R. Barnacle, 'Gut Instinct: The Body and Learning', *Educational Philosophy and Theory*, Vol. 41, No. 1, 2009, pp. 22-33; L. Bresler, *Knowing Bodies. Moving Minds*, Kluwer, Dordrecht, 2004; G. Dall'Alba and R Barnacle, 'Embodied Knowing in Online Environments', *Educational Philosophy and Theory*, Vol. 37, No. 5, 2005, pp. 719-744; and K. M. Leander and J. F. Lovvorn, 'Literacy Networks: Following the Circulation of Texts, Bodies, and Objects in the Schooling and Online Gaming of One Youth', *Cognition and Instruction*, Vol. 24, No. 3, 2006, pp. 291-340.

[9] K. J. Gergen, 'The Challenge of Absent Presence', in *Perpetual Contact, Mobile Communication, Private Talk, Public Performance*, J. E. Katz and M. A. Aakhus (eds), Cambridge University Press, Cambridge, 2002, pp. 227-241; Bull, op. cit; B. Wellman, 'Physical Place and Cyberplace: The Rise of Personalized Networking'. *International Journal of Urban and Regional Research*, Vol. 25, No. 2, 2001, pp. 228-252.

[10] T. Cresswell, *Place: A Short Introduction*, Blackwell, Oxford, 2004.

[11] For examples see R. Barnett, 'Recapturing the Universal in the University', *Educational Philosophy and Theory*, Vol. 37, No. 6, 2005, pp. 785-797; Barnacle, op. cit.; A. Mol, *The Body Multiple: Ontology in Medical Practice*, Duke University Press, Durham, 2002.

[12] See K. Simonsen, 'Place as Encounters: Practice, Conjunction and Co-existence', in *Mobility and Place: Enacting Northern European Peripheries*, J. O. Bærenholdt and B. Granås (eds), Ashgate, Burlington, VT, 2008, pp. 13-25.

[13] J. E. Katz, 'Mobile Communication and the Transformation of Daily Life: The Next Phase of Research on Mobiles', in *Thumb Culture: The Meaning of*

Mobile Phones for Society, P. Glotz, S. Bertschi, C. Locke (eds), Transcript Verlag, Bielefeld, 2005, pp. 171-184.

[14] D. Ihde, *Bodies in Technology*, University of Minnesota Press, Minneapolis, 2002.

[15] A. Feenberg, 'Active and Passive Bodies: Comments on Don Ihde's Bodies in Technology', *Techné*, Vol. 7, No. 2, 2003, pp. 102-109.

[16] Ibid.

[17] Bull, op. cit.

[18] Ibid.

[19] Freenberg, op. cit., p. 103.

[20] R. Al-Mahmood, 'Spatialities and Online Teaching: To, From and Beyond Academy', in *Proceedings of the 25th ASCILITE Conference: In Hello! Where Are You in the Landscape of Educational Technology?*, Melbourne, Australia, December 2008, pp. 11-22.

[21] J. Clifford, 'On Ethnographic Allegory', in *The Postmodern Turn: New Perspectives on Social Theory*, S. Siedman (ed), Cambridge University Press, Cambridge, 1994.

[22] Ibid., p. 206.

[23] Al-Mahmood, 'Spatial Imaginings: Learning and Identity in Online Environments', in *Proceedings of the 23rd Annual ASCILITE Conference: Who's Learning? Whose Technology?*, Sydney, Australia, December 2006, pp. 43-54.

[24] C. Paechter, R. Edwards, R. Harrison, P. Twining (eds), *Learning, Space and Identity*, Paul Chapman Pub. in association with the Open University, London, 2001.

[25] Al-Mahmood, op. cit, p. 43; Al-Mahmood, 'Spatialities and Online Teaching', p. 11.

[26] Al-Mahmood, op. cit.

[27] Ibid., p. 13.

[28] Ibid., p.18.

[29] Ihde, op. cit.

[30] Feenberg, op. Cit.

[31] Bull, op. cit.

[32] Gergen, op. cit.

[33] Wellman, op. cit.

[34] Bull, op. cit.

[35] Urry, op. cit., p. 47.

[36] Bull, op. cit; A. Lasen, *The Social Shaping of Fixed and Mobile Networks: A Historical Comparison*, University of Surrey, DWRC, 2002.

[37] Bull, op. cit.

[38] Wellman, op. cit., p. 240.

[39] R. Sennett, *The Conscience of the Eye*, Faber, London, 1990.
[40] Bull, op. cit.
[41] Ibid.
[42] S. Douglas, *Listening in, Radio and the American Imagination*. University of Minnesota Press, Minneapolis, 2004.
[43] Dall'Alba and Barnacle, op. cit.

Bibliography

Al-Mahmood, R., 'Spatial Imaginings: Learning and Identity in Online Environments', in *Proceedings of the 23rd Annual ASCILITE Conference: Who's Learning? Whose Technology?* Sydney, Australia, December 2006, pp. 43-54.

——, 'Spatialities and Online Teaching: To, From and Beyond the Academy', in *Proceedings of the 25th ASCILITE Conference: In Hello! Where Are You in the Landscape of Educational Technology?* Melbourne, Australia, December 2008, pp. 11-22.

Barnacle, R., 'Gut Instinct: The Body and Learning'. *Educational Philosophy and Theory*, Vol. 41, No. 1, 2009, pp. 22-33.

Barnett, R., 'Recapturing the Universal in the University'. *Educational Philosophy and Theory*, Vol. 37, No. 6, 2005, pp. 785-797.

Bresler, L., *Knowing Bodies. Moving Minds*. Kluwer, Dordrecht, 2004.

Bull, M. *Sound Moves: iPod Culture and Urban Experience*. Routledge, London, 2007.

Callon, M. and Law, J., 'Absent Presence: Localities, Globalities and Methods'. *Environment and Planning D: Society and Space*, Vol. 22, No. 1, 2004, pp. 3-11.

Clifford, J., 'On Ethnographic Allegory', in *The Postmodern Turn: New Perspectives on Social Theory*, S. Siedman (ed), Cambridge University Press, Cambridge, 1994, pp. 205-228.

Crang, M., 'Public Space, Urban Space and Electronic Space: Would the Real City Please Stand Up?' *Urban Studies*, Vol. 37, No. 2, 2000, pp. 301-317.

——, 'Qualitative Methods: Touchy, Feely, Look-see?' *Progress in Human Geography*, Vol. 27, No. 4, 2003, pp. 494-504.

Cresswell, T., *Place: A Short Introduction*. Blackwell, Oxford, 2004.

Dall'Alba, G., and Barnacle, R., 'An Ontological Turn for Higher Education'. *Studies in Higher Education*, Vol. 32, No, 6, 2007, pp. 679-691.

——, 'Embodied Knowing in Online Environments'. *Educational Philosophy and Theory*, Vol. 37, No. 5, 2005, pp. 719-744.

Donath, J. S., 'Identity and Deception in the Virtual Community', in *Communities in Cyberspace*. M. A. Smith and P. Kollock (eds), Routledge, London, 1999. pp. 29-59.

Douglas, S., *Listening in. Radio and the American Imagination*. University of Minnesota Press, Minneapolis, 2004.

Feenberg, A., 'Active and Passive Bodies: Comments on Don Ihde's Bodies in Technology'. *Techné*, Vol. 7, No. 2, 2003, pp. 102-109.

Gergen, K. J., 'The Challenge of Absent Presence', in *Perpetual Contact, Mobile Communication, Private Talk, Public Performance*. J. E. Katz and M. A. Aakhus (eds), Cambridge University Press, Campbridge, 2002, pp. 227-241.

Geser, H., 'Towards a (Meta-)Sociology of the Digital Sphere'. Zurich, December 2002, <http://socio.ch/intcom/t_hgeser13.htm>.

——, 'Towards a Sociological Theory of the Mobile Phone'. Online Publications, Zurich, March 2004 (Release 3.0), <http://socio.ch/mobile/t_geser1.htm>.

Glotz, P., Bertschi, S., Locke, C. (eds), *Thumb Culture: The Meaning of Mobile Phones for Society*. Transcript Verlag, Bielefeld, 2005.

Ihde, D., *Bodies in Technology*. University of Minnesota Press, Minneapolis, 2002.

Katz, J. E. and Aakhus, M. A., *Perpetual Contact: Mobile Communication, Private Talk, Public Performance*. Cambridge University Press, Cambridge, 2002.

Katz, J. E., 'Mobile Communication and the Transformation of Daily Life: The Next Phase of Research on Mobiles', in *Thumb Culture: The Meaning of Mobile Phones for Society*. P. Glotz, S. Bertschi, C. Locke (eds), Transcript Verlag, Bielefeld, 2005, pp. 171-184.

Lasen, A., *The Social Shaping of Fixed and Mobile Networks: A Historical Comparison*. University of Surrey, DWRC, 2002.

Leander, K. M. and Lovvorn, J. F., 'Literacy Networks: Following the Circulation of Texts, Bodies, and Objects in the Schooling and Online Gaming of One Youth'. *Cognition and Instruction*, Vol. 24, No. 3, 2006, pp. 291-340.

Mol, A., *The Body Multiple: Ontology in Medical Practice*. Duke University Press, Durham, 2002.

Paechter, C., Edwards, R., Harrison, R., Twining, P. (eds), *Learning, Space and Identity*. Paul Chapman Pub. in association with the Open University, London, 2001.

Sennett, R., *The Conscience of the Eye*. Faber, London, 1990.

Simonsen, K., 'Place as Encounters: Practice, Conjunction and Co-existence', in *Mobility and Place: Enacting Northern European Peripheries*. J. O. Bærenholdt and B. Granås (eds), Ashgate, Burlington, VT, 2008, pp. 13-25.

Strathern, M., *Partial Connections*. Rowman & Littlefield, Savage, MD: Rowman & Littlefield, 1991.

Urry, J., *Mobilities*. Polity, Cambridge, 2007.

Wellman, B., 'Physical Place and Cyberplace: The Rise of Personalized Networking'. *International Journal of Urban and Regional Research*, Vol. 25, No. 2, 2001, pp. 228-252.

Judith Guevarra Enriquez probes and puzzles over literacy practices, bodily issues in (dis)located spaces, oxymoronic arrangements of (im)mobilities and simply meddles with 'softer' and more organic alternatives (closer to our 'guts') for mediated research approaches, articulated through actor-network theory, sociology, organisation science, computer-supported collaborative work, critical literacy studies and cultural studies.

Part 3

Cybercultures and the Public Sphere

Post-Fordist Communities and Cyberspace: A Critical Approach

Jernej Prodnik

Abstract
This chapter approaches from a critical perspective questions regarding so-called 'virtual communities.' Because the origins of every community arise from language and communication it is impossible to distinguish between 'genuine,' communities and imaginary, or even 'fake,' communities. It is, however, possible to discern both their (changing) stability and solidity within specific social conditions and the ways in which these communities are imagined. This social-constructivist approach is further developed by proposing a three-fold construction of community while simultaneously demonstrating the falsehood of the 'virtual' versus 'real' dichotomy. Throughout the chapter, determinist paradigms are questioned and demystified by demonstrating how both optimistic and pessimistic *technologistic* currents fail to acknowledge wider structural changes in capitalism, and attempt to depoliticise these developments by providing escapist or unitary solutions to social antagonisms. Because technology is neither autonomous nor neutral, and always develops within a complex conjuncture of power relationships, there is a need to look beyond views that solely blame technology for social transformations. In the time of 'liquid modernity' and post-Fordist capitalism, temporary *cloakroom* communities have become a rule, and this chapter aims at revising our understanding of their role in society.

Key Words: Capitalism, post-Fordism, imagined communities, liquid modernity, language, myth, pseudo-environment, worldliness, virtual.

*****

1.   Introduction

In this chapter I approach questions regarding cyberspace and changes concerning communities from a critical perspective. My analysis is aimed at re-conceptualising communities, including 'virtual' ones, by demonstrating how they are always socially constructed through the use of language. This enables me to illustrate the non-existence of a 'virtual' community as such, or at least at its lack of separation from a 'real' social environment. The fluidity and temporariness of contemporary communities, or in some cases even pronouncements of the end of communities as we know them, that are commonly blamed on new technology, will be discussed with respect to the social transformations of recent decades, in particular the structural changes in capitalism. Capitalism needs the constant and rapid revolutionising of technology, as this is often the driving force for its reproduction and growth.

When analysing new technologies, including the Internet, we are able to see a common pattern seen in previous technological revolutions.[1] Technology, in relation to some social practice or social actor, is subtly regarded either as a potential saviour or, in a more pessimistic view, as something that will aggravate social conditions or disintegrate communities further.[2] I want to reject both these views as inadequate; I will however acknowledge them as important indicators of where society stands and what may be seen as the main social antagonisms within it. It will be argued that these antagonisms can be tackled only by political means in the broadest and most democratic sense of these words. When approaching these antagonisms from other perspectives, such as the above-mentioned paradigms, there is a danger of somehow mythologising them and providing inappropriate, even reactive, solutions.

What is crucial at this point is to distinguish these approaches from the early utopian and dystopian attempts that have historically also accompanied new communication technologies, but that usually are fairly limited at elaborating changes in society. This is the case with journalistic discourse, the e-utopianism of virtual agorae, political discourses such as Al Gore's concerning global community and prosperity, and the hopes that the Internet will overcome social inequalities of all forms. Such approaches are easily identified as being socially ignorant, ideologically questionable, or politically motivated in their very *explicit* emphasis on technology and technological revolution as the sole agent of social change, particularly as new technologies are normalised. Consequently, they are quickly and rightly questioned.

The two paradigms I oppose in this chapter are primarily regarded as important additions in the academic sphere, as in most cases they enable in-depth studies of social life. Their emphasis on the autonomy of technology is very much *implicit* and hidden, as the presence of technology is much less visible and at most regarded as only *one* of the factors in social changes. Nevertheless, in the last instance we are able to see that this is still by far the most important factor, hidden behind others.

My approach is of a different nature, and can perhaps be best summarised with Armand Mattelart's words that 'each historical period and each type of society has the communicational configuration it deserves.'[3] Technology never develops or comes into existence in a vacuum, outside of society and social relations, which requires us to look beyond simple technological developments that are repeatedly featured in deterministic arguments. Technology can be used, misused, and abused by those in power. Its development always depends on the outcome of social struggles rather than some quasi-natural evolution/development.[4]

It also has to be noted that conceptualising 'community' has always been a slippery terrain, which is one of the reasons why I will not be offering any 'proper' definitions of what this term should mean. I am, however, opposed to any communitarian understanding that, at least implicitly, regards community as some kind of homogeneous amalgam. I contend that this is a regressive response to the dangers of the 'world': in this case the instabilities and dangers accompanying life in contemporary societies. We can also see another, optimistic conceptualisation of the 'virtual' community and, like the first type, it goes hand in hand with the two aforementioned paradigms. According to this view, the 'virtual' is somehow separated from the 'real,' thus completely creating another world. As this can in fact never be realised, this view at the end of the line avoids tackling (or at least properly approaching) the same problems as the communitarian view.

2.   From Pseudo-Communities to Imagined Communities

James R. Beniger's concept of 'pseudo-community' is often reckoned to be a pessimistic outlook on the consequences of the new media for traditional communities. His concept, in essence, questions impersonal communication and idealises face-to-face relationships, while claiming that the mass media and other developments in technology have eroded the intimate community relationships, the sincerity, and the authentic proximity distinctive of the *Gemeinschaft*.[5] Interpersonal relationships are suddenly confused with mass messages and, for Beniger, 'the change constitutes nothing less than a transformation of traditional community into impersonal association - toward an unimagined hybrid of the two extremes that we might call *pseudo-community*.'[6]

Beniger reproduces quite a few of the fears that have been articulated by other contemporary technological pessimists, even though he wrote before the rise of the Internet and cyberspace. Apart from being completely outdated because of the interactivity integral to digital communication)[7] - which opened up the optimistic paradigm of *community renaissance* and in part influenced an often mentioned transformation from mass to network society - Beniger's theory should be subjected to scrutiny because of its technological determinism. Technology, as such, is not autonomous; therefore there is a need to look at the wider structural changes in society that stimulate (or at least parallel) developments in technology, influence it, and define its use.

It should be noted that the alleged consequences of technology, and the supposed in-authenticity of social relations that are mediated through it, still determine how people understand the Internet and virtual spaces (promoted especially by popular and journalistic discourses). As I attempt to point out in this chapter, however, the virtual-real dichotomy is in fact completely false, and this question should be approached from a different perspective. Speaking of a *virtual* community can also be viewed as somehow odd and brings to the fore many paradoxes, which so commonly plague different conceptions of 'community' as they centre around false questions.

To talk about community is first and foremost to talk about language and communication. As the philosopher John R. Searle has demonstrated, human reality is created and maintained by speech acts, and thus exists in and through language. Language and social cooperation enable the creation of institutional reality and structures that enable the construction of a social and political environment that achieves the status of objective social fact.[8] The reproduction of social institutions through language was perhaps best illustrated by Benedict Anderson in his seminal historical study, *Imagined Communities*.[9] His discussion is well-known amongst authors writing about virtual communities. Harris Breslow and Ilhem Allagui in this volume, amongst others, base their arguments on it and are paving the way for the comprehension of communities as constructs that have their origins in communication. For Anderson, 'the most important thing about language is its capacity for generating imagined communities, building in effect *particular solidarities.*'[10] A useful term for describing this process is 'communification'; according to this view communication can be formative of a community. People without direct interpersonal relations imagine themselves as members of a community through the communication of symbols and cultural artefacts of a particular kind, which can arouse deep and strong attachments.[11] All communities are imagined, according to Anderson, perhaps even those that are most tightly knit together, and they should be distinguished by the style in which they are imagined, not by their authenticity or falsity.[12]

However, 'imagined' should not be confused with 'imaginary,' and Anderson points out that 'the imagined world is visibly rooted in everyday life … fiction seeps quietly and continuously into reality, creating that remarkable confidence of community in anonymity which is the hallmark of modern nations.'[13] Anderson was not the first person to stress the importance of language and communication to human beings, as this question has preoccupied both philosophers and social theorists since the beginnings of the twentieth century. Charles H. Cooley, for example, argued that 'the achievement of speech is commonly and properly regarded as the distinctive trait of man [sic], as the gate by which he emerged from his pre-human state,' while at the same time acknowledging the flexibility of human nature.[14] John Dewey, another pragmatist, went even further when he directly connected 'communities' with 'communication' and the things that people have in common, stating that there is more than a verbal tie between them, while also pointing out the necessity of human agency in relation to the construction of social institutions.[15] Anderson's study was nevertheless significant because he demonstrated that one of the most commonly naturalised and de-historicised examples of the processes discussed above - national identity and its derivatives - is actually formed through communication.

All of the aforementioned approaches can be regarded as proceeding from social constructionism, similar to Anthony Cohen's, who outlined his views on the concept of 'community' in his book *The Symbolic Construction of Community*.[16] According to Graham Day,

> the social constructionist spotlight is turned more on the ways in which communities are brought into being through the interpretive activities of their members, and registered among the concepts which they use in everyday talk and interaction.[17]

This is an important argument, as the subjective dimensions of community creation and existence are brought to the fore. Cohen also insisted in his approach that there should be no assumptions regarding homogeneity of individual meanings concerning certain communities.

3.   A Threefold Construction of Community?

Approaches that emphasise the subjective dimensions of communities and the necessities of everyday life in their reproduction, both of which can be clearly seen in Anderson's study, are of considerable importance when we approach problems concerning cyberspace and the 'virtual' versus 'real' dimensions of communities. We can presuppose that there cannot be a community that, on the one hand, has no chance of seriously changing one's everyday life and, on the other hand, does not reproduce itself through this same everyday lifestyle. There also cannot be a community that at least potentially has no effect on the material conditions of one's life and common being with (and of) other people. Furthermore, no community can exist without communication in the broadest sense of this word, imparting its symbolic meaning to every single person. These inseparable dimensions can form a threefold construction of community, namely: a) subjective (symbolic) dimension; b) lived practice and everyday life (e.g. linguistic context, experience, daily *living*, the community etc.); c) objective material structures and their manifestation.

I have quite forcefully separated these dimensions to make my argument clearer; in reality they are always closely knit together and interdependent and cannot in fact be separated, as one dimension would not exist without the others, at least not in the same manner. Even though different social institutions, which are a necessary prerequisite for the existence of communities, may (for example) objectively and even materially exist, they cannot be separated from language (which enables them) and symbolic meaning, or their (subjective) everyday use. We can take, for example, the national flag of Slovenia or a flag of an English football club, as they are all, like many other institutions, material manifestations of certain types of (imagined) communities. Even though both their existence and the existence of communities are widely recognised objective facts, they have no meaning without people subjectively recognising them as such. People inside or outside of a certain community may at the same time have different subjective perceptions of these artefacts and their perceptions can also depend on the social context of these artefacts' use. To sum up the argument: we can say that communities, just like social institutions, must exist subjectively (members of community believe in it and 'know' that others share this belief) in order to exist objectively; at the same time communities need different social institutions that manifest themselves in everyday life - and their constant daily or ritual use - for them to exist.

A.   Subjective Dimension: There Is No 'Virtual' Community
Following Cohen, many boundaries of different communities exist only in the eyes of their members, as they share the same symbols within certain cultures, and give these symbols particular meanings. These meanings may or may not be seen by people 'outside' of the community, or even in the same way amongst members of the same community. The meanings of these symbols can be of particular importance to every member and consequently help to maintain the existence of a particular community. Boundaries, which are constituted through symbols and concepts, form what we could call 'special' communities, as there is something special about every particular community that makes it distinctive from other communities for its members as they internalise its life and culture. Communities are therefore largely based on the subjective experiences of their members, on language and the communication of symbols that keeps communities alive. Members of a given community more often than not naturalise its existence, even though it depends on their symbolic communication to actually keep this community alive, and their subjective experience and recognition of it as in fact existing.[18]
It is therefore disputable to debate 'virtual' communities as such, or even more so to debate their separation from 'real' social conditions. Nobody can be part of something that is 'virtual,' but rather of a certain, very specific kind of a community, as we can elaborate following Cohen. Either there is in fact no such thing as a *virtual community* or we are simply talking about special communities, which are *imagined* through a specific medium or technology. 'Virtual' community is presently, to the contrary, perceived and named after this same *product* enabling the imagination. Further, if one follows this reasoning, a 'virtual' community should be, after all, nothing more than a community in its own world, somewhere on the Internet. How

could these communities be under any circumstances real, if they are apparently *virtual*, which is almost the opposite of the real, the (so to say) non-real, and fictionalisation-of-the-real? The word alone carries with itself an obvious connotation of something that is at worst imaginary, or at best not genuine (enough) when comparing it to some 'natural' notion of actually existing and *real-life* living.

It should be stressed that all communities are subject to processes of imagination. In fact, we can say that the Internet is just an upgraded apparatus of the imagination, enabling new ways for this process of imagination to work. One can also say that it is cyberspace that can serve as the best example of the power of communication itself, for if communication is to carry any force, it *must* have some direct 'material,' real-life consequences.

We should be careful, however, not to reduce community only to symbolic identification, but to acknowledge the two aforementioned aspects of its existence. Furthermore, according to Žižek, the bond linking members of communities always implies a relationship towards the Thing, which can be for example 'our way of life' accessible only to 'us', and which 'others' cannot grasp. 'They' even want to steal this Thing, which is materialised through different social practices as rituals or ceremonies, and further reproduced in myths, if we are discussing a very stable community. Community and its symbolic existence are therefore materialised both as (daily, ritualised, etc.) practices and also in artefacts. Members can see these manifestations as defining Us against some outside Other.[19]

B.   The 'Virtual' Versus the 'Real' Opposition

As already discussed, no community can be separated from 'real' social circumstances. Community life might try to somehow avoid this 'outer' reality, or suppress it in the background, but that does not mean that it is, in fact, ever fully detached. On the contrary, if such a separation is wished-for, then this tells us quite a lot about social life itself. The artificial contrast between two supposedly distinct 'worlds' is a dangerous illusion and lays claims to a fundamental mistake in perception: a virtual, or any other supposedly imagined world, is never fully autonomous, for it is always dependent upon socio-economic and socio-cultural processes, physical structures, languages, everyday life, human existence, etc.[20] It is merely another part, aspect, or extension of everyday life, and not in contradiction with our common 'reality.'

As with any other space, cyberspace is a social construct, produced by a dynamic relationship amongst material and semiotic processes.[21] In many ways, social relations in cyberspace (including communities imagined primarily through this new medium) are only a consistent continuation of corresponding relations in the 'real' world, quite similar to the description of communities. As Nunes eloquently puts it, cyberspace is not where we go with technology, but something that we live, 'the user interacts with networked technology as a medium, rather than as a computational device.'[22]

This becomes more obvious first with the normalisation and then with the naturalisation of particular technologies in people's lives, when their use becomes invisible, and a technology is (furthermore) not consciously thought about anymore. Computers and the Internet have already become invisible to their users in their everyday use, and many of the latest social events should serve as evidence of how internalised this new technology and computer mediated communication has already become. One only needs to look at many of the chapters in this volume, a prime example perhaps being Fidele Vlavo's reassessment of a form of civil disobedience that has also spread via the use of the Internet. But this, as she further demonstrates, has in fact brought little change to the existing power relations or inequalities that are constantly reproduced through social structures, therefore proving that problems arise when we try to somehow detach the 'virtual' from the 'real.'

According to Vincent Mosco, it is exactly 'when technologies ... cease to be sublime icons of mythology and enter the prosaic world of banality - when they lose their role as sources of utopian visions - that they become important forces for social and economic change.'[23] As the so-called Iranian 'Twitter revolution' in the summer of 2009 and the recent Wikileaks controversies have illustrated, new technology is already widely used in such a manner. Again, one should be careful not to over-emphasise the role played by technology - a paradigm that is constantly reproduced, especially in journalistic discourse. To give special credit to technology in such events demonstrates an historical blindness; social uprisings have not, after all, originated with the rise of the Internet. Resistance in Iran, for example, did not occur because of some 'digital miracle,' but because of social conditions that pushed people over the edge; and technology was not the main cause for its spread, it was only used as a convenient ready-made tool. It was available, there, and at the end even much more useful for those on 'the outside' than for the organisation of the protesters themselves.

Approaches that place their focus strictly on technology as a rule neglect not only history but, as I contend in the following sections, they also ignore the fact that the rise of specific technologies is always socially dependent. This means that the use of technology and changes to its development are never natural, but the result of complex social relations and, above all, in the interests of power. To put it in Daniel Cohen's terms, 'one cannot grasp the full significance of new technology without understanding how it gets to interact with the organisation of labour and without understanding the consumer society it feeds.'[24] Through an expansion of this type of analysis we are able to go beyond technological determinism in understanding the changes in contemporary society and, consequently, contemporary communities.

As I have discussed, communities are socially constructed through language and communication. We cannot, therefore, decide whether they are in fact genuine or not, and it is also impossible to differentiate them hierarchically with claims that some of them are false and others natural, because they are all social products. We can, however, try to comprehend the ways in which they are imagined, as how communities are mediated has historically changed; or why they have become so fragile and changeable, because it seems an obvious fact that most communities will never be as strongly connected and taken-for-granted as the communities of the past were.

4.   'All Those Communities Melt into Air'

Theoretical understandings of what is meant by 'community' are always in a process of continuous transition, and changes to community life have consequently always echoed changes in society. It should be acknowledged that there has never been a fixed definition of community, or at least a common understanding amongst theoreticians of what an ideal type of community is. Even for the earliest sociologists writing on this question, community in its traditional sense had been in a state of decline and crisis; they generally agreed that this was because of capitalist industrialisation and modern society's propensity for a less tightly connected city life. Their response to these developments was not one-sided, however; for Tönnies the decline of a pre-given *Gemeinschaft* was a pre-requisite for the creation of a public opinion, and hence a public sphere.

It can be noted that, at least since the onset of modernity, interpersonal relationships have been separated from large-scale social formations, going beyond the previous foundational necessity of physical and geographical connection. Indirect relationships by means of markets, politics, social organisations, and communication systems (from railroads to specific use of new types of media), have enabled people to continue to conceive of themselves as part of large collectivities.[25]

Because of these changes, a 'real' sense of community has been pronounced as dead more than once in the past century or so, and this mythological loss of community life and its constant idealisation has been, amongst other things, constantly usurped by an ideology of consumption that appeals to this past through the sale of products that are intended to compensate for this loss.[26] However, 'community' has always revived and, through re-conceptualisations, survived these apocalyptic visions, demonstrating that it is impossible to just dismiss it because society has undergone vast changes. Furthermore, this also demonstrates that it is impossible to fix an ideal-type of community, not least because of authors' ideological differences. Changing means of communication and the spread of new media, especially the rise of the Internet, have indeed offered new ways to imagine and construct both a community and its identity. However, it is necessary to offer a more detailed overview of the ways in which these technological developments corresponded to social transformations since the second part of the twentieth century, especially in relation to structural changes in capitalism.

The latest communication revolution was largely preceded by changes in the social structure, and through further developments the evolution of both technology and society became extremely interdependent and inseparable. Technology came to serve as an important source of legitimation for the social processes that led to the neo-liberal turn, by neutralising and depoliticising them through the naturalisation of these processes as unavoidable facts that are a necessary response to the changes in technology. It is no accident that political questions are often presented as technical, benevolent, and above any ideology. Changes to the social structure since the sixties were, however, influenced both by the so-called cultural shift towards post-modernist practices and vast transformations in capitalism and capitalist states that were in need of restructuring. The latter led to vast changes in modes of production and consumption, from Taylorist and Fordist standardised production to post-Fordist configurations, emphasising the diversification and 'personalisation' of commodities and the creation of other post-industrial products for consumption. These changes were mirrored by new working conditions, which came to be characterised by flexibility, the high volatility of the market-place, temporary and self-employment, part-time contracts, low social security, and deregulation. As a result, an entirely new regime of accumulation emerged, flexible and disorganised, accompanied by new systems of political and social regulation. This became manifest especially throughout the nineties, with the Internet and the so-called 'new economy' in the United States, but actually started to slowly unfold, in most Western nation-states, in the seventies.

These changes (i.e. legitimation, profitability etc.) followed both the crisis of previous configurations of political-economic power of the Keynesian welfare state, and the socio-cultural rebellions against the 'old' system of big state, mass society, hierarchical relationships, and modern meta-narratives. These changes were also, and perhaps most importantly, a reactionary response of the middle classes against the exceptional power of the working classes in the previous system. This conservative response was masked by a rhetoric about individual freedom and empowerment, liberty, and personal responsibility, which largely echoed socio-cultural claims against unification by the new social movements at the end of the sixties, but in fact led to the restoration and consolidation of middle-class power over labour. As Eran Fisher brilliantly demonstrated in his study on 'The Spirit of Networks,' the hegemonic digital discourse concerning network technology assisted this radical switch by providing a critique of Fordist society, transforming the argument of individual liberty and other promises of postmodernity into naturalised technologised legitimation.

> This techno-social constellation of a strong market, a weak state, an empowered individual, and a privatised social sphere is presented as the pinnacle of human progress and as an apolitical situation that has no political alternatives.[27]

To put it in other words; a new network revolution, largely also emerging from the ideals of the new social movements, found its logical compatriot in a neo-liberal project that readily assimilated it, leaving out ideas that could undermine it.[28]

This complex set of relationships that led to the break-up of the old system - having its origins in the sixties and evolving throughout recent decades - brought rapid change and uncertainty, meaning that solid and durable structures were neither wanted nor possible anymore. Zygmunt Bauman's sociology can be seen as a prime example of laying the groundwork for understanding these vast social transformations and their meaning for contemporary societies and communities. Even though Bauman started his work in the last decade of the previous century adopting the concept of post-modernity, he more or less refuted this arguably bankrupt notion later, and denied most of the emancipatory possibilities of post-modern authors, while also acknowledging that 'capitalism and modernity live on, rather, in the permanent revolution of liquid modernity.'[29]

Constant revolutionising in Bauman's theory could be seen as an apt reaction to, and a continuation of, the modern paradigm. He has pointed out that when Marx and Engels famously wrote 'all that is solid melted into air,' we should also acknowledge that the goal was not to remove solids once and for all, but to 'clear a site for new and improved solids.'[30] This argument has been further developed by Mark Fisher who claims that in capitalism, 'all that is solid melts into PR, and late capitalism is defined at least as much by this ubiquitous tendency towards PR-production as it is by the imposition of market mechanisms.'[31] Fisher's claim reveals one of the most important characteristics of post-Fordist capitalism, its constant need for language-production that is instrumentalised for market (ab)use. What used to be an often-unintentional product of state institutions (producing national community and its identity), as Harris Breslow and Ilhem Allagui demonstrate in their chapter, has now been appropriated and instrumentalised by capitalist institutions for the production of consumer identities and communities. The question of the tight connection between language and capitalism is of extreme importance in post-Fordist capitalism, as communication is structurally present both in the sphere of production, of distribution of goods/services, and also the financial sphere; I return to this problem in the next section.[32]

Bauman embraced this new state of things by adopting the metaphor of 'liquidity,' while still stressing much of the same urgency for individual freedom and social plurality as he had in the past. His later work is perhaps best represented by his book *Liquid Modernity*, where Bauman acknowledges that revolutionising is not a break with routines like it has been in the past, but has become a normal practice of contemporary society. It is indicated by flexibility, insecurity, uncertainty, a lack of safety, and precariousness. Stable orientation points and reliable reference frames have, according to Bauman, become almost non-existent: 'the destination of individual self-constructing labours is endemically and incurably undetermined, is not given in advance, and tends to go numerous and profound changes.'[33]

This means that most people do not know where exactly they stand; it is much easier to change form, much like liquids, than to keep the planned life-patterns in linear paths towards certain goals. Bauman insists that these changes in social structure also leave very visible marks on communities and identities. Identities have become the centre of attention for individuals in liquid modernity, they have become a personal project; people buy them in identity-supermarkets and try to avoid any fixations, carrying them 'like a light cloak ready to be taken off at any time.'[34] Similar arguments can be made for communities that are becoming more and more connected (via memberships) to personal identities. Following Bauman's argument, we can say they are surrogates of communities, which are metaphorically named 'cloakroom communities,' fulfilling the need for a spectacle of either ecstasy or panic for a very short time. Their temporality and brevity means that they add little new quality to life as they last as long as the excitement of a certain performance. Their quantity therefore replaces any possibility of quality.[35]

> These are ghost communities, phantom communities, ad hoc communities, carnival communities - the kinds of communities one feels one joins simply by being where others are present, or by sporting badges or other tokens of shared intentions, style or taste … it is the "momentary *experience* of community" that counts.[36]

Even though communities are becoming more and more like projects, this short discussion of Bauman should not be seen as an overtly pessimistic prospect for the future. As a robust critic of modernity, Bauman defies the oppressiveness of traditional conceptions of communities that are very commonly idealised as some lost model that should be retrieved. Unity, homogeneity, and sameness cannot be found in his conceptual repertoire; on the contrary, this is by no means the type of ideal community we should be searching for. It should consist of reflection, criticism, experimentation, and it should never be immune to criticism; no agreement should ever be 'natural' and 'self-evident.' Changes in the consumer society are therefore not necessarily a regression within a community, according to Bauman. They are just a different type of something that we ought to avoid in our quest for a safer and liberated life.[37]

> Community of common understanding, even if reached, will therefore stay fragile and vulnerable, forever in need of vigilance, fortification and defence. People who dream of community in the hope of finding a long-term security which they miss so painfully in their daily pursuits, and of liberating themselves from the irksome burden of ever new and always risky choices, will be sorely disappointed.[38]

5. Human Nature between the 'Environment' and the 'World'

The connections of this increasingly 'liquid' state of social conditions to both political economy outlined in the previous section, and the human dependence on language for constructing socio-cultural life, discussed at the start of this chapter, enables us to trace the deeper roots of contemporary distress and the wider meaning of these structurally conditioned imbalances. The rapid repetition of creative destruction recurrently throws human beings in the 'world,' where they indeed belong by their very nature. Paolo Virno maintains that human beings are separated from other animals by its openness to the 'world' by a high degree of undefined potentiality that originates from the unspecialised character of Homo Sapiens. The human animal, which is in its foundation a *linguistic* animal, can be seen in essence as an undetermined being with no predefined instincts, unlike other animals. While environments are more or less closed and stable, worldliness is a state of potentiality, 'a vital context that always remains partially undetermined and unpredictable.'[39] Human beings, by their very nature, lack a fixed, univocal environment, so they can at the utmost build themselves pseudo-environments of automatism and repetition. This naturally risky instability of a disoriented animal without stable frames of reference can bring to the fore both dangers as well as freedom and creativity.

> There is always something indefinite about the world; it is laden with contingencies and surprises; it is a vital context which is never mastered once and for all; for this reason, it is a source of permanent insecurity. While relative dangers have a "first and last name," absolute dangerous-ness has no exact face and no unambiguous content.[40]

Human potentiality means that 'evil' is derived from the same biolinguistic conditions as 'virtue'; from the human's emptiness, his *openness*; it is what separates man from animal and enables human beings to envision different possibilities. Contemporary changes in capitalism, and other wider social transformations, have brought these basic human virtues of language and communication to the fore, meaning that the subject/worker and his entire life, together with the life of the linguistic community, is put to work. The biological invariant is now exploited, while the centrality of language means that we can talk about the semiotisation of production and social relations in production processes, and in the selling of goods, and consequently of semio-capital; at the same time this became a possible territory of social conflicts.[41]

This is a vast change since the advent of industrial capitalism and the Fordist/Taylorist work constellation, which was full of pseudo-environments that were of exceptionally limited impact (and also possibilities) brought by the potentiality of 'worldliness.' E. P. Thompson long ago understood that the repeating rhythm of the Fordist factory life shifted those (working) habits and discipline to the rest of the labourer's life, coming to a similar conclusion as Antonio Gramsci in his essay on Americanism and Fordism, where Gramsci noted that Fordism is an effort to create a new type of man and human life through purposeful social design.[42] Limiting the human being to repetitive tasks, almost reducing him to a robot, almost deprives him of his humanity. Today, on the contrary, people are continuously exposed to all the risks and uncertainties of the world because of the incredible mutability of the forms of life, the wild flexibility of work, and the needs of production.[43] This is demonstrated by Richard Sennett, for whom the main motto of this new capitalism has become 'No long term.' This does not only produce weak social bonds, it can also corrode trust, loyalty, and commitment. 'What is peculiar about uncertainty today is that it exists without any looming historical disaster; instead, it is woven into the everyday practices of vigorous capitalism. Instability is meant to be normal.'[44] Or, to put it in Virno's terms, once again:

> The biological non-specialisation of *Homo sapiens* does not remain in the background, but gains maximal historical visibility as the universal *flexibility* of labour services. The only professional talent that really counts in post-Fordist production is the habit not to acquire lasting habits, that is the capacity to react promptly to the unusual.[45]

It should come as no surprise that it has become increasingly difficult to talk about substantial, solid communities under such conditions; they once offered important reference points that we can describe as pseudo-environmental niches, where people could find shelter and a hiding place. In the conditions of buoyant laissez-faire capitalism, influencing and combining with liquid social structures and an information glut, what remains are only extremely temporary pseudo-environment niches. People are constantly and forcefully oscillating between them and the world, which is best illustrated by the ever-present possibility of a state of exception or blurring of the line between what is still 'legitimate' and what is 'illegal' (demonstrated for example by the financial meltdown, Guantanamo Bay, etc.).

Robert Putnam, one of the leading advocates of community restoration in America, could not, therefore, be more wrong, when he writes that we cannot search for answers in capitalism. 'A constant can't explain a variable,' he claims, when describing a supposedly faltering American community life,[46] as if there had been no major changes to capitalism in the past decades, or indications that this 'constant' had been completely changed. Moreover, exhibiting a blatant determinism, Putnam goes on to attribute most of the problems to television, which is supposed to be the primary cause for low community involvement, adding that we should kindly ask those wonderful people producing TV programmes to encourage people to get out of their homes. Besides being obviously ignorant to the motives leading owners of the (monopolised) media system, Putnam is also seemingly uninterested in asking *why* it is that this technology has developed in such a direction to 'encourage lethargy and passivity.' Having a 'hunch' that 'the link between channel surfing and social surfing is more than metaphorical' is ludicrous, to say the least.[47]

Social imbalance is, in its essence, inherent to capitalism, and particularly so in capitalism's latest incarnation. A neo-liberal capitalism with extremely flexible working conditions has more or less completely substituted Fordist and Taylorist capitalism, with their jail-like pseudo-environment factories and a Keynesian welfare state, which provided people with at least a basic safety net. Communication is a quintessential part of post-Fordist capitalism and society; its production has become the most important source of capitalist profit and it is used and abused on all possible levels. Most contemporary online communities are condemned to profit-making and capitalist extortion, while they are at the same time quite often themselves a product of such socio-cultural commodification.

Constant disruptions leading to human exposure to unorganised, frequently nonsensical, information and a ceaseless stream of intensive stimuli, which are characteristic of being exposed to the 'world' while also demonstrating the needs of post-Fordist capitalism can, from a different perspective, be seen in Aris Mousoutzanis's discussion of trauma, driven by observations concerning information overload. His findings can, in the context of this discussion, be connected both to Fredric Jameson's observations about post-modernity as the cultural logic of late capitalism, and

Georg Simmel's seminal essay 'The Metropolis and Mental Life,' written at the start of the twentieth century. Simmel drew attention to the 'unexpectedness of violent stimuli' in metropolitan life, which creates a psychological foundation for the rationalistic calculability of modern man, his indifference to all things personal, and primarily instrumentalist relationships. The human subject is 'dealing with persons as with numbers' by creating a 'protective organ for itself against profound disruptions' of the modern city - the seat of the money economy, commercial activity, and the market.[48]

It is crucial to point to the historical dimension here, as Simmel's observations came before the welfare state or the combination of the Fordist and Taylorist organisation of work, when ruthless *laissez-faire* capitalism was in full swing, resting upon the social Darwinist exploitation of ideas of 'the survival of the fittest,' leaving workers with few or no social rights. This was a time when labour was poorly organised, although workers' movements played a highly antagonistic part in social relations, when labour unions had not yet been incorporated into the capitalist state that later became a model of a social, political, and economic partnership. When this settlement between labour and capital came to fruition it, on the one hand, neutralised and depoliticised class struggles and, on the other hand, assured workers of social stability and safety. These characteristics are, in most Western countries, decaying under the wild flexibility of working conditions and the deprivation of social rights. It is obvious that in many ways Simmel's time was very similar to ours.

6.   **The End of Community (...Myth)?**

We encounter several profound problems here. Problems regarding the ideal type of community have already been indicated. Closed, limited communities, with no real reflexivity - those that are at least implicitly proposed by a number of communitarian authors, such as Amitai Etzioni - can in my view be seen as a reactionary and regressive response to the social antagonisms discussed above, an attempt to recover some never-achieved, mythological, community life of a once-upon-a-time dream where everyone got along. Such a vision of community is, of course, repressive of difference and fails to grasp where these antagonisms actually stem from. As Barry Wellman wrote three decades ago; 'for those who seek solidarity in tidy, simple hierarchical group structure, there may *now* be a lost sense of community.'[49] Over the past couple of decades Wellman has been continuously suggesting that we move beyond a conception of community that takes as its starting point local primary bonds, territorial units, and solidarity (i.e., a naturalistic, unitary perspective). His network analytic perspective of a 'community liberated' is closely related to the social constructionist perspective and these are what we could today call 'communities as networks.'

As several authors have argued, it is a distinctive contradiction to search for freedom in a unitary community of a communitarian type.[50] But this is still nevertheless continuously seen as some kind of saviour that could provide everything: liberation, safety, and salvation for a declining democratic life. We could easily reject these propositions as nonsense, but we would neglect important messages arising from these paradigms. 'To understand a myth involves more than proving it to be false. It means figuring out why the myth exists, why it is so important to people,' claimed Vincent Mosco.[51] Even though myths fall short of reality, they are more than 'fabrications of truth,' as they help people deal with the contradictions of life that are, in fact, never resolvable in their entirety. Myths are also embraced and encouraged by those in power, in their desire to mystify social antagonisms; a prime example of this is the simplistic logic explaining that if there really are problems, they are of course produced by technology, this autonomous, natural, unstoppable force.

The recipe prescribed by communitarian authors is a reactionary response to the 'world,' inadvertently exemplified by an implicit promotion of religious communities as simply one-of-the-many-others. Because people are repeatedly exposed to the 'world' and its 'dangers,' there needs to be some sort of solution. But this solution always involves myths, which materialise in social practices, and divide 'Us' from 'the Other' through social homogeneity and an exclusion of supposed deviancy. What is peculiar about this proposition is the fact that it *can* solve the problem of human exposure to the 'world.' In its mild version this means a return to the Keynesian nation-state, a historic model of political unity (the People) *par excellence*, which is today allegedly disintegrating in the wake of Empire, and was from its start robbed of a public sphere.[52] In a more radical version, this can be seen as a plea for an autocratic, 'purebred,' ethnic nation. It is worth acknowledging that both versions, most alarmingly the latter one, are currently on the rise.

Even more interestingly, an alternative conception of virtual technological optimism may also provide some sort of a solution, but instead mystifies the actual problems while avoiding the answers. Howard Rheingold, one of the above-mentioned prophets of the wonders of 'virtual' communities, said a great deal about this in a recent interview. In answering the question about on-line relationships, he pointed out that one needs to think critically about them and curb one's enthusiasm, but that they can, in many instances, improve lives; an example being the people that live 'in a scary part of town, where they don't want to leave their apartment at night.'[53] Even though this is a banal example, it is absolutely necessary to reiterate how this separation never actually occurs; these authors propose to turn a blind eye to certain aspects of social life, which in this particular example lie outside of virtual spaces. This is an escapist 'solution' that solves nothing of particular relevance.

7.   Concluding Remarks

At a fundamental level, what connects both of these problematic paradigms is their attempt to resolve political questions without recourse to politics. They completely avoid politics by riding the wave of anti-political currents and by excluding people from political participation and action. Moreover, they also attempt to avoid the 'world' as such by building pseudo-environmental niches, which serve as hiding places, while the first analysed 'camp,' the communitarian, is able to provide solid pseudo-environmental niches. While it is engaged in a fight over social antagonisms, it is at the same time constructing a unitary sovereign or similar homogeneous amalgams. The second current of thought concerning possibly 'lifesaving' technology does not even address these conditions, instead promoting a virtual quasi-separation, enabling antagonisms to constantly pressure these created niches, making them extremely temporary and unstable, hardly providing any stable boundaries or appearances of safety. 'Lacking access to an environmental niche that would prolong its body like a prosthesis, the human animal exists in a state of insecurity even where there is no trace of specific dangers.'[54] To be precise, pseudo-environmental niches fundamentally defer political action, as they offer hiding places from the scary dangers of the 'world.' Such niches are ignorant substitutes for direct and inclusive political activity.

When talking about myths, we should note they are not only post-political, but also pre-political, sometimes pointing to the right direction of where the problems lie. Myths cannot, however, offer real ways to solve these problems. It is, for example, an illusion that both freedom and safety can be simultaneously achieved without recourse to politics. It is therefore of special importance for us to embrace the question of why 'worldliness' could be so problematic when Hannah Arendt wanted to preserve it at all costs, expressing an urgent need to stay open to the world. There are a few reasons for this peculiarity, one being of prime importance: Arendt was writing about the common world being a prerequisite for political action and a robust public sphere, which would both relate and separate human beings at the same time.[55]

We are able to discern that the real public world, where humans gather together, was impossible under the conditions of mass society and the Keynesian nation-state, as politics was reduced to interest-group negotiations, while workplace repetition excessively restricted exposure to the world. Today what is at hand is a simulacrum of the public world and worldliness - it is being transformed into a spectacle, privatised for prompt profit making.

The human animal is not exposed to the world because of a search for the commons, out of a desire to disrupt quasi-natural social developments with political interventions, or because of built environments inhabited and influenced by all, but because of the brute force of capital, often simply out of existential need. The public world has at the same time become extremely personalised or, to put it in Marazzi's terms, 'the private has become public, and the public has become economic.'[56]

The potentiality of human beings does not mean that a unitary project like the sovereign State or a communitarian type of community that automatically forces homogeneity and represses differences should be desired. Nor do we need authoritarian, non-democratic institutions that are not subject to direct political control. This kind of perspective *a priori* presupposes humans not as harbouring potential, but as dangerous beings, as if this potentiality is necessarily problematic, indeed evil, even though it is a pre-condition for the creation of a genuinely democratic society. From this perspective, the question of community in its essence becomes a political question of creating friendships without familiarity - friendship without brotherhood, as Virno or Arendt would put it, of primarily creating commons, not unity.

Notes

[1] See for example V. Mosco, *The Digital Sublime: Myth, Power, and Cyberspace*, The MIT Press, Cambridge and London, 2005; D. J. Czitrom, *Media and the American Mind: From Morse to McLuhan*, University of North Carolina Press, Chapel Hill, 1982.

[2] The most often cited optimistic early work is probably H. Rheingold, *The Virtual Community: Homesteading on the Electronic Frontier*, Addison-Wesley Pub. Co, Reading, MA, 1993. For more pessimistic outlines see S. Doheny-Farina, *The Wired Neighborhood*, Yale University Press, New Haven-London, 1996; R. D. Putnam, *Bowling Alone: The Collapse and Revival of American Community*, Simon and Schuster, New York, London, Toronto and Sidney, 2000; see also Mosco, op. cit., pp. 13-16.

[3] A. Mattelart, *The Invention of Communication*, University of Minnesota Press, Minneapolis, London, 1996.

[4] For struggles regarding the Internet and communication technologies see, for example, R. McChesney, *Communication Revolution: Critical Junctures and the Future of Media*, The New Press, New York and London, 2007.

[5] J. R. Beniger, 'Personalisation of Mass Media and the Growth of Pseudo-Community', *Communication Research*, Vol. 14, No. 3, 1987, pp. 352-371; J. R. Beniger, 'The Control Revolution', in *Technology and the Future*, A. H. Teich (ed), 5th Edited, St. Martin's Press, New York, 1990, pp. 51-76; S.

Jones, 'Understanding Community in the Information Age', in *Computer Media and Communication: A Reader*, A. P. Mayer (ed), Oxford University Press, Oxford, 1999, pp. 226-233.

[6] J. R. Beniger, 'Personalisation of Mass Media', p. 354.

[7] See for example the discussion by Gundelsweiler and Filk in this volume.

[8] J. R. Searle, *Making the Social World: The Structure of Human Civilization*, Oxford University Press, Oxford and New York, 2010.

[9] B. Anderson, *Imagined Communities*, Verso, London, 1991.

[10] Ibid., p. 133.

[11] C. Calhoun, 'Indirect Relationships and Imagined Communities: Large-Scale Social Integration and the Transformation of Everyday Life', in *Social Theory for a Changing society*, P. Bourdieu and J. S. Coleman (eds), Westview Press, Boulder, San Francisco and Oxford, 1991, pp. 108-109.

[12] Anderson, op. cit., p. 6.

[13] Ibid., pp. 35-36.

[14] C. H. Cooley, *Social Organization/Human Nature and the Social Order*, Free Press, Glencoe, 1956, p. 70. See also D. J. Czitrom, op. cit., pp. 93-102.

[15] D. J. Czitrom, op. cit., pp. 102-112. See also J. Dewey, *The Public and its Problems*, Ohio University Press, Ohio, 1989 [1927].

[16] G. Day, *Community and Everyday Life*, Routledge, New York, 2006, pp. 154-163.

[17] Ibid., p. 156.

[18] See A. P. Cohen, *The Symbolic Construction of Community*, Routledge, New York, 1985.

[19] S. Žižek, 'Eastern Europe's Republic of Gilead', in *Dimensions of Radical Democracy: Pluralism, Citizenship, Community*, C. Mouffe (ed), Verso, London and New York, 1996, pp. 194-199.

[20] J. Malpas, 'On the Non-Autonomy of the Virtual', *Convergence*, Vol. 15, No. 2, pp. 135-139. For a similar argument see also M. Nunes, *Cyberspaces of Everyday Life*, University of Minnesota Press, Minnesota and London, 2006.

[21] See Nunes, op. cit.

[22] Ibid., p. xiii.

[23] Mosco, op. cit., p. 6.

[24] D. Cohen, *Our Modern Times: The New Nature of Capitalism in the Information Age*, The MIT Press, Cambridge and London, 2003, p. 3.

[25] Calhoun, op. cit.

[26] See Czitrom, op. cit., p. 88; H. Hardt, *Myths for the Masses: An Essay on Mass Communication*, Blackwell Publishing, Malden, 2004, pp. 38-44.

[27] E. Fisher, *Media and New Capitalism in the Digital Age: The Spirit of Networks*, Palgrave MacMillan, New York, 2010.

[28] On these structural changes see Cohen, op. cit.; Fischer, op. cit.; D. Harvey, *The Condition of Postmodernity*, Blackwell Publishing, Malden and Oxford, 1990; D. Harvey, *The Enigma of Capital and the Crises of Capitalism*, Profile Books, London, 2010, pp. 1-40; C. Offe, *The Contradictions of the Welfare State*, The MIT Press, Cambridge, 1984, pp. 179-206; C. Offe, 'Challenging the Boundaries of Institutional Politics: Social Movements since the 1960s', in *Changing Boundaries of the Political*, C. S. Maier (ed), Cambridge University Press, Cambridge, 1987, pp. 63-105; C. Marazzi, *Capital and Language: From the New Economy to the War Economy*, Semiotext(e), Los Angeles, 2008.

[29] Z. Bauman, 'The 20th Century: The End or the Beginning?', *Thesis Eleven*, No. 70, 2002, p. 15.

[30] Z. Bauman, *Liquid Modernity*, Polity Press, Cambridge, 2000, p. 3.

[31] M. Fischer, *Capitalism Realism: Is There No Alternative?*, O Books, Winchester and Washington, 2009, p. 44.

[32] Marazzi, op. cit.

[33] Bauman, *Liquid Modernity*, p. 7.

[34] Z. Bauman, *Identity: Conversations with Benedetto Vecchi*, Cambridge, Polity Press, 2004, p. 30.

[35] Bauman, *Liquid Modernity*, pp. 199-201.

[36] Z. Bauman, *Consuming Life*, Polity Press, Cambridge, 2007, pp. 111-112.

[37] Z. Bauman, *Community: Seeking Safety in an Insecure World*, Polity Press, Cambridge, 2001.

[38] Ibid., p. 14.

[39] P. Virno, *Multitude Between Innovation and Negotiation*, Semiotext(e), Los Angeles, 2008, p. 17.

[40] P. Virno, *A Grammar of the Multitude: For an Analysis of Contemporary Forms of Life*, Semiotext(e), Los Angeles and New York, 2004, p. 32.

[41] Ibid. See also P. Virno, 'Natural-Historical Diagrams: The "New Global" Movement and the Biological Invariant', *Cosmos and History: The Journal of Natural and Social Philosophy*, Vol. 5, No. 1, 2009, pp. 92-104.

[42] E. P. Thompson, 'Time, Work-Discipline, and Industrial Capitalism', *Past and Present*, No. 38, 1967, pp. 56-97; A. Gramsci, *Selections from the Prison Notebooks*, Lawrence and Wishart, London, 1971, pp. 277-318.

[43] Several authors have taken into account the questions relating changes in working conditions, either from the perspective of wider structural changes in the contemporary societies, for example, U. Beck, *The Brave New World of Work*, Polity Press, Cambridge, 2000; Cohen, op. cit.; Harvey, *The Condition of Postmodernity*, or its more personal consequences, for example, M. Fischer, op. cit.; R. Sennett, *The Corrosion of Character: The Personal*

Consequences of Work in the New Capitalism, W.W. Norton & Company, New York, 1999.

[44] Sennett, op. cit., p. 31.

[45] Virno, 'Natural-Historical Diagrams', p. 101.

[46] Putnam, op. cit., p.282.

[47] Ibid., pp. 216-246, and Ibid., pp. 277-284.

[48] See G. Simmel, 'The Metropolis and Mental Life', in _The City Reader_, G. Bridge and S. Watson (eds), Blackwell, Oxford, 2002 [1905], pp. 11-19.

[49] B. Wellman, 'The Community Question', _The American Journal of Sociology_, Vol. 84, No. 5, 1979, p. 1227. Emphasis mine.

[50] For example, Z. Bauman, _Community: Seeking Safety in an Insecure World_; Sennett, op. cit., pp. 136-148; R. Sennett, _The Fall of Public Man_, Penguin Book, London and New York, 2002, pp. 219-256; M. Hardt and A. Negri, _Multitude: War and Democracy in the Age of Empire_, The Penguin Press, New York, pp. 202-208..

[51] Mosco, op. cit., p. 29.

[52] On the political model of Empire, see M. Hardt and A. Negri, _Empire_, Harvard University Press, Cambridge, MA, 2000.

[53] H. Rheingold (interviewee), 'Howard Rheingold Interview - USA'. <http://www.bbc.co.uk/blogs/digitalrevolution/2009/10/title.shtml>.

[54] Virno, 'Natural-Historical Diagrams', p. 97.

[55] H. Arendt, _The Human Condition_, 2nd Edition, The University of Chicago Press, Chicago and London, 1998 [1958].

[56] Marazzi, op. cit., p. 44.

Bibliography

Anderson, B., _Imagined Communities_. Verso, London, 1991.

Arendt, H., _The Human Condition_, 2nd Editon. The University of Chicago Press, Chicago and London, 1998 [1958].

Bauman, Z., _Intimations of Postmodernity_. Routledge, London and New York, 1992.

——, _Liquid Modernity_. Polity Press, Cambridge, 2000.

——, _Community: Seeking Safety in an Insecure World_. Polity Press, Cambridge, 2001.

——, 'The 20th Century: The End or the Beginning?'. *Thesis Eleven*, No. 70, 2002, pp. 15-25.

——, *Identity: Conversations with Benedetto Vecchi*. Cambridge, Polity, 2004.

——, *Consuming Life*. Polity Press, Cambridge, 2007.

Beck, U., *The Brave New World of Work*. Polity Press, Cambridge, 2000.

Beniger, J. R., 'Personalisation of Mass Media and the Growth of Pseudo-Community'. *Communication Research*, Vol. 14, No. 3, 1987, pp. 352-371.

——, 'The Control Revolution', in *Technology and the Future*, 5th Edition, A. H. Teich (ed), St. Martin's Press, New York, 1990, pp. 51-76.

Calhoun, C., 'Indirect Relationships and Imagined Communities: Large-Scale Social Integration and the Transformation of Everyday Life', in *Social Theory for a Changing Society*. P. Bourdieu and J. S. Coleman (eds), Westview Press, Boulder, San Francisco and Oxford, 1991, pp. 95-121.

Cohen, A. P., *The Symbolic Construction of Community*. Routledge, New York, 1985.

Cohen, D., *Our Modern Times: The New Nature of Capitalism in the Information Age*. The MIT Press, Cambridge and London, 2003.

Cooley, C. H., *Social Organization/Human nature and the Social Order*. Free Press, Glencoe, 1956.

Czitrom, D. J., *Media and the American Mind: From Morse to McLuhan*. University of Carolina Press, Chapel Hill, 1982.

Day, G., *Community and Everyday Life*. Routledge, New York, 2006.

Dewey, J., *The Public and its Problems*. Ohio University Press, Ohio, 1989 [1927].

Doheny-Farina, S., *The Wired Neighborhood*. Yale University Press, New Haven-London, 1996.

Fischer, M., *Capitalism Realism: Is There No Alternative?* O Books, Winchester and Washington, 2009.

Gramsci, A., *Selections from the Prison Notebooks*. Lawrence and Wishart, London, 1971.

Hardt, H., *Myths for the Masses: An Essay on Mass Communication*. Blackwell Publishing, Malden, 2004.

Hardt, M. and Negri, A., *Empire*. Harvard University Press, Cambridge, MA, 2000.

——, *Multitude: War and Democracy in the Age of Empire*. The Penguin Press, New York, 2005.

Harvey, D., *The Condition of Postmodernity*. Blackwell Publishing, Malden and Oxford, 1990.

——, *The Enigma of Capital and the Crises of Capitalism*. Profile Books, London, 2010.

Jones, S., 'Understanding Community in the Information Age', in *Computer Media and Communication: A Reader*. A. P. Mayer (ed), Oxford University Press, Oxford, 1999, pp. 226-233.

Malpas, J., 'On the Non-Autonomy of the Virtual'. *Convergence*, Vol. 15, No. 2, pp. 135-139.

Marazzi, C., *Capital and Language: From the New Economy to the War Economy*. Semiotext(e), Los Angeles, 2008.

Mattelart, A., *The Invention of Communication*. University of Minnesota Press, Minneapolis and London, 1996.

McChesney, R., *Communication Revolution: Critical Junctures and the Future of Media*. The New Press, New York and London, 2007.

Mosco, V., *The Digital Sublime: Myth, Power, and Cyberspace*. The MIT Press, Cambridge and London, 2005.

Nunes, M., *Cyberspaces of Everyday Life*. University of Minnesota Press, Minnesota and London, 2006.

Offe, C., *The Contradictions of the Welfare State*. The MIT Press, Cambridge, 1984.

——, 'Challenging the Boundaries of Institutional Politics: Social Movements since the 1960s', in *Changing Boundaries of the Political*. C. S. Maier (ed), Cambridge University Press, Cambridge, 1987, pp.: 63-105.

Putnam, R. D., *Bowling Alone: The Collapse and Revival of American Community*. Simon & Schuster, New York, London, Toronto and Sidney, 2000.

Rheingold, H., *The Virtual Community: Homesteading on the Electronic Frontier*. Addison-Wesley Pub. Co, Reading, MA, 1993.

——, (interviewee), 'Howard Rheingold Interview - USA'. <http://www.bbc.co.uk/blogs/digitalrevolution/2009/10/title.shtml>.

Searle, J. R., *Making the Social World: The Structure of Human Civilization*. Oxford University Press, Oxford and New York, 2010.

Sennett, R., *The Corrosion of Character: The Personal Consequences of Work in the New Capitalism*. W.W. Norton & Company, New York, 1999.

——, *The Fall of Public Man*. Penguin Books, London and New York, 2002.

Simmel, G., 'The Metropolis and Mental Life', in *The City Reader*. G. Bridge and S. Watson (eds),. Blackwell, Oxford, 2002 [1905], pp. 11-19.

Virno, P., *A Grammar of the Multitude: For an Analysis of Contemporary Forms of Life*. Semiotext(e), Los Angeles and New York, 2004.

——, *Multitude: Between Innovation and Negotiation*. Semiotext(e), Los Angeles, 2008.

——, 'Natural-Historical Diagrams: The "New Global" Movement and the Biological Invariant'. *Cosmos and History: The Journal of Natural and Social Philosophy*, Vol. 5, No. 1, 2009, pp. 92-104.

Wellman, B., 'The Community Question'. *The American Journal of Sociology*, Vol. 84, No. 5, 1979, pp. 1201-1231.

Žižek, S., 'Eastern Europe's Republic of Gilead', in *Dimensions of Radical Democracy: Pluralism, Citizenship, Community*. C. Mouffe (ed), Verso, London and New York, 1992, pp. 193-207.

Jernej Prodnik works at the Social Communication Research Centre at the Faculty of Social Sciences, University of Ljubljana. His research interests include the potential of new information and communication technologies and wider structural changes in the post-Fordist capitalist societies.

The Internet, Fixity, and Flow:
Challenges to the Articulation of an Imagined Community

Harris Breslow and Ilhem Allagui

Abstract
This paper uses the results from the first annual Emirates Internet Project survey to address the effect of the Internet upon the articulation of social and national communities in the UAE. The UAE is in the process of defining its 'imagined community' and the Internet is affecting the articulation of this community in the following ways. 1. Pressure upon the national lingua franca: although Arabic is the UAE's national language, web use in the UAE amongst young Emiratis in particular and Arabs in general overwhelmingly occurs in English. 2. Pressure upon heretofore-traditional patterns of social networks: Arab societies and their resultant social networks are organised within layers of private space, around the family, and within the home. The Internet plays a role in rearticulating the nature, location, and membership of social networks. 3. The role of the Internet in the articulation of a post-national culture: the articulation of an Emirati nation is always already problematic because of the fragmenting role played by historical tribal identities in Emirati commerce and politics, and the fact that four in five residents do not have citizenship. Internet use in the UAE intensifies this by enabling the propagation of social networks that exceed or circumvent national identity and space.

Keywords: Internet use, UAE, survey, national community, social networks, national polity.

*****

1. Introduction

The Emirates Internet Project (EIP) is a longitudinal survey research project of patterns of Internet usage amongst residents of the United Arab Emirates (UAE). The EIP is a participating partner in the World Internet Project (WIP), a consortium of institutions researching Internet usage in 22 countries. Partners survey a basket of common questions used for comparative analysis and local survey questions to gain additional insight of local Internet usage.

One set of results that is important relates to the role of the Internet in the articulation of stress to Emirati culture and polity. Like any nation state, the UAE signifies the articulation of a sense of a singular community fashioned from a set of heretofore-disjunctive components of political institutions, language, and culture, thus enabling the articulation of common traditions and common identity.[1]

We examine three of these - language, social networks, and a sense of national polity - as they articulate to one another in the UAE, and the pressure that they face from Internet usage. We argue that the patterns of Internet usage in the UAE pose a challenge to the Emirati national project.

Our examination is couched within a discussion of a theory of supermodern 'flow.'[2] It is our contention, following Appadurai, that the spaces within which modern states and their attendant nations were historically articulated - spaces that were relatively fixed and bounded in nature - are undergoing a period of rupture within which 'nation-states are struggling to retain control over their populations in the face of a host of subnational and transnational movements and organisations.'[3]

2.   States, Fixity, and Flow in the Supermodern World

States have many functions. One key function is the creation of social and spatial fixities.

> The state must create both social and spatial fixities; the former, as stricture, channel activity into areas that are both profitable to the group and predetermined by the forms of enunciative codes of the state itself. The latter channel movement through a series of conduits necessary to bleed off the excess and heterogeneous energy of the social in its day-to-day activities.[4]

In this respect the nation-state should be read as a static phenomenon. It is based on, and promotes, a regime of fixity: the nation-state is located within a particular physical space, and is both created and maintained by juridical, social, economic and communications technologies that have, in the past, served to preserve this stability and permanence. The nation-state functions within fixed borders that both determine and define the population that comprises the nation. An army maintains these fixed borders, defends the nation and protects the state. A juridical state apparatus, whose jurisdiction extends to the very edges of these borders and within which it is sovereign, governs the nation and preserves and maintains the relationships therein. A national market regulated by the state creates and distributes wealth for and among those within its borders, thereby funding the state, enriching the nation, and enlisting its members as stakeholders in the state's ongoing existence. A national mass media apparatus produces and distributes fictional and nonfictional cultural content within the national marketplace. This content functions to naturalise, legitimate, and substantiate the existence of both nation and state by establishing a sense of autochthony, narrating a history and ascribing a particular relationship and an enduring set of characteristics to these entities.[5]

Lim and Kann have argued that Habermas's work on the public sphere was, in many ways, a eulogy.[6] In a similar vein, our description of the state as a regime of fixity should be seen as a eulogy for the fixed and frozen relationships once found in the nation-state and that are productive of the sense of subjectivity, community, and locale that those who write of postmodern subjects, locales, and meaning often lament its 'death.'[7] Appadurai has argued that one can fundamentally characterise the twentieth century in terms of the articulation of an apparatus of flows of five distinct entities - technology, money/finance, images, ideas, and people - that exceed the ability of the contemporary state to channel and contain their movement. Although the state has arguably not withered away and died, its ability to contain and channel (in particular) political and cultural phenomena such as nationalism, communal identity, and subjectivity within its own space has become severely limited.[8]

We want to point to three consequences of the developments that Appadurai charts. The first is that, freed from any ontological 'obligation' to the borders of the nation state, these once bounded phenomena are now set in motion and become free to move and to relocate. In this respect, notions such as 'home,' 'polity,' 'culture,' etc., must be seen 'as primarily relational and contextual as opposed to scalar or spatial.'[9] The second consequence is that the relationship between space, culture, and the production of subjectivity, between locale and ritual - which had heretofore been seen as essentially localised phenomena[10] - becomes fluid.[11] The third consequence is the now fluid dimension to national politics and their location. Freed from the constraints of space, subjects can articulate themselves to, and have an effect upon, polities that exist at great distance.[12]

We want to argue - and we shall return to this discussion later - that within this apparatus of movement the social conceptions of space and place are themselves no longer tied to locale, to a concrete place. Rather, space and place become much more fluid concepts, articulated to movement, tenuous in nature, and momentary in duration - what Augé has described as non-spaces.[13] This tendency has always been present in modernity;[14] what makes this moment in time so interesting is the degree to which that which we here term 'flow' - following Appadurai - simultaneously exists within, and is articulated across, so many socio-structural dimensions.

It is our thesis that the Internet plays a key role in the disarticulation of the nation-state's ability to establish, maintain, and enforce boundaries, and thus to contain the activities that contain therein. IP technology breaches this regime of fixity by imposing a form of transmissive transparency upon and across the borders of the nation-state apparatus. All modern mass media have exhibited this characteristic to some extent. Radio and television networks have transmitted their content across national borders since the very beginning of their existence; newspapers have long been available across the world within a short period of their printing and often have same-day international publishing, as is the case with *The New York Times*, *Le Monde* and *The Financial Times*; films have long been released internationally and increasingly require international markets for their economic viability; and telephone networks have long been used for both mass and interpersonal communication regardless of distance or political boundaries, easily, instantaneously, and economically.

The effect of the Internet upon the nation-state apparatus is one of disaggregation. Indeed, the Internet is the *ne plus ultra* apparatus of national cultural, social, political and economic disaggregation. The phenomenology of the Internet is the emphasis of individual experience over that of the group. It disaggregates the mass audience in favour of an endless series of recombinant groups of individuated users. The Internet rearticulates both social space and social networks; indeed, our very conception of both what and where it is to be social. It displaces the articulation of national politics and its aggregate of local political concerns and polities in favour of networks of individuals concerned with single issues that traverse local spaces, national borders, polities and governments. The Internet has a profound effect on commerce; whether it is B2B or B2C commercial activities, banking, or the purchase of stocks and bonds, the Internet is fundamentally reorganising the marketplace. The Internet marginalises the use of a whole host of national languages in favour of a simplified form of English as the lingua franca of the digerati.

We want to argue that the UAE is the nation-state of flow *par excellence*. Consider the five dimensions of flow described by Appadurai and enumerated above: people, finance, technology, images and ideas. Some eighty percent of the country's population is comprised of resident migrant workers; individuals who by definition will not live and die in country, but rather who flow through the country, pausing to work, contribute to the economy, and then move on. The country is the region's leading financial services hub, and although a fair percentage of the money that cycles through Dubai's International Finance Centre (DIFC) remains in country for investment in one project or another, the country's financial community specialises in the international transmigration of - the flow of - money from one part of the world to another. The UAE is one of the largest transhipment ports in the world, specialising in the management of the international flow of goods. Although the country has an advanced telecommunications infrastructure, including its own nationally based satellite and terrestrial television and radio channels as well as two 3G/GSM mobile phone networks, an overwhelming degree of its mass media consumption and virtually *all* of the online media content accessed in the UAE flows through the country from elsewhere.

3.   Stresses to the National Language

A fundamental structure of any national community is its shared language, the most complex, and most important medium through which members of a nation gain their sense of common identity.[15] In the UAE this language is Arabic. Arabic occupies a central role in the cultural history of the region. Emiratis view themselves as heirs to 6000 years of human habitation on the Arabian peninsula, and Arabic is the historical language through which Emiratis gain their distinctive identities.

And yet, English is the language most commonly spoken by residents of the UAE. There are many complex reasons for this, and it is beyond this paper to discuss these at length. We will point to the somewhat unique political economies of Gulf Cooperation Council (GCC) countries, where expatriates hold both high value occupations and low paying positions. The majority of these - 70% of the total population - do not speak Arabic. Typically, migrant labourers and high-value employees both view English as a requisite skill for overseas work, thus predisposing this population towards speaking English.[16] English has thus become the national lingua franca, used by residents of the UAE as 'a contact language used among people who do not share a first language.'[17]

In this respect one can argue that the spread of English as the international language of commerce, the mass media, science, and technology, is a phenomenon of flow over fixity. We can understand this in two ways. On the one hand, there are the political, economic, and sociocultural economies of the UAE, which, as we discussed above, are phenomena of flow. On the other hand, there is a growing detachment of English from its formerly rigid rules of use, which we can also describe as a phenomenon of flow. The extent to which a national language's rules of use and deployment - its grammar and syntax, its rules of pronunciation - are taught and socioculturally enforced, regardless of where the teaching and enforcement occur, is an indicator of the degree to which a given nation-state can be said to exist within a complex conjuncture that may be characterised by either fixity or flow.

Here then, the current debates over, and the teaching of, English as a Lingua Franca (ELF) offer strong evidence of flow and the escape of national cultures from the boundaries within which a given nation-state could enforce their deployment. There are two salient points to our discussion that need to be made with respect to ELF. The first is that, unlike English as a Second Language (ESL) teaching, or World English (WE) teaching, ELF does not attempt to promote strict adherence to the fundamental rules of grammar, syntax and pronunciation: the objective is to enable non-native speakers to be able to make themselves understood to other non-native speakers and to understand their interlocutors in turn. English, then, is freed from strict adherence to its rules of understanding and use that were produced within the bounded geographical constraints from within which the language coalesced into its modern form.[18]

Skutnabb-Kangas points to the fact that native languages often decline in the adoption of formal education systems.[19] In the UAE private education stresses the teaching and use of English as a Lingua Franca (ELF), whether because it is the language of commerce, the language of science, or simply because English is the 'world's language.'[20] Online communication reinforces this phenomenon; English has become the language of Internet use in general and the web in particular.

Language of Websites Most Often Visited by Nationality and Age

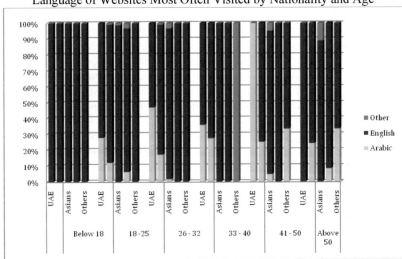

Clearly, the younger one is, the more likely one is to report most frequently visiting English language websites. A majority of Emirati respondents under the age of 41, large majorities of Emirati respondents aged 18-25, and *every* Emirati respondent under the age of 18, report that they most often visit English language websites.[21]

This assertion is made more compelling by the figure below.

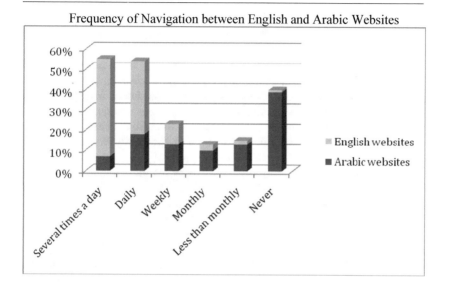

Frequency of Navigation between English and Arabic Websites

Here we see that:

> a respondent navigates to an English website, and then remains within the English web universe. The opposite, where one navigates to an Arabic website and remains within the Arabic web universe, occurs so rarely - less than three percent of respondents do so - that it may be said to not be occurring at all.[22]

The use of English while online functions as an ELF bridge builder through which members of disparate linguistic and cultural communities communicate. This places non-native speakers of English in a loop that propagates and reinforces western cultural values among online users of ELF. Here the use of ELF occurs within a technological environment, and if 'we assume … it "brings forth a world", and that the social organisation of this world is rooted in the worlds which gave rise to it … the Internet embodies the values of its creators.'[23]

4. Pressure upon Traditional Patterns of Social Networks.

The social construction of families on the Arabian Peninsula is based on clan and tribe. Families are central to one's social relationships, and are consulted on both major and minor issues. Halimi describes the ideal of the Arab family as 'a central socioeconomic unit' in the sense that 'all members contribute to secure its livelihood and improve its standing in the community.'[24] He adds that the Arab family 'constitutes the dominant social institution through which persons and groups inherit their religious, social class, and cultural identities.'[25]

Arabs share a set of values, beliefs and traditions. The Arab Thought, a research project produced by the Zogby Institute, surveyed 3800 Arab adults in eight Arab countries (Egypt, Lebanon, Israel, Jordan, Kuwait, Morocco, UAE and KSA) and found that personal concerns related to family, job security, and religion are most important to Arabs' lives.[26] The same research showed that Arab values are centred on the family first and the self; such as self-respect, health, hygiene, and responsibility.

While the family certainly seems to be the most important of one's social networks, neighbours and other relationships of friendship also exist and are developed through schools and other meeting institutions and locales. The scope for extra-familial relationships has grown mainly with the popularisation of education (education was made mandatory for all school age children in the majority of Arab countries during the 1970s), the development of women's social and legal status (women were guaranteed the right to go to school and to enter the labour force in most Arab countries during the late seventies), as well as with the development of media and new information and communication technologies. For instance, the development of the mass media in the Arab Middle East has strengthened these relationships. The usage patterns of both radio and television embraced the place of the family. Radio was listened to in family circles of and amongst neighbours. Watching television was a family activity, be it for *musalsalat* (Egyptian drama series), or football matches. 'Traditional' mass media were not only a good fit for the pre-existing structure of social networks and community, they also strongly articulated to and reinforced this structure.

The development of the new media, however, tends to articulate itself to an individuated usage pattern, causing a shift from physical community to virtual community and potentially reconfiguring Arab space. Van Dijk notes this transposition, and argues that

> The history of the 20th century reveals a disintegration of traditional communities … into associations which … are declining in size (caused by privatisation and individualisation) and … are extending as they become more diffused and spread over greater distances. In the eyes of many social scientists, planners and citizens, we are dealing with a "lost" community.[27]

This trend is intensified by the development of the new media. With the advent of the Internet a new set of relationships occurs, displacing the family for the 'equilibrium' of individuals (specifically in Arabic societies).

For example, Arab couples get to meet each other nowadays on the Internet and, in some cases, they even develop long-term relationships via and through the Net. Wheeler, for example, discusses the Internet's role as matchmaker among young Kuwaitis.[28] This would have been unacceptable just few years ago because marriage is supposed to be arranged by the family and relatives. Now girls and boys take advantage of this restructuring of social space, as a result of the adoption of NICT to restructure their own lives. The Internet seems to have enabled a shift from a family-centric Arabic society to a self-centric one where individuals are no longer under the 'control' of, and reigned in by, their elders. Rather, young Arab people are primarily on their own, free from any traditional boundaries they might have encountered; in other words, they are free to meet whomever they like in cyberspace.

Individual choices of identity are, from now on, an option for these Internet users who were previously under the reign of families and boundaries of the 'horizontal' society as described by Lawrence Friedman.[29] The new generation of Arab youth are web users who are eager to discover the new media that offer a new opportunity of forging other relationships, web-social relationships. Indeed, social networking was found to be a main reason for using the Net by Arab Internet users. For instance, Alfhoneiz finds that the first need Arabic language Internet visitors seek to satisfy is to 'facilitate and extend social contacts through emails and chat.'[30] Furthermore, other recent research analysing the most visited Arabic websites finds that the most appealing websites for Arab users are those that offer entertainment and social interaction.[31] This is just one of many examples where Arab web surfers have discovered a new kind of relationship where they keep in touch with others, virtually and regularly, and thus belong to a new structure of family and social networks, the 'virtual community.'

The literature concerning the concept of virtual communities has been abundant since the late eighties, when what was a new set of computer-mediated-communications was the object of study. The concept of virtual community was made popular by Rheingold, a utopian of virtual communities.

> People in virtual communities do just about everything people do in real life, but we leave our bodies behind. You can't kiss anybody and nobody can punch you in the nose, but a lot can happen within those boundaries.[32]

As an advocate of virtual communities, Rheingold suggested that virtual communities replace whatever is lost with the decline of traditional communities. Long before Rheingold, however, Pool discussed the opportunities afforded by computer-mediated-communication, and regarded the Internet as a technology that helps to liberate the self from localities and boundaries, creating new opportunities for personal relationships.

Opposed to this utopian position is a number of sociologists such as Fernback, and Wellman and Gulia, who attenuate the effects of technology upon society.[33] Jankowski highlights the difference between early sociology and that after the Internet as a 'redirection of emphasis from geographic place to a feeling or sense of collectivity.'[34] This sense of collectivity happens to be outside the family, but to what extent does this occur in the UAE? In this collection, Fidele Vlavo reminds us that one can situate discussions of virtual communities - whether utopian or otherwise - within the discourse surrounding the Internet *Imaginaire*, as developed by Patrice Flichy. As Vlavo notes, one aspect of the Internet *Imaginaire* is the notion that technology 'is the foundation of social progress and the improvement of the human condition ... [directing us] towards the creation of a new digital society.'[35]

The Emirates Internet Project (EIP) found a moderate impact from the adoption of the Internet upon UAE society.

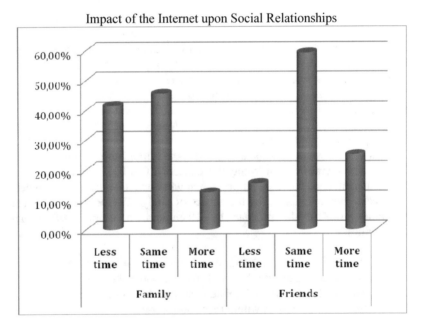

Impact of the Internet upon Social Relationships

More than half the Internet users in the UAE spend the same time with their friends since adopting the Internet, and about 40% spend the same time with their families. However, one could also note that about 40% say they spend less time with the family since their adoption of the Internet. The advent of the Internet has not *yet* drastically changed the social habits of Internet users. However, there are indications of a shift from time spent with families to time spent with friends, and thus a shift in the construction of these networks. This is most noticeable among Emirati youth, those UAE nationals below age of 18, 66.7% of whom declared that they spend less time with their families since the adoption of the Internet.

This shows that Emiratis are not different from any other youth population around the world, be it Chinese or Swedish, who have also been found to restructure their social networks thanks to their time spent on and the social ties made through the Net, extending their social networks across a global reach. For example, when studying Kuwaiti youth Internet usage, Wheeler found that traditional gatherings are affected by Internet adoption. Young people 'find it more enjoyable to surf the net in the evenings instead of participating in traditional social rituals.'[36]

Impact of the Internet on Time Spent with Friends

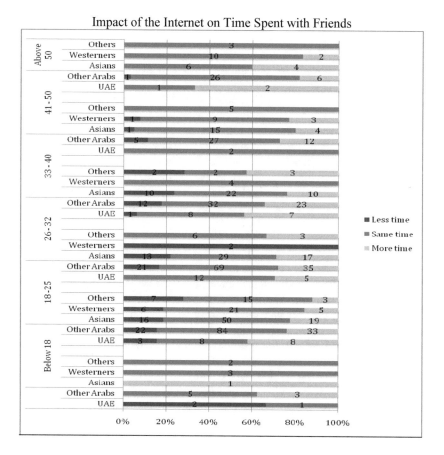

When asking respondents about the impact of the Internet on the quality of the relationships they have with their families, we note a positive trend. 66% of respondents report that the quality of their relationship with their family has either somewhat or greatly increased. This is explained by the fact that the UAE is a multiethnic population; most of its residents are expatriates who use the Internet as a channel to communicate with their families while saving communication fees. The Internet offers efficiency while improving the quality of one's relationships with family; Internet users save on telephone call fees and keep in touch with families and friends over great distances and eventually at a higher frequency of communications, as discussed by Hampton and Wellman.[37] They discuss Robertson's theory of 'glocalisation,' wherein the Internet binds global social networks to the local area.[38] By developing and investing time within these expanded social networks, users are not necessarily taking time from their local relationships. Stern found that the physical centrality is no longer core to social relationships. He states

> The fact that the local area remains central to people's social network is no longer true and technology has evolved to accommodate this reality. The findings from this study show clearly that people use email primarily, yet not exclusively, as the mode of communication with those social ties outside the local area. Email is largely an asynchronous form of contact and thus is suited particularly well to long distance communication, because regardless of time zones and availability of the recipient, a person can send a message quickly. Further, whereas there are fees for long distance on the telephone, there are no additional costs for long distance emails.[39]

One might add that the positive trend regarding the quality of relationships with family observed for UAE respondents is suspected to apply mainly to expatriates, as discussed above, but with consideration to ethnicity and race. For instance, Westerners, in general, have a long history of experience using the Net and the majority of Western countries have high household Internet penetration rates. However, this might not be true for other nationalities where the Internet is not yet widely adopted in the household.

When looking at the figure below, 'Impact of the Internet on Families' Relationships,' cross-tabbed according to ethnic groups, one can see that there is no significant change on time spent with the family after Internet adoption.

Impact of the Internet on Families' Relationships

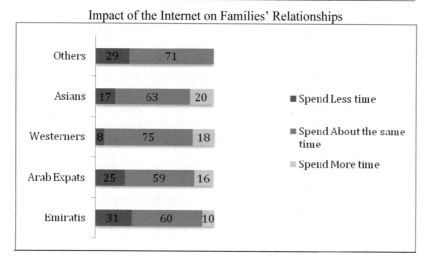

Furthermore, the results confirm the above discussion in the sense that most Internet users in the UAE said they spend either the same time with their families or less time; only 10% said that the Internet improved the quality of their relationships with their families. Thus, the Internet did not significantly change respondents' relationships with their families, however time spent on the Internet has probably reduced the time using other media or hanging out in malls as is the practice in the UAE culture. Furthermore, 20% of Asians, 18% of Westerners and 16% of Arab expatriates declared that the Internet improved their relationships with their families regardless of their gender, age or income.

5.   Heading towards a Post National Culture?

Finally, we examine the effect of the Internet upon political participation in the UAE, which is a constitutive and measurable component of any national culture. Typically, when one thinks of a national polity one thinks of the several components of fixity that we discussed at the start of this paper: a bounded space within which the polity exists; a spatially bounded and determined population from which the polity is comprised; a set of common media channels/outlets within this space that provide the community qua polity with information regarding affairs of national concern; and a set of laws that determine who amongst the members of the population will comprise the polity and the legitimate means by which the political franchise may be exercised - in other words a set of strictures determining political actors and the channels through which political efficacy will be exercised. Of course, this is also the model of the public sphere, and to the extent that Habermas described the constituent components of the public sphere, he also described the key elements in what one could describe as an apparatus of fixity; a fixed space, a specific population, a nascent mass media apparatus, and a set of laws governing political behaviour. Indeed, the ideal locale within which the rational critical public would come to congregate - the city square - is a perfect metaphor for the fixity of the public sphere. Bounded in space, governed by laws, and inhabited by assembled members of the public, the city square is that place where people come to congregate. It is that space where the public literally fixes itself and from this enunciates itself in a rationally critical fashion.[40] It is this last point that we want to concentrate on in this final section.

Vlavo's analysis of a virtual public sphere, couched within the framework of cyber-*imaginaires*, is an important aside to our discussion of the Internet, flow and politics. For Vlavo, the idealised description of the public sphere as an environment that facilitates the free exchange of ideas and thus fosters the rational critical stance necessary of individuals within a public sphere, finds an analogous home in the Internet. 'It is ... no surprise that the faster and broader communication channels provided by the Internet have brought forward the assumption that virtual environments can and will expand the potential for democracy.'[41] However, this is not guaranteed, but rather serves the function of a fortuitous coincidence amongst network topology, theories of democracy couched within language, and the adoption of the philosophical framework of Deleuze and Guattari, whose work on rhizomatic logics and topographical structures lends itself to this debate.[42]

In the same vein as Jernej Prodnik's chapter in this collection, Vlavo does not believe that this invalidates the potential for cyberspace to function as a political environment or as a discursive environment within which politically efficacious discourse may occur.[43] Prodnik views cyberspace in terms that are quite similar to those used by Appadurai. For Prodnik, cyberspace is a dynamic social process 'produced by a dynamic relationship of material and semiotic processes ... a consistent continuation of corresponding relations of the "real" world ... .'[44] Although the epiphenomena that Prodnik examines are similar to Appadurai, the conclusions that he draws are most assuredly not. Reading the nature of cyberspace through Bauman's work on 'liquid modernity,' Prodnik argues that the high degree of movement amongst commodities, messages, finance and individuals does *not* signal a new moment in late modernity, where meaning, subjectivity and community are able to rearticulate somewhat free of the nation state, but rather signal a somewhat triumphant moment of the mass media where identity has 'become the centre of attention for individuals in liquid modernity ... people buy them in identity-supermarkets and try to avoid any fixations ... .'[45] In this respect, the ability to articulate *any* form of public sphere - whether online or in real life - becomes highly problematic; one of the key elements to the constitution of a public sphere, stable subject positions from which individual subjects may articulate themselves as members of a rational critical public, is no longer assigned any ontological permanency.

To our minds, this lack of permanency - the liquidity of modernity - characterises the political economy of the UAE. We will argue, however, that although this means that the public sphere in the UAE becomes a problematic construct, this does not meant that individuals cannot enact some form of political efficacy. It just means that they will not be able to enact it within the bounded confines of this particular state. We begin by noting that, in the UAE, non-national residents' visas are, in effect, *temporary* residence visas. This has a profound effect on the results of our survey: People without the ability to politically participate will generally display a distinct lack of affect regarding local political affairs.

Impact of the Internet upon Politics

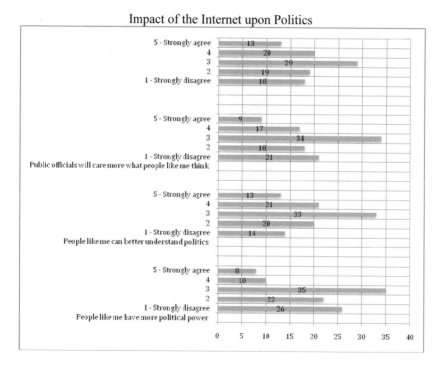

This last point is, predictably, what we find in one set of results from our survey.

Amongst the aggregate responses the mean varies between 2.5 and 3 (where 2 means disagree and 3 means Neutral) for each of the following statements; "people like me have more political power," "people like me can better understand politics," "public officials will care more about what people like me think," and "people like me have more say about what the government does."[46]

This does not, however, mean that people are entirely apolitical. It means that their political concerns may be directed elsewhere. In this vein the figure, below, is of great interest.

Importance of Media as Source of Information

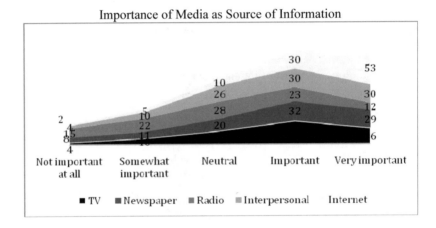

Our results indicate that the Internet has clearly supplanted all other mass media as the most important source of information in the UAE. More than four in five respondents (83%) state that the Internet is either an important or very important source of information. This is significantly greater (29%) than the percentage of respondents who rank television as either important or very important (64%), the second highest rated medium in terms of importance.[47]

We postulate several causes to these results. Amongst them are the predominance of expatriate residents in the UAE; a lack of local media sources in expatriates' native languages, regardless of the use of ELF; and the dearth of investigative print and/or electronic media in the UAE, which will drive expatriates and citizens alike to seek other sources of information, online.

We can also, however, point to the idea of a post-national culture in the UAE. It is our belief that, in the UAE, one does not find a single national community articulating itself as a polity. In this respect we wholeheartedly agree with Appadurai's discussion of the production of locales. In discussing the ontological constitution of locality Appadurai notes that it is a phenomenon of a complex conjuncture that has little to do with any specific space and much more to do with the contingent intersection of the five flows that we enumerated above. For Appadurai this intersection produces a sense of subjectivity, community, and polity - his term, following Raymond Williams, is a 'structure of feeling' - and (at times) political action that *may* be articulated to the space within which this structure of feeling is effected, but whose efficacy may also be articulated to other similarly articulated locales that *need not be contiguous.*[48]

Rather, one finds a series of sociopolitical national circuits within which residents of the UAE 'travel.' At times and places these circuits come into contact - such as at the mosque, or the mall. In terms of politics, however, these circuits almost never come into contact. The Canadian engineer living in the UAE who is committed to Canadian politics and keeps abreast of political developments back home via the web, and who votes at the embassy in Dubai, does not occupy a common, fixed, public space with the Indian IT worker who is involved with Indian politics, writes a political blog in Hindu, and maintains a shared database of electoral resources to help his 'local' political party in Kerala; or the German marketing executive who helps to write political speeches for a member of the Christian Democratic Union, and who does so by exchanging a large number of daily emails, text messages and VoIP calls with her counterparts in Germany.

For the majority of residents in the UAE there is a turning away from the concept of a unified polity within a fixed and contiguous locale in favour of a series of parallel political circuits whose existence is enabled by a variety of telecommunications media, but most importantly those channels found online. These circuits are comprised of the structures of feeling that serve to articulate non-contiguous locales into common political spaces. In these circuits one can communicate with others in one's native language, discuss events of common political importance and concern, and effect a sense of political efficacy within a polity that is no longer coextensive with a specific bounded space and its population.

In this case one finds not a national dialogue, but rather a series of private conversations. ELF use, then, bridges the above-mentioned circuits, but it does not function to integrate the UAE's residents into a common community or polity, be it in English or Arabic. Rather, ELF functions to disaggregate the various resident national groups found in the UAE. In so doing non-national residents - regardless of the duration of the time in country - do not occupy a single national space, but rather move through social circuits that are akin to Moebius strips; two dimensional spaces that enable the flow of information, participation and structures of feeling that are enabled by ELF, articulated across the Internet, but which have no social efficacy or permanency within the UAE.

Notes

[1] B. Anderson, *Imagined Communities: Reflections on the Origin and Spread of Nationalism*, Verso, London, 1991, Chapters 2 and 3; E. Hobsbawm, 'Introduction: Inventing Traditions', in *The Invention of Tradition*, E. Hobsbawm and T. Ranger (eds), Cambridge University Press, Cambridge, 1983, pp. 1-14; T. Bennett, *The Birth of the Museum: History, Theory and Politics*, Routledge, London, 1995, Chapter 4.

[2] On the notion of the contemporary period as one of 'supermodernity' as opposed to postmodernity or hypermodernity, and the relationship of this to the dynamics of flow, see M. Augé, *Non-Places: Introduction to an Anthropology of Supermodernity*, Verso, London, 2000, Chapter 3, *passim*, and in particular pp. 77-80.

[3] A. Appadurai, *Modernity at Large: Cultural Dimensions of Globalization*, University of Minnesota Press, Minneapolis, 1996, p. 189.

[4] H. Breslow, 'Spatial Narratives and Political Space', in *Philosophical Streets: New Approaches to Urbanism*, D. Crow (ed), Maisonneuve Press, Washington DC, 1990, p. 135.

[5] See Anderson, op. cit., Chapters 3 and 10; Appadurai, op. cit., pp. 28-29, pp. 190-191; J. Everard, *Virtual States: The Internet and the Boundaries of the Nation-State*, Routledge, London, 2000, pp. 4-5 and pp. 45-48.

[6] M. Lim and M. Kann, 'Politics: Deliberation, Mobilization, and Networked Practices of Agitation', in *Networked Publics*, K. Varnelis (ed), MIT Press, Cambridge, MA, 2008, p. 78.

[7] On the relationship of fixity to the state and its production of subjectivity, see Everard, op. cit., p. 7 and pp. 48-49.

[8] Appadurai, op. cit., pp. 33-37.

[9] Ibid., p. 178.

[10] See Everard, op. cit., p. 53.

[11] Appadurai, op. cit., pp. 188-193.

[12] Everard, op. cit., pp. 4-8; K. Varnelis and A. Friedberg, 'Place: The Networking of Public Space', in *Networked Publics*, in Varnelis, op. cit., pp. 16-30; T. Eriksen, 'Nationalism and the Internet', *Nations and Nationalism*, Vol. 13, No. 1, 2007, pp. 2-3.

[13] Augé, op. cit., pp. 84-86.

[14] See, for example, Breslow, op. cit., pp. 133-134.

[15] Anderson, op. cit., Chapters 4 and 5.

[16] A. Pennycook, 'Beyond Hegemony and Heterogeny: English as a Global and Worldly Language', in *The Politics of English as a World Language:*

New Horizons in Postcolonial Cultural Studies, C. Mair (ed), Editions Rodopi, Amsterdam, 2005, pp. 6-7.

[17] J. Jenkins, *English as a Lingua Franca: Attitude and Identity*, Oxford University Press, Oxford, 2007, p. 8.

[18] A. James, 'New Englishes as Post-Geographic Englishes in Lingua Franca Use: Genre, Interdiscursivity and Late Modernity', *European Journal of English Studies*, Vol. 12, No. 1, 2008, pp. 99-100 and p. 109; M. Dewey, 'English as a Lingua Franca and Globalization: An Interconnected Perspective', *International Journal of Applied Linguistics*, Vol. 17, No. 3, 2007, pp. 334-337.

[19] T. Skutnabb-Kangas, 'Linguistic Diversity and Biodiversity: The Threat from Killer Languages', in C. Mair (ed), op. cit., pp. 40-42.

[20] R. Zaltsman, 'The Challenge of Intercultural Electronic Learning: English as Lingua Franca', in *Cyber Culture and New Media*, F. Ricardo (ed), Amsterdam, Editions Rodopi, 2009, p. 99.

[21] I. Allagui and H. Breslow, *The Internet and the Evolving UAE: Year One of the Emirates Internet Project*, Unpublished MS, 2009, p. 40.

[22] Ibid., p. 39.

[23] M. Chase, L. Macfayden, K. Reeder, J. Roche, 'Intercultural Challenges in Networked Learning: Hard Technologies Meet Soft Skills', *First Monday*, Vols. 7 and 8, 2002, viewed on 1 February, 2010, <http://firstmonday.org/htbin/cgiwrap/bin/ojs/index.php/fm/article/view/975/896>, p. 9.

[24] B. Halimi, 'The Arab Family and the Challenge of Social Transformation', in *Women and Islam: Critical Concepts in Sociology*, Volume 2, H. Moghissi (ed), Routledge, London, 2004.

[25] Ibid.

[26] J. Zogby, *What Arabs Think: Their Values, Beliefs and Concerns*, Zogby International Graphics, Utica, NY, 2002, p. 7.

[27] J. Van Dijk, *The Network Society*, Sage, London, 2006, p. 165.

[28] D. Wheeler, 'The Internet and Youth Subculture in Kuwait', *Journal of Computer-Mediated-Communication*, Vol. 8, No. 2, 2003, viewed on 10 July 2010, <http://jcmc.indiana.edu/vol8/issue2/wheeler.html>.

[29] See, L. Friedman, *The Horizontal Society*, Yale University Press, New Haven CT, 1999.

[30] A. Hofheinz, 'Arab Internet Use: Popular Trends and Public Impact', in *Arab Media and Political Renewal: Community, Legitimacy and Public Life*, N. Sakr (ed), I.B Tauris, London, 2007, p. 70.

[31] See I. Allagui, 'Multiple Mirrors of the Arab Digital Gap', *Global Media Journal*, Vol. 8, No. 14, Spring 2009.

[32] H. Rheingold, *The Virtual Community: Homesteading on the Electronic Frontier*, MIT Press, Cambridge, MA, 2000, p. 3.
[33] N. Jankowski, 'Creating Community with Media: History, Theories and Scientific Investigations', in *Handbook of New Media*, M. Lievrouw and S. Livingstone (eds), Sage, London, 2006, p. 60.
[34] Ibid., p. 60.
[35] F. Vlavo, '"Click Here to Protest": Electronic Civil Disobedience and the Future of Social Mobilisation', in this volume.
[36] Wheeler, op. cit.
[37] K. Hampton and B. Wellman, 'Long Distance Community in the Network Society: Contact and Support Beyond Netville', *American Behavioral Scientist*, Vol. 45, No. 3, 2001, pp. 477–496.
[38] K. Hampton and B. Wellman, 'Neighboring in Netville: How the Internet Supports Community and Social Capital in a Wired Suburb', *City & Community*, Vol. 2, No. 3, 2003, pp. 277–311.
[39] M. J. Stern, 'How Locality, Frequency of Communication and Internet Usage Affect Modes of Communication Within Core Social Networks', in *Information, Communication & Society*, Vol. 11, No. 5, 2008, p. 610.
[40] See J. Habermas, *The Structural Transformation of the Public Sphere: An Inquiry into a Category of Bourgeois Society*, P. Burger (trans), MIT Press, Cambridge, MA, 1984; see also, Appadurai, op. cit., p. 189.
[41] F. Vlavo, '"Click Here to Protest". Electronic Civil Disobedience and the *Imaginaire* of Virtual Activism', in this volume, op. cit., p. 130.
[42] Ibid.
[43] See Ibid.; J. Prodnik, 'Post-Fordist Communities and Cyberspace: A Critical Approach', in this collection, pp. 75-100.
[44] Prodnik, op. cit., p. 81.
[45] Ibid., p. 86.
[46] Allagui and Breslow, op. cit., p. 68.
[47] Ibid., p. 42.
[48] Appadurai, op. cit., pp. 188-189.

Bibliography

Allagui, I., 'Multiple Mirrors of the Arab Digital Gap'. *Global Media Journal*, Vol. 8, No. 14, Spring 2009, viewed on 25 January, 2010, <http://lass.calumet.purdue.edu/cca/gmj/sp09/gmj-sp09-allagui.htm>.

Allagui, I. and Breslow, H., *The Internet and the Evolving UAE: Year One of the Emirates Internet Project*. Unpublished MS, n.d.

Appadurai, A., *Modernity at Large: Cultural Dimensions of Globalization*. University of Minnesota Press, Minneapolis, 1996.

Anderson, B., *Imagined Communities: Reflections on the Origin and Spread of Nationalism*. Verso, London, 1991.

Augé, M., *Non-Places: Introduction to an Anthropology of Supermodernity*. Verso, London, 2000.

Bennett, T., *The Birth of the Museum: History, Theory and Politics*. Routledge, London, 1995.

Breslow, H., 'Spatial Narratives and Political Space', in *Philosophical Streets: New Approaches to Urbanism*. D. Crow (ed), Maisoneuve Press, Washington DC, 1990, pp. 133-155.

Chase, M., Macfayden, L., Reeder, K., Roche, J., 'Intercultural Challenges in Networked Learning: Hard Technologies Meet Soft Skills'. *First Monday*, Vols. 7 and 8, 2002, viewed on 1 February, 2010, <http://firstmonday.org/htbin/cgiwrap/bin/ojs/index.php/fm/article/view/975/896>.

Dewey, M., 'English as a Lingua Franca and Globalization: An Interconnected Perspective'. *International Journal of Applied Linguistics*, Vol. 17, No. 3, 2007, pp. 332-354.

Eriksen, T., 'Nationalism and the Internet'. *Nations and Nationalism*, Vol. 13, No. 1, 2007, pp. 1-17.

Everard, J., *Virtual States: The Internet and the Boundaries of the Nation-State*. Routledge, London, 2000.

Friedman, L., *The Horizontal Society*. Yale University Press, New Haven CT, 1999.

Habermas, J., *The Structural Transformation of the Public Sphere: An Inquiry into a Category of Bourgeois Society*. Trans. P. Burger. MIT Press, Cambridge, MA, 1984.

Halimi, B., 'The Arab Family and the Challenge of Social Transformation', in *Women and Islam: Critical Concepts in Sociology*. Volume 2, H. Moghissi (ed), Routledge, London, 2004.

Hampton, K. and Wellman, B., 'Long Distance Community in the Network Society: Contact and Support Beyond Netville'. *American Behavioral Scientist*, Vol. 45, No. 3, 2001, pp. 477-496.

——, 'Neighboring in Netville: How the Internet Supports Community and Social Capital in a Wired Suburb'. *City & Community*, Vol. 2, No. 3, 2003, pp. 277-311.

Hobsbawm, E., 'Introduction: Inventing Traditions', in *The Invention of Tradition*. E. Hobsbawm and T. Ranger (eds), Cambridge University Press, Cambridge, 1983, pp. 1-15.

——, *Nations and Nationalism Since 1780: Programme, Myth, Reality*. Cambridge University Press, Cambridge, 1990.

Hofheinz, A., 'Arab Internet Use: Popular Trends and Public Impact', in *Arab Media and Political Renewal: Community, Legitimacy and Public Life*. N. Sakr (ed), I.B Tauris, London, 2007, pp. 56-79.

James, A., 'New Englishes as Post-Geographic Englishes in Lingua Franca Use: Genre, Interdiscursivity and Late Modernity'. *European Journal of English Studies*, Vol. 12, No. 1, 2008, pp. 97-112.

Jankowski, N., 'Creating Community with Media: History, Theories and Scientific Investigations', in *Handbook of New Media*. L. Lievrouwand and S. Livingstone (eds), Sage, London, 2006, pp. 55-74.

Jenkins, J., *English as a Lingua Franca: Attitude and Identity*. Oxford University Press, Oxford, 2007.

Lim, M. and Kann, M., 'Politics: Deliberation, Mobilization, and Networked Practices of Agitation', in *Networked Publics*. K. Varnelis (ed), MIT Press, Cambridge, MA, 2008, pp. 78-105.

Pennycook, A., 'Beyond Hegemony and Heterogeny: English as a Global and Worldly Language', in *The Politics of English as a World Language: New*

Horizons in Postcolonial Cultural Studies. C. Mair (ed). Amsterdam, Editions Rodopi, 2005, pp. 3-18.

Rheingold, H., *The Virtual Community: Homesteading on the Electronic Frontier*. MIT Press, Cambridge, MA, 2000.

Skutnabb-Kangas, T., 'Linguistic Diversity and Biodiversity: The Threat from Killer Languages', in *The Politics of English as a World Language: New Horizons in Postcolonial Cultural Studies*. C. Mair (ed). Rodopi, Amsterdam, 2005, pp. 31-52.

Stern, M. J., 'How Locality, Frequency of Communication and Internet Usage Affect Modes of Communication Within Core Social Networks'. *Information, Communication & Society*, Vol.11, No. 5, 2008, pp. 591-616.

Van Dijk, J., *The Network Society*. Sage, London, 2006.

Varnelis, K. and Friedberg, A., 'Place: The Networking of Public Space', in *Networked Publics*. K. Varnelis (ed), MIT Press, Cambridge, MA, 2008, pp. 15-42.

Wheeler, D., 'The Internet and Youth Subculture in Kuwait'. *Journal of Computer-Mediated-Communication*, Vol. 8, No. 2, 2003, viewed on 10 July 2010, <http://jcmc.indiana.edu/vol8/issue2/wheeler.html>.

Zaltsman, R., 'The Challenge of Intercultural Electronic Learning: English as Lingua Franca', in *Cyber Culture and New Media*. F. Ricardo (ed), Amsterdam, Editions Rodopi, 2009, pp. 99-113.

Zogby, J., *What Arabs Think: Their Values, Beliefs and Concerns*. Zogby International Graphics, Utica, NY, 2002.

Harris Breslow is an Associate Professor in the Department of Mass Communication, American University of Sharjah.

Ilhem Allagui is an Associate Professor in the Department of Mass Communication, American University of Sharjah.

'Click Here to Protest'
Electronic Civil Disobedience and the *Imaginaire* of Virtual Activism

Fidele Vlavo

Abstract
For more than a decade, the praxis of electronic civil disobedience has developed to represent a potential redefinition of contemporary socio-political activism. This chapter considers the concept of electronic civil disobedience as a new form of protest derived from cyber-*imaginaires*. The term defines a range of shared conceptions that promote the redemptive role of digital technology. One of these *imaginaires* sees cyberspace as a new public sphere and the stage for radical social change. In this chapter, I examine the problematic repositioning of Habermas's model of civic engagement with the virtual world. I also outline the challenges posed by online activism through an analysis of electronic civil disobedience and a reassessment of Henri David Thoreau's original formulation of civil disobedience. Raising questions related to the legitimacy of digital resistance, I illustrate how the proposition for radical virtual protest discursively reinforces social domination and inequality in its attempt to assert cyberspace as the exclusive place for socio-political activism.

Key Words: Cyberspace, cyber-*imaginaire*, socio-political activism, virtual public sphere, Critical Art Ensemble, electronic civil disobedience, Electronic Disturbance Theater, Swarm project.

*****

1.   Virtual Activism

In September 1998, the website of Mexican president Ernesto Zedillo became the target of a virtual attack along with the sites of the US Pentagon and the Frankfurt Stock Exchange. The event was organised by artists and activists from Electronic Disturbance Theater and, to this day, it is recognised as the first actual case of electronic civil disobedience: The Electronic Disturbance Theater drew its inspiration from the writings of the American group of media theorists and artists, Critical Art Ensemble, who created the first theoretical texts on electronic civil disobedience in the mid 1990s.[1] Influenced by, amongst other themes, Deleuze and Guattari's concepts of deterritorialisation and nomadicity, Critical Art Ensemble developed an historical account that drew attention to the relocation of institutions of power and governance in cyberspace. Arguing that past models

---

of opposition were no longer successful in the 'physical' world, the group suggested the development of a form of virtual resistance based on computer hacking. The practice entails the re-staging of civil disobedience protests, previously performed during the American civil rights and anti-war movements, in cyberspace in order to disrupt governing bodies in their so-called virtual locations: 'nomadic power must be resisted in cyberspace rather than physical space.'[2]

At first, the idea of a new form of protest that encompasses digital technologies seems to offer great potential for the reconsideration of social and political inequality worldwide. The advent of the Internet promotes the resurgence of ideals and discourses on the democratic and transformative power of technology. Cyberspace, the 'new' virtual world is often presented as a borderless and unified space that supersedes nation states and geographical frontiers.[3] In this context, utopian visions of global democracy and citizenship encourage the view of cyberspace not only as the new virtual public sphere but also as a space for radical dissent. The Internet has revived the collective dream of universal social change and egalitarian societies.

However, a closer examination of this view of cyberspace reveals that the principles and arguments framing online activism are actually reproducing patterns of discrimination and social control. In this chapter, I retrace some of the narratives framing the concept of virtual activism and discuss the contradictions located at the core of the theory of electronic civil disobedience. My principal argument is that, far from offering a radical form of protest, the praxis of electronic civil disobedience replicates existing models of socio-political domination and cultural imperialism. These models, I contend, have been so far ignored in most assessments of the relationship between cyberspace and contemporary activism.

2.   Cyber-*Imaginaires*

The positioning of cyberspace as a unique location for social protest corresponds to a representation of the virtual environment that can be related to a 'cyber-*imaginaire.*'[4] Patrice Flichy uses the term to refer to a phenomenon that sees any major technological development as representative of a collective utopian project. The particularity of this trend is that it often occurs within disparate social groups. As Martin Lister *et al* explain, 'some tendencies that may have been originally posited (in psychoanalytical theory) as belonging to individuals are also observed to be present at the level of social groups and collectivities.'[5] As such, technological developments are regularly interpreted as positive transformations that are due to reverse the failures and deficiencies of contemporary society. Digital technology is attributed a new redeeming function, usually disseminated through distorted narratives that promise new social order, fair economic growth and democratic political structures.[6]

In *The Internet Imaginaire*, Patrice Flichy identifies two main forms of cyber-*imaginaires*, both traced to contemporary American society. One relates to the innovations of digital technology and is mainly based on utopias produced by politicians, industrialists, computer scientists, and hackers. This *imaginaire* serves the digital economy and develops the production and consumption of electronic commodities. The other cyber-*imaginaire*, in contrast, is not associated with specific projects or directed towards a particular audience. Flichy describes it as a 'complete imaginary construction encompassing all aspects of the new digital society: individual life, relations between body and mind, micro and macro social management of society, and production and distribution of wealth.'[7] These two *imaginaires* envision technology as the foundation of social progress. Additionally, the second *imaginaire* is directed towards the creation of a new digital society. Flichy connects the project with a conceptual shift promoted by early writings on digital technology. In particular, Howard Rheingold's book *Virtual Community* is considered central to the transition of digital technology from the scientific framework to the sphere of 'ordinary sociability.'[8]

Rheingold is often named as the leading figure of the cyber-hype trope. Since his notoriously eloquent narration of virtual reality, his highly deterministic publications have been the foundation for the visualisation of cyberspace as the ultimate space for infinite global communication.[9] Writing in the early 1990s, Rheingold attempted to demonstrate how technology had evolved from the prehistoric age to prosper in the era of the digital. At the time, his views encouraged a new generation of computer users to experiment with the Internet and form new social networks. The *imaginaire*, which was cultivated through the development of the PC, encompassed the creation of a new digital environment, free and open to all; a space where users could extend their knowledge to the community but also strive to build a better society.

John Perry Barlow, who portrayed cyberspace as a new virtual state, developed Rheingold's narrative even further. Barlow's 'Declaration of the Independence of Cyberspace' is perhaps one of the most eloquent examples of the utopian and distorted constructions made about cyberspace.[10] Former lyricist for the rock band The Grateful Dead, Barlow is the digital media activist who co-founded the Electronic Frontier Foundation (EFF), a US-based organisation dedicated to the protection of free speech online. In the early days of February 1996, Barlow declared the independence of cyberspace in response to the publication of the then new US 1996 Telecommunications Act. This act included a Communications Decency Act directed towards the regulation and sanction of indecent and obscene material circulating on the Internet. It infuriated many groups of Internet users who denounced infringements on their right to free speech.[11] Commenting on his declaration, Barlow explains:

> This bill was enacted on us by people who haven't the
> slightest idea who we are or where our conversation is
> being conducted ... . Well fuck them. Or more to the point,
> let us now take our leave of them. They have declared war
> on cyberspace. Let us show them how cunning, baffling
> and powerful we can be in our own defense.[12]

Barlow's text has become a seminal piece in the articulation of cyberspace as
a free, autonomous and self-governable environment. What is more, it
explicitly calls for a restriction of state control and the protection of
cyberspace through radical action.

This idea that cyberspace can be declared an independent state is
related to a highly problematic, yet dominant, view of the virtual as an
'electronic frontier.'[13] This is the most powerful and pervasive metaphor that
has been used to shape preliminary understandings of the Internet. The
concept of the frontier enables the portrayal of cyberspace as a self-sufficient
entity, independent from existing political and economic structures. To a
large extent, it is this view that enables the discursive construction of
cyberspace as an adequate sphere for political opposition. The genesis of the
electronic frontier imagery directly relates to the thesis of the Western
frontier developed by American historian Frederick Jackson Turner during
the late nineteenth century. Turner's conception of early America is based on
a binary divide that sees the East of the country as a reflection of modern
Europe and the West as representing the untamed territory of boundless
opportunities and riches.[14] In Turner's formulation, the West signified the
possibility of freedom and economic prosperity for new settlers; an
assumption reinforced by the apparent absence of official structures and the
limitation of governmental interference in public affairs. This distorted vision
which, amongst other omissions, ignored the existence of an indigenous
population, has been re-appropriated by a number of cyber-enthusiasts,
including Barlow, to create early descriptions of cyberspace:

> Imagine discovering a continent so vast that it may have no
> other side. Imagine a new world with more resources than
> all our future greed might exhaust, more opportunities than
> there will ever be entrepreneurs enough to exploit, and a
> peculiar kind of real estate which expands with
> development.[15]

What Barlow effectively produced is a stirring representation of cyberspace
as a free digital land, removed from governmental control; a new territory
where anyone can potentially prosper and gain social and economic

independence. This is the cyberspace that has come to be defended by most cyber-utopians.

The point of reference for Rheingold and Barlow's visions is an early online social community project set up in the mid 1980s. The Whole Earth 'Lectronic Link, commonly known as the WELL, was one of the first virtual projects that allowed public users to communicate on the Internet. The concept was inspired by the Whole Earth Catalog project, an American counterculture publication started in the late 1960s. Technically, the WELL functioned as a bulletin board system where users could post items using, at the time, dial-up Internet connections. The main instigator of the project was Steward Brand, a Stanford graduate who frequented San Francisco's circles of bohemian artists, homesteading ecologists, and business entrepreneurs. Brand used the WELL to set up publications, social networks, and virtual meetings where members of different communities could converse and collaborate. Fred Turner identifies the creation of the WELL as a shifting point in the conceptual understanding of the potential of computer technology:

> Over time, the network's members and forums helped redefine the microcomputer as a "personal" machine, computer communication networks "virtual communities" and cyberspace itself as the digital equivalent of the western landscape into which so many communards set forth in the late 1960s, the "electronic frontier."[16]

With this project, Brand succeeded in bringing together members of previously disparate social groups. Discussions on the online bulletin boards varied from topics on science and computing to counterculture movements, to homesteading ecology, to mainstream consumption culture. Turner suggests that the WELL enabled the merging of countercultural movements and the idea of a virtual community, thus promoting the possibility for social transformation through digital technologies.[17] Barbrook and Cameron also retrace the emergence of cyber utopias to the Californian counterculture of the 1960s.[18] They suggest that idealistic views of digital technology emerged from the remains of the collective desires for social change and equality promoted by activists and artists based in the Bay Area. According to Barbrook and Cameron, to revive their unfulfilled socio-political dreams, these groups turned to the fast-developing digital communication technologies. Hence, the story of the WELL signifies the potential of the digital era for the creation of an online world; a space that apparently can offer a universal means of communication and the possibility to build networks that are inexistent or failing in the physical world. This includes the creation of a virtual community removed from state control, in other words, a new virtual public space.

3.   The Virtual Public Sphere

In a philosophical inquiry about the Internet, Gordon Graham questions the democratic power attributed to digital technology.[19] Graham notes that new means of communication and interaction tend to bring new ideas and new hopes for social equality. It is therefore not surprising that the faster and broader communication channels provided by the Internet have propagated the assumption that virtual environments can, and will, expand the potential for democracy. However, whilst he recognises the important role of virtual communication in public debate, Graham raises a controversial question regarding our persisting aspiration for greater democracy.

> Is democracy a good thing, and does what we know about the Internet give us good reason to think that this is the way to realise it? So powerful are the democratic presuppositions of the present age that it is difficult to persuade people to take [the question] seriously and approach it in a genuine spirit of critical inquiry.[20]

The question entails complex philosophical issues that are beyond the focus of this chapter. However, it should be pointed out that this interrogation is closely related to the dilemma associated with cyber-*imaginaires*. The desire to achieve better democracy through digital technology is linked to the belief that technology inherently, and autonomously, holds the means to improve society. As I have discussed so far, there is a series of conflicting elements in this assumption, and the question then becomes whether the strength of this idealistic desire for universal consensus should allow for the construction of distorted narratives or the redeployment of past utopian projects.

Such a project is the re-consideration of Habermas's concept of the public sphere in relation to cyberspace. In *The Structural Transformation of the Public Sphere*, Habermas produced an historical and sociological account of the origins of the public sphere.[21] Habermas associates the emergence of the bourgeois public sphere with the new social order created by early capitalism. According to him, this political and economic shift allowed for the rise of the public sphere or 'in the modern sense of the term: the sphere of public authority.'[22] The public sphere becomes the place for the voluntary and free expression of ideas. Whilst scholars have for a long time challenged Habermas's empirical claims, Andrew Chadwick confirms that the theoretical model of the public sphere has re-emerged as a normative ideal against which current communication structures are examined and evaluated.[23]

The *imaginaire* that encourages the construction of cyberspace as the new public sphere is partially related to its apparent decentralised structure. The historical view of the Internet as a series of independent nodes of networked computers plays a dominant role in the view that cyberspace is a universal system of communication. In addition, the concepts of the rhizome and deterritorialisation, as theorised by Deleuze and Guattari in their seminal book, *A Thousand Plateaus*, are regularly used to theorise the independent and seemingly borderless quality of the Internet.[24] Cyberspace is often represented as a deterritorialised space that enables the formation of autonomous zones of communication removed from state surveillance and corporate control. For Stefan Wray the coincidental link between the release of Gibson's metaphorical vision of cyberspace and Deleuze and Guattari's model of the rhizome may have served as 'an important marker in the history of ideas about the rhizomatic nature of cyberspace.'[25] In particular, the conception of cyberspace as a non-linear or rhizomatic system encourages the assumption that online information is always shared in an instantaneous and non-hierarchical mode. Yet again, this clearly dismisses the history of the Internet infrastructure and, by the same token, the materiality of technology.

Following the example of the WELL, cyberspace has witnessed a consistent growth in social organisation through countless discussion groups, forums, bulletin boards, chat rooms, and so on. These interactive spheres seem to offer a space for civic engagement and reinforce the idea that cyberspace is, in fact, the most unrestricted and egalitarian environment for the development of a public sphere. Hubertus Buchstein produces a list of some of the early arguments supporting the idea of online democracy.[26] The 'Optimists,' as Buchstein presents them, suggest that the Internet provides an immunisation against authoritarian power and promotes democratic virtual communities. Access to the technology is easy and universal. This enables the emergence of a critical public sphere where interaction and exchange 'subvert traditional power structures by enhancing citizens' independence from government agencies and big business.'[27] However, Buchstein warns against this discourse of online democracy, arguing that, far from constituting a domain for the new public sphere, the Internet can actually distort the very concept of citizenship. The point is that, by now, Habermas's original model of the public sphere has received important criticisms that the virtual environment does not begin to resolve.

According to Lister et al., many critics have qualified Habermas's public sphere as neither democratic nor public.[28] In his analysis, Finlayson provides a clear summary of the criticism formulated against the bourgeois public sphere:

> [In] practice, the participation in the public sphere that existed in the coffee houses, salons, and the literary

> journals of 18th century Europe was always restricted to a
> small group of educated men of means. Property and
> education were the two unspoken conditions of
> participation. In reality, the majority of poor and
> uneducated people, and almost all women, were
> excluded.[29]

Indeed, the so-called democratic practices taking place within such parameters are more than likely to have prevented undesired genders, sexualities, ethnicities or classes from equal participation. The new virtual forums of communication that have emerged with the Internet appear to resolve the shortcomings of the bourgeois public sphere. However, the ideas of open interaction, social diversity and inclusion are still embedded in a cyber-*imaginaire* that considers cyberspace to be disconnected from the offline world. One of the recurrent tropes is the belief that the dynamics of socio-cultural discrimination and inequality no longer operate in the virtual world. Yet, past research has illustrated that practices of racism, sexism and intolerance are easily replicated in cyberspace.[30]

Returning to the WELL project, which could be considered as a first template for a virtual community, it must be stated that most of the initial participants belonged to a close circle of Internet enthusiasts. Despite its presence in cyberspace, and thus the belief in its deterritorialised nature, the project was based in the US and developed in the mid 1980s, a time when access to online technology was still very limited. Despite the discourse of its elite users, which included Howard Rheingold, John Perry Barlow, and the editor-in-chief of WIRED magazine, Kevin Kelly, the WELL was a confined global village where the dream of egalitarian and open communication was hardly materialising. As Flichy explains, 'in the case of The Well, where the community was not linked to a geographic territory, very few people expressed themselves and the vast majority simply observed the debate (read messages) as in most online communities.'[31] What is more, those who did participate tended to reproduce the dominant discourse of the ideal virtual community promoted by the founders.[32]

The point here is not to dismiss the potential of online interaction and online communities. As Jernej Prodnik rightly argues, the view of virtual communities as inauthentic and impersonal is clearly limited.[33] Ironically, Beniger's idea of pseudo-community, as described by Prodnik, discursively reinforces a problematic dichotomy between real and virtual by suggesting that online interactions are of lesser relevance and value. Rather, the dynamics of online communities should be examined in direct relation to existing structures of communication. This is because of the intrinsic connections between offline and online environments. In the first instance, the formation of online communities could not have occurred outside of

existing models and patterns of communication. As such, Prodnik's
preference for Benedict Anderson's 'imagined communities' is a useful shift
away from the misreading of online communities. However, while Prodnik
warns against the temptation to confuse 'imagined' and 'imaginary,' I would
argue that this is a fine, if not invisible, line to draw. It implies the existence
of a system according to which narratives about digital technology and
cyberspace can easily be sorted into 'imagined' or 'imaginary' boxes. On the
contrary, this distinction is at the core of the difficult examination of
discourses regarding online interactions. This is clearly illustrated by the case
of the cyber-imaginaire that 'imagined' cyberspace as the decisive site for
socio-political protest, and by the complex task of disputing this view.

4.   Electronic Civil Disobedience
        The role given to cyberspace in the emergence of radical forms of
protest is based on the series of problematic conceptions that have been
discussed above. The vision of cyberspace that Critical Art Ensemble
articulates to introduce electronic civil disobedience is also rooted in the
concepts of the rhizome and borderlessness. However, Critical Art
Ensemble's account diverges from a crucial viewpoint: the assumption that
cyberspace is still a free, self-governed environment. For the group, this view
may have been accurate at some point in time, but it is no longer valid.
Critical Art Ensemble's argument is that power forces have relocated and
taken control of cyberspace:

> The location of power - and the site of resistance - rest in
> an ambiguous zone without borders. How could it be
> otherwise, when the traces of power flow in transition
> between nomadic dynamics and sedentary structures -
> between hyperspeed and hyperinertia?[34]

Critical Art Ensemble re-appropriates Deleuze and Guattari's account of
nomadicity and deterritorialisation, but this time in order to portray
cyberspace as a conquered place. The formulation of 'nomadic power' is
based on the argument that power has redeployed the tactics of ancient
nomadic tribes to command from and within cyberspace. Consequently, the
group argues, an online form of resistance must be developed to counter
nomadic power. Critical Art Ensemble effectively creates a cyber-*imaginaire*
that promotes the development of an electronic resistance. The rationale is
that previous means of resistance (including mass demonstrations) can no
longer be effective in the digital era. Therefore, there needs to be a digital
form of protest. The concept of electronic civil disobedience (ECD) is thus
theorised as a new online form of political dissent and Critical Art Ensemble
places it in line with the practice of civil disobedience (CD): 'blocking

information conduits is analogous to blocking physical locations; ... ECD is CD reinvigorated. What CD once was, ECD is now.'[35]

Since the publication of the pamphlets that lay down the grounds for electronic civil disobedience, many scholars have been caught up in Critical Art Ensemble's narrative. The typical research on electronic civil disobedience investigates the concept as a potentially new form of socio-political activism. It is focused on practical aspects and compares and evaluates apparent successes and shortfalls. In his classification of online political activism, Sandor Vegh contends that electronic civil disobedience is a promising form of 'hacktivism,' that is a form of online activism that moves beyond information and advocacy to direct practices of resistance.[36] Wray also praises the practice of electronic civil disobedience for its use of cyberspace as a site for communication *and* active protest.[37] Generally, these early critics rarely consider or question the definitions and conceptual assumptions at the core of electronic civil disobedience.

More recently, Mathias Klang has attempted to relate online activism to the concept of civil disobedience. His research concentrates substantially on the definitions and conceptual representations of online and offline protest using semantic and philosophical frameworks.[38] Similarly, Graham Meikle's research is relevant for its analysis of electronic civil disobedience and the discourses of symbolic power, 'netwar' and activism. Meikle draws some important conclusions that allow a subtle distinction between electronic civil disobedience and other forms of online activity.[39] A recurring shortfall in these studies, however, is the absence of a critical discussion of the philosophical and practical legacy of civil disobedience. Despite the explicit reference made by Critical Art Ensemble, the examination of the relationship between the two concepts is a process that is too often neglected in the discussion of online activism. Yet, it is essential not only for the assessment of online activism but also for understanding some of the current contradictions and failures of electronic civil disobedience. In what follows, I provide an overview of this relation and highlight some of the problems related to the direct transposition of social protest in cyberspace.

The term 'civil disobedience' was coined by American author Henry David Thoreau in a title essay published in 1849.[40] Thoreau wrote the text as part of his official opposition to the slave trade and the Mexican war. *Civil Disobedience* is a direct attack on the American government, which Thoreau considered to have been abused and perverted by a few individuals against the will of the American citizens. In his account, Thoreau describes the government's deficiency as an institution that 'does not keep the country free. It does not settle the West. It does not educate.'[41] The essay criticises the government's lack of actions as well as the limited consensus within oppositional and reformist groups: 'Unjust laws exist; shall we be content to obey them, or shall we endeavour to amend them, and obey them until we have succeeded, or shall we transgress them at once?'[42] While Thoreau's text later became favoured by many anarchist movements, it must be stated that his call was not for the suppression of the government but rather for the establishment of a better government.

Nevertheless, the essay has been the subject of many divergent interpretations, mainly due to the fact that it does not actually contain a definition of the term 'civil disobedience.'[43] Ever since, there have been ongoing debates regarding the definitions and practices of civil disobedience. For example, theorists have argued that the term 'civil' implies the existence of a formal legal structure. Jeffrie Murphy offers a definition of what he considers the '*necessary* conditions' for civil disobedience:

> An act A is properly called an act of civil disobedience only if there is some law L according to which A is illegal, L is believed by the agent to be immoral, unconstitutional, irreligious, or ideologically objectionable, and this belief about L motivates or explains the performance of A.[44]

The act of civil disobedience thus consists of the infringement of a law found to be unfair or immoral, but it also implies obedience to the overall legal system and its representatives. This is what effectively differentiates civil disobedience from anarchism and disobedient citizens from revolutionaries or criminals.

The second element considered central to the philosophy of civil disobedience is the notion of public announcement. As Bay notes, 'one would have to state in public that one does not intend to comply with the particular law: typically but not necessarily, one would publicly encourage others too, to disobey.'[45] Civil disobedience aims to draw public attention to social inequalities and to instigate changes in legislation; as such a full disclosure of intention and action seems essential. Leading figures of civil disobedience protests such as Mohandas Gandhi or Martin Luther King have argued that by making public their intention to disobey, protesters confirm their decisions and demonstrate their full awareness of the law and the consequences for breaching it.[46] The non-violent opposition to British rule that led India to its independence and the tactics of pacifist demonstrations during the US civil rights movement are often used as emblematic examples in the evaluation of civil disobedience as an appropriate form of socio-political protest.

As mentioned earlier, Critical Art Ensemble positions electronic activism in the direct legacy of civil disobedience. According to the group, due to the alleged relocation of power to the virtual world, civil disobedience is no longer an appropriate form of social or political resistance:

> Nothing of value to the power elite can be found on the
> streets, nor does this class need control of the streets to
> efficiently run and maintain state institutions. For CD to
> have any meaningful effect, the resisters must appropriate
> something of value to the state. Once they have an object of
> value, the resisters have a platform from which they may
> bargain for (or perhaps demand) change.[47]

Critical Art Ensemble's account clearly acknowledges the past efficiency of
civil disobedience strategies. Physical blockades and sit-ins are praised for
their innovation and non-violence. Some disrupted power institutions led to
major social and political transformations. Nevertheless, Critical Art
Ensemble defends the progressive dismissal of traditional civil disobedience
in favour of a more appropriate strategy. According to the group, social
protest must take place in cyberspace:

> These outdated methods of resistance must be refined, and
> new methods of disruption invented that attack power (non)
> centres on the electronic level. The strategy and tactics of
> CD can still be useful beyond local actions but only if they
> are used to block the flow of information rather than the
> flow of personnel.[48]

However, this suggestion for a seamless transition from civil disobedience to
digital protest is not without obstacles. In theory, Critical Art Ensemble
suggests the formation of small cells of resistance constituted by a few people
with varied experience in activism. The idea is that each cell, with the support
of a computer hacker, organises its own online disturbance activity according
to a pre-selected social or political agenda. Clearly, this basic transposition of
practice raises questions that the current praxis of electronic civil
disobedience does not begin to address. For instance, the questions of access,
legality and legitimacy resurface as part of the organisation and evaluation of
virtual protest. Yet, far from taking into consideration the philosophical and
practical heritage of civil disobedience and its implications for the Internet,
cyber utopians, including Critical Art Ensemble, cyberculture theorists and
political activists, continue to promote cyberspace as the most suitable
environment for social mobilisation.

5.   Protest in Cyberspace
The first practical manifestation of electronic civil disobedience was
organised in September 1998. Artists and activists from Electronic
Disturbance Theater arranged for a virtual protest against the website of
Ernesto Zedillo, at the time the President of Mexico, the Frankfurt Stock

Exchange and the US Department of Defense.[49] The Swarm protest was coordinated in support of the Zapatista movement that rose up against the Mexican authorities during the early 1990s. Formed of indigenous Maya people from the Chiapas region, the Zapatistas entered into an armed conflict to oppose their domination by the Mexican government. With their charismatic leader, Commandant Marcos, the Zapatistas developed an unprecedented political campaign using the Internet and the World Wide Web to gain international media coverage. The strategy evolved as a global movement, *Zapatismo,* which Manuel Castells considers to be 'the first informational guerrilla movement.'[50]

As part of the virtual project, Electronic Disturbance Theater set up a website that provided information about the event and invited Internet users to participate. The homepage contained the full details and schedules of the Swarm protest including a brief statement on the purpose of the event:

> To demonstrate our capacity for simultaneous global electronic actions and to emphasise the multiple nature of our opponents, FloodNet will target three web sites in Mexico, the United States, and Europe representing three important sectors: government, military, and financial. [51]

Electronic Disturbance Theater presented the targets as part of a process of rational selection: the Mexican government was targeted for its oppression of the Zapatistas and the US Pentagon site for its military and intelligence involvement in Mexico. Although the attack of the Frankfurt Stock Exchange was less evident, the group defended its decision as 'a less obvious choice, but one that makes sense as it is a key European financial site with high symbolic value and as Germany is a major player in the global neoliberal economy.'[52] Incidentally, this foretells the subsequent virtual attacks organised against the World Trade Organisation in 1999.

For the Swarm project, Electronic Disturbance Theater created FloodNet, a computer application designed to temporary block access to websites. As envisioned by Critical Art Ensemble, the concept of FloodNet replicates the practice of civil disobedience. In the same way that activists staged sit-ins to physically block access to buildings, the FloodNet application enables the temporary blocking of digital information using DoS (Denial of Service). The project required that participants simultaneously connect to the Internet and reload the pages of targeted websites every three seconds for the duration of the event. The hosting servers were expected to slow down or even crash under the excess of requests. During the Swarm strike, it was reported that the Mexican government website experienced a reduction of its activity.[53] Yet, no evidence suggests that the site was ever at risk of shutting down. The Frankfurt Stock Exchange website was built to cope with large amounts of online requests and did not experience any dysfunction. As for the virtual sit-in of the US Pentagon website, the Department of Defense retaliated by setting up Hostile, a counterattack application that responded with empty browser windows, and which temporarily disabled protesters' computers. Ricardo Dominguez, leader of Electronic Disturbance Theater, considered the Department of Defense's decision to counter attack as 'the first offensive use of information war by a government against a civilian server.'[54] Although the information available regarding the virtual sit-in is limited, the organisers claim that thousands of protesters took part in the event.[55] Wray states that the project drew substantial attention and estimates the number of participants connected to FloodNet between the ninth and tenth of September 1998 to have been 20,000.[56]

Whilst the virtual attacks did not cause noticeable damage, the Swarm project remains the first official application of electronic civil disobedience. At such, it brings to the forefront several contradictions that have remained unresolved, with the questions of access and participation being central. The well-rehearsed discourses of digital divides are useful in drawing attention to the limitation of a form of social protest that exclusively relies on Internet technology. However, the point is not just that hardware and specialist knowledge are essential to the organisation of an event such as Swarm. More importantly, the exclusive practice of online activism raises the problem of legitimacy, that is the question of *who* can and does protest, for *what* causes, and on behalf of *whom*.

On this matter, several human right activists have voiced their concerns and objected to electronic civil disobedience, considering it to be an illegal and non-justifiable practice.[57] These activists question the impact of the virtual attacks and the response of the Mexican authorities, not against the so-called cyber-protesters but towards the dissident local populations. At present there is no means of gaining information regarding the location of the thousands of virtual protesters who participated in the Swarm project, however, it can be safely assumed that with the Internet penetration levels of the time, very few participants were located in the conflict area of Chiapas, or indeed, in Mexico.[58]

The point made here is not that socio-political movements need to remain localised and self-contained. Rather, my intent is to draw attention to the idealised possibilities of digital technology and the limiting view of an exclusive form of activism. Clearly, with an event such as the Swarm project, those with digital access are the only citizens with a say and an opportunity to act. Electronic Disturbance Theater effectively set up a resistance project in which those directly affected could not readily participate. In this case, electronic civil disobedience becomes a form of resistance, whereby global participants can select social movements online and 'click to protest' from the comfort of their secured environment, unaware of and unaffected by the possible outcomes of their virtual engagement. Ironically, the visions of so-called transnational solidarity and global mobilisation actually seem to deny, or minimise, the importance of local populations and their distinctive struggle.

In an open email to Electronic Disturbance Theater, Miguel Garcia Ramirez, member of the Mexican human rights organisation AME LA PAZ, shared his views of what he considers to be 'a dirty war.'[59] Ramirez discusses the underlying discourses of electronic civil disobedience and the danger of a remote, and paradoxically disengaged, form of resistance. Referring to the Swarm project, he asks:

> Did somebody ask the Zapatistas or Marcos? Did somebody tell us let's encourage hackers and mail bombers? Did somebody ask us, webmasters in Mexico that are dealing not one but various sites linked to the social movement, whether we considered such an action convenient? Did they consult it with anyone? Was their action supported by the NCDM in USA? It is not that we think a permission is necessary to take actions, but there must be a consensus about what can affect us all and especially if they are going to be taken in the name of the Zapatistas. Did anyone say: let's suggest without breaking the law actions that break the law or could destroy or saturate important segments of the Mexican state, banks and the stock market information system? Who can benefit from such actions when with antiterrorist laws in the USA whose target is foreigners? We, the Mexicans, need the world's solidarity, imagination and skills. We do not need to resurrect the monster of the metropolis and colony; an action such as the one suggested had to be consulted both with the Zapatistas and the organisations that have sites from Mexico. Or perhaps, immersed in the colonial perception, we are considered unable babies?[60]

At the time when Critical Art Ensemble was formulating the concept of electronic disturbance, less than one percent of the world's population had access to the Internet. By the time of the first manifestation of electronic civil disobedience, the worldwide penetration rate had risen to 3.2 percent.[61] Internet usage in Mexico can only compare to these figures. Certainly, the central nerve of the Zapatistas based in the poorest region of Chiapas created links with the virtual world. This is how the Zapatistas' struggle achieved global awareness. However, it seems unlikely that the militants would make use of this access to engage in virtual attacks against the American and Mexican government sites. As Ramirez rightly points out, this would have probably jeopardised the resistance movement and given the authorities the opportunity to intensify their strike. However, the more contentious issue in Ramirez's plea is the association made between electronic civil disobedience and Western imperialism. This corroborates the main point that I contend regarding the current praxis of electronic civil disobedience that, despite contemporary beliefs, reproduces and reinforces political inequality and socio-cultural domination. The Eurocentric interpretations of the potential of digital technologies need to be reassessed within informed understandings of digital technology and socio-political activism worldwide.

As an example, it is difficult to ignore the impact of online activism in the more recent political events in Burma. Following the uprising of the Buddhist monks in August 2007, it was reported that the Burmese military regime had shut down the Internet, claiming that the country's unique network had been damaged.[62] In fact, the authorities had detected that Burmese citizens were using the web to alert international communities of their violent repression, in the same way that the Zapatista revolutionaries had done ten years earlier. This time, recognising the potential threats, the military state reacted by disconnecting the entire public communication network. This suggests an increasing awareness of the potential use of cyberspace for virtual mobilisation, and it equally demonstrates governments' unrestricted control and authority to 'switch off' the Internet. This point is too often swept away by the dominant constructions of cyberspace as the free and autonomous electronic frontier. Far from being self-governed and borderless, cyberspace is actually a highly territorialised and controlled environment. As such, the repositioning of social debates and the so-called public sphere online does not escape latent practices of discrimination and power struggle.

6.   Rethinking Online Activism

Since its conception, cyberspace has been promoted as the most promising platform for freedom of expression and global democracy. The influence of the technological-*imaginaire* plays an important role in this vision of the Internet as the answer to inequality and socio-political hegemony. Despite contradictory evidence and challenges, the view that cyberspace offers a revolutionary platform for social change remains persistent. In his praise of online activism, Wray declares that, 'unlike the participant in a traditional civil disobedience action, an ECD actor can participate in virtual blockades and sit-ins from home, from work, from the university, or from other points of access to the Net.'[63] This comment illustrates a disconcerting and narrow grasp of the meaning of protest and political dissidence.

Critical Art Ensemble's early discussion of electronic resistance fails to critically engage with the contradictions of narratives that idealise technology. The group suggests the development of a global resistance strategy without considering the materiality of the Internet as well as the technical constraints of online resistance. Furthermore, the premise of online activism is based on the assumption that the 'digital divide' gap will eventually close, resolving the issue of access at once. In the meantime, those with ready access to the Internet, that is, those living in the most industrialised countries, can and should organise remote protests on behalf of the less fortunate, regardless of the consequences of these actions. These contradictions that emerge from the practice of electronic civil disobedience increasingly show that the idea of a socio-political dissidence exclusive to the Internet is indeed an oblivious project.

By retracing some of the conceptual arguments and visions that form the basis of contemporary online activism, I have aimed to bring attention to the disregard of the moral, political and legal implications of virtual resistance. My main point is that no meaningful political protest can or should rely exclusively on digital technology. As it is formulated, the concept of electronic civil disobedience corresponds to a utopian and distorted conception of cyberspace. This approach will need to be addressed and renegotiated, if indeed cyberspace is to play a predominant role in the future of global socio-political mobilisation.

Notes

[1] See Critical Art Ensemble, *The Electronic Disturbance,* Autonomedia, New York, 1994; Critical Art Ensemble, *Electronic Civil Disobedience,* Autonomedia, New York, 1996.

[2] Critical Art Ensemble, *The Electronic Disturbance*, p. 25.

[3] For examples see M. L. Benedikt (ed), *Cyberspace: First Steps*, The MIT Press, Cambridge, MA, 1991.

[4] P. Flichy, *The Internet Imaginaire*, MIT Press, London, 2007, p. 89.

[5] M. Lister et al, *New Media: A Critical Introduction*, Routledge, London, 2003, p. 60.

[6] For an account of early predictions on digital technology, see V. Mosco, *The Digital Sublime*, MIT Press, London, 2004.

[7] Flichy, op.cit., p. 107.

[8] Ibid., p. 90.

[9] H. Rheingold, *Virtual Reality*, Summit Books, New York, 1991.

[10] J. P. Barlow, 'A Declaration of Independence of Cyberspace', in *Crypto Anarchy, Cyberstates, and Pirate Utopias*, P. Ludlow (ed), MIT Press, Cambridge, MA, 2001, p. 27.

[11] A year later, the US Supreme Court overruled the Communication Decency Act on the ground that it violated the First Amendment.

[12] J. P. Barlow, 'Declaring Independence', *WIRED*, Vol. 4, No. 6, June 1996, viewed on 8 September 2010, <http://www.wired.com/wired/archive/4.06/independence.html>.

[13] For a discussion of the 'electronic frontier' metaphor, see A. C. Yen, 'Western Frontier or Feudal Society? Metaphors and Perceptions of Cyberspace', *Berkeley Technology Law Journal*, Vol. 17, December 2002, pp. 1207-1263.

[14] F. J. Turner, *The Frontier in American History*, Holt, New York, 1921.

[15] J. P. Barlow 'Decrypting the Puzzle Palace', *Communications of the ACM*, Vol. 35, No. 7, July 1992, pp. 25-31.

[16] F. Turner, *From Counterculture to Cyberculture: Stewart Brand, the Whole Earth Network and the Rise of Digital Utopianism*, Chicago University Press, Chicago, 2006, p. 6.

[17] Ibid., p. 141.

[18] R. Barbrook and A. Cameron, *California Ideology*, 1995, viewed on 8 September 2010, <www.hrc.wmin.ac.uk/theory-californianideology-main.html>.

[19] G. Graham, *The Internet: A Philosophical Inquiry*, Routledge, London, 1999.

[20] Ibid., p. 62.

[21] J. Habermas, *The Structural Transformation of the Public Sphere: An Inquiry into a Category of Bourgeois Society*, Polity Press, London, 1989.

[22] Ibid., p. 18.

[23] A. Chadwick, *Internet Politics: States, Citizens, and New Communication Technologies*, Oxford University Press, New York, 2006, p. 83.

[24] G. Deleuze and F. Guattari, *A Thousand Plateaus: Capitalism and Schizophrenia*, University of Minnesota Press, Minneapolis, 1987.

[25] S. Wray, *Rhizomes, Nomads, and Resistant Internet Use*, Thing.net, 1998, viewed on 8 September 2010, <http://www.thing.net/~rdom/ecd/rhizomatic.html>.

[26] H. Buchstein, 'Bytes that Bite: The Internet and Deliberative Democracy', *Constellations*, Vol. 4, No. 2, October 1997.

[27] Ibid., pp. 250-251.

[28] Lister et al., op. cit., p. 178.

[29] J. G. Finlayson, *Habermas: A Very Short Introduction*, Oxford University Press, Oxford, 2005, p. 12.

[30] For example see B. Kolko et al. (eds), *Race in Cyberspace*, Routledge, New York, 2000.

[31] Flichy, op. cit., p. 87.

[32] Ibid., p. 74.

[33] Prodnik, 'Post-Fordist Communities and Cyberspace', in this volume, pp. 75-100.

[34] Critical Art Ensemble, *The Electronic Disturbance*, p. 11.

[35] Critical Art Ensemble, *Electronic Civil Disobedience*, p. 18.

[36] S. Vegh, 'Classifying Forms of Online Activism: The Case of Cyberprotests against the World Bank', in *Cyberactivism: Online Activism in Theory and Practice*, M. McCaughey and M. D. Ayers (eds), Routledge, New York, 2003, p. 91.

[37] S. Wray, 'Electronic Civil Disobedience and the World Wide Web of Hacktivism', *Switch*, 1998, viewed on 8 September 2010, <http://switch.sjsu.edu/web/v4n2/stefan/>.

[38] M. Klang, 'Virtual Sit-Ins, Civil Disobedience and Cyberterrorism', in *Human Rights in the Digital Age*, M. Klang and A. Murray (eds), Cavendish Publishing, London, 2005, pp. 135-146.

[39] G. Meikle, 'Electronic Civil Disobedience and Symbolic Power', in *Cyber-conflict and Global Politics*, A. Karatzogianni (ed), Routledge, London, 2008, pp. 177-187.

[40] H. D. Thoreau, *The Writings of Henry David Thoreau*, Houghton Mifflin Co., Boston, 1894.

[41] Ibid., p. 132.

[42] Ibid., p. 144.

[43] Thoreau's essay was initially titled *Resistance to Civil Government*. Some doubts remain as to whether or not Thoreau himself changed it to *Civil Disobedience* at a later point.

[44] J. G. Murphy (ed), *Civil Disobedience and Violence*, Wadsworth Publishing, Belmont, 1991, p. 1.

[45] C. Bay, 'Civil Disobedience Theory', in *Civil Disobedience: Theory and Practice*, C. Bay and C. Walker (eds), Black Rose Books, Montreal, 1975, p. 15.

[46] See K. M. Gandhi, 'Non-violence', in *Civil Disobedience and Violence*, J. G. Murphy (ed), Wadsworth Publishing, Belmont 1991; M. L. King Jr., 'Letter from Birmingham City Jail', in *Civil Disobedience in Focus*, A. H. Bedau (ed), Routledge, London, 1991.

[47] Critical Art Ensemble, *Electronic Civil Disobedience*, p. 11.

[48] Ibid., p. 9.

[49] See Electronic Disturbance Theater, 'Advance News Release', Thing.net, 25 Aug 1998, viewed on 8 September 2010, <http://www.thing.net/~rdom/ecd/September9.html>.

[50] M. Castells, *The Power of Identity*, Blackwell Publishers, Oxford, 1997, p. 79.

[51] Electronic Disturbance Theater, op. cit.
[52] Ibid.
[53] C. Fusco, *Electronic Disturbance Ricardo Dominguez* (interview), Subsol, 25 November 1999, viewed on 8 September 2010, <http://subsol.c3.hu/subsol_2/contributors2/domingueztext2.html>.
[54] M. Bond and R. Frank, *Ricardo Dominguez, Artist and Electronic Civil Disobedience Pioneer*, (interview), The gothamist.com, 29 November 2004, viewed on 8 September 2010, <http://gothamist.com/2004/11/29/ricardo_dominguez_artist_and_electronic_civil_disobedience_pioneer.php>.
[55] Fusco, op. cit.
[56] S. Wray, 'On Electronic Civil Disobedience', *Peace Review*, Vol. 11, No. 1, March 1999, p. 110.
[57] See M. G. Ramirez, *A Dirty War in Internet (analysis)*, Thing.net, 27 April 1998, viewed on 8 September 2010, <http://www.thing.net/~rdom/ecd/amelapaz.html>.
[58] According to ITU reports, in 1998, the estimated number of Internet users in Mexico was 1,350 m. The figures was 8,000 m in the UK and 60, 000 m in the US. ITU, *Yearbook of Statistics: Telecommunication Services Chronological Time Series 1989-1998*, International Telecommunication Union, Geneva, 2000.
[59] Ramirez, op. cit.
[60] Ibid.
[61] ITU, op. cit.
[62] J. Booth, *Internet Access 'Cut Off' in Attempt to Silence Burma*, Time Online, 28 Sept 2007, viewed on 8 September 2010, <http://www.timesonline.co.uk/tol/news/world/asia/article2549404.ece>.
[63] S. Wray, 'Electronic Civil Disobedience and the World Wide Web of hacktivism', *Switch*, 1998, viewed on 8 September 2010, <http://switch.sjsu.edu/web/v4n2/stefan/>.

Bibliography

Barbrook, R. and Cameron, A., *The California Ideology*. August 1995, viewed on 8 September 2010, <www.hrc.wmin.ac.uk/theory-californianideology-main.html>.

Barlow, J. P., 'Decrypting the Puzzle Palace'. *Communications of the ACM*, Vol. 35, No. 7, July 1992, pp. 25-31.

——, 'Declaring Independence'. *WIRED*, Vol. 4.06, June 1996, viewed on 8 September 2010, <http://www.wired.com/wired/archive/4.06/independence.html>.

——, 'A Declaration of the Independence of Cyberspace', in *Crypto Anarchy, Cyberstates, and Pirate Utopias*. P. Ludlow (ed), MIT Press, Cambridge, MA, 2001, pp. 27-30.

Bay, C. and Walker, C., *Civil Disobedience: Theory and Practice*. Black Rose Books, Montreal, 1975.

Benedikt, L. M. (ed), *Cyberspace: First Steps*. MIT Press, Cambridge, MA, 1991.

Bond, M. and Frank, R., 'Ricardo Dominguez, Artist and Electronic Civil Disobedience Pioneer (interview)', *The gothamist.com*, 29 November 2004, viewed on 8 September 2010, <http://gothamist.com/2004/11/29/ricardo_dominguez_artist_and_electronic_civil_disobedience_pioneer.php>.

Booth, J., 'Internet Access "Cut Off" in Attempt to Silence Burma'. *Time Online*, 28 September 2007, viewed on 8 September 2010, <http://www.timesonline.co.uk/tol/news/world/asia/article2549404.ece>.

Buchstein, H., 'Bytes that Bite: The Internet and Deliberative Democracy'. *Constellations*, Vol. 4, No. 2, October 1997, pp. 248-263..

Castells, M., *The Power of Identity*. Blackwell Publishers, Oxford, 1997.

Chadwick, A., *Internet Politics: States, Citizens, and New Communication Technologies*. Oxford University Press, New York, 2006.

Critical Art Ensemble, *The Electronic Disturbance*. Autonomedia, New York, 1994.

——, *Electronic Civil Disobedience*. Autonomedia, New York, 1996.

Deleuze, G. and Guattari, F., *A Thousand Plateaus: Capitalism and Schizophrenia*. University of Minnesota Press, Minneapolis, 1987.

Electronic Disturbance Theater, 'Advance News Release', *Thing.net*, 25 August 1998, viewed on 8 September 2010, <http://www.thing.net/~rdom/ecd/September9.html>.

Finlayson, J. G., *Habermas: A Very Short Introduction*. Oxford University Press, Oxford, 2005.

Flichy, P., *The Internet Imaginaire*. MIT Press, London, 2007.

Fusco, C., 'Electronic Disturbance Ricardo Dominguez (interview)'. *Subsol*, 25 November 1999, viewed on 8 September 2010, <http://subsol.c3.hu/subsol_2/contributors2/domingueztext2.html>.

Gandhi, K. M., 'Non-violence', in *Civil Disobedience and Violence*. J. G. Murphy (ed), Wadsworth Publishing, Belmont, 1991, pp.93-102.

Graham, G., *The Internet: A Philosophical Inquiry*. Routledge, London, 1999.

Gibson, W., *Neuromancer*. Harper Collins, London, 1986.

Habermas, J., *The Structural Transformation of the Public Sphere: An Inquiry into a Category of Bourgeois Society*. Polity Press, London, 1989.

ITU, *Yearbook of Statistics: Telecommunication Services Chronological Time Series 1989-1998*. International Telecommunication Union, Geneva, 2000.

King, M. L. Jr., 'Letter from Birmingham City Jail', in *Civil Disobedience in Focus*. A. H. Bedau (ed), Routledge, London, 1991, pp. 68-84.

Klang, M., 'Virtual Sit-Ins, Civil Disobedience and Cyberterrorism', in *Human Rights in the Digital Age*. M. Klang and A. Murray (eds), Cavendish Publishing, London, 2005, pp. 135-146.

Kolko, B., Nakamura, L., Rodman, G. B. (eds), *Race in Cyberspace*. Routledge, New York, 2000.

Lister, M., Dovey, J., Giddings, S., Grant, I., Kelly, K., *New Media: A Critical Introduction*. Routledge, London, 2003.

Meikle, G., 'Electronic Civil Disobedience and Symbolic Power', in *Cyber-conflict and Global Politics*. A. Karatzogianni (ed), Routledge, London, 2008, pp. 177-187.

Mosco, V., *The Digital Sublime*. MIT Press, London, 2004.

Murphy, J. G. (ed), *Civil Disobedience and Violence*. Wadsworth Publishing, Belmont, 1991.

Prodnik, J., 'Post-Fordist Communities and Cyberspace', in *Cybercultures: Mediations of Community, Culture, Politics*. H. Breslow and A. Mousoutzanis (eds), Rodopi, Amsterdam and New York, NY, 2012, pp. 75-100.

Ramirez, M. G., 'A Dirty War in Internet (analysis)', *Thing.net*. 27 April 1998, viewed on 8 September 2010, <http://www.thing.net/~rdom/ecd/amelapaz.html>.

Rheingold, H., *Virtual Reality*. Summit Books, New York, 1991.

Thoreau, H. D., *The Writings of Henry David Thoreau*. Mifflin Co., Boston, 1894.

Turner, F., *From Counterculture to Cyberculture: Stewart Brand, the Whole Earth Network and the Rise of Digital Utopianism*. Chicago University Press, Chicago, 2006.

Turner, F. J., *The Frontier in American History*. Holt, New York, 1921.

Vegh, S., 'Classifying Forms of Online Activism: The Case of Cyberprotests against the World Bank', in *Cyberactivism: Online Activism in Theory and Practice*. M. McCaughey and M. D. Ayers (eds), Routledge, New York, 2003, pp. 71-96.

Wray, S., 'Electronic Civil Disobedience and the World Wide Web of Hacktivism'. *Switch*, 1998, viewed on 8 September 2010, <http://switch.sjsu.edu/web/v4n2/stefan/>.

——, *Rhizomes, Nomads, and Resistant Internet Use*, Thing.net, 7 July 1998, viewed on 8 September 2010, <http://www.thing.net/~rdom/ecd/RhizNom.html>.

——, 'On Electronic Civil Disobedience'. *Peace Review*, Vol. 11, No. 1, March 1999, pp. 107-111.

Yen, A. C., 'Western Frontier or Feudal Society? Metaphors and Perceptions of Cyberspace'. *Berkeley Technology Law Journal*, Vol.17, December 2002, pp. 1207-1263.

Fidele Vlavo is a Visiting Lecturer in the Department of Arts and Media at London South Bank University, UK. Her research work focuses on new media theory, cyberculture discourses and online activist art.

Part 4

Mediatisation of Memory

Diverging Strategies of Remembrance in Traditional and Web-2.0 On-Line Projects

Heiko Zimmermann

Abstract
This paper focuses on the conditions for using on-line media as means of remembrance, memory and achieving. Starting from a diverse theoretical basis that does not only include theorists like Halbwachs and Assmann but also older metaphorical literary descriptions of processes of remembrance, the paper will compare projects like *Facebook* and *GayRomeo* with less interactive Web 1.0 projects in terms of their aptitude for the described processes. As a result, it will have to be questioned whether traditional on-line media can serve to (re-)construct memory at all or how they will have to be adapted to obtain this ability. For Web 2.0 projects, there are other implications that are related to the level of subjectivity vs. collectivity and public vs. private memory.

Key Words: Social network sites, memory, collective memory, communicative memory, remembrance, Web 2.0, Web 1.0, Facebook, GayRomeo, Find a Grave.

*****

1.   Typology of Memories

Memory is always collective.[1] Taking the example of a tourist's walk trough London, the French philosopher and sociologist Maurice Halbwachs has shown very clearly that '[o]ur memories [are] collective, however, and are recalled to us through others even though only we were participants in the events or saw the things concerned. In reality, we are never alone.'[2] The tourist is never alone as they have heard about London from others, as they might have a map created by others, or just because they are putting themselves into the point of view of the land surveyor who had designed the layout of the city.[3] The German egyptologist Jan Assmann distinguished two types of collective memory: cultural and communicative memory.[4] For him, cultural memory is 'a collective concept for all knowledge that directs behaviour and experience in the interactive framework of a society and one that obtains through generations in repeated societal practice and initiation.'[5] It has to be distinguished from the above-mentioned communicative or everyday memory, that lacks cultural characteristics, and from science.[6] Communicative memory

includes those varieties of collective memory that are based
on everyday communication ... . Typically, it takes place
between partners who can change roles. Whoever relates a
joke, a memory, a bit of gossip, or an experience becomes
the listener in the next moment.[7]

Cultural memory, in contrast, 'is characterised by its distance from
the everyday. ... Cultural memory has its fixed points; its horizon does not
chance with the passing of time. These fixed points are fateful events of the
past.'[8]

To what extent can one talk then about individual or subjective
memory at all? Halbwachs explains, 'remembrances are organised in two
ways, either grouped about a definite individual who considers them from his
own viewpoint or distributed within a group for which each is a partial
image.'[9] The individual, thus, participates in two types of memory:

[H]e places his own remembrances within the framework
of his personality, his own personal life; he considers those
of his own that he holds in common with other people only
in the aspect that interests him by virtue of distinguishing
him from others.[10]

Therefore, individual memory is a vital part of personal identity
construction that goes hand in hand with the knowledge of the differences
from others. It is a form of othering. Collective memory is constructed
through the interaction of people as members of a group. It comprehends the
individual memories of the group members while remaining distinct from
them.[11] If one were to describe the relation in terms of set theory, one could
understand collective memory to be a superset of the involved individual
memories. These notions of individual - augmented by subjective evaluations
of mere events and, thus, called subjective memory - and collective memory
shall be used in the following analysis.

2.   A Metaphorical Literary Description

The idea of an active construction of memory by remembrance is
not new. In the second book of his epic *The Fairie Queene*, written in 1596,
Edmund Spenser describes a library as the metaphor for processes of
remembrance and memory. This metaphor distinguishes an active and a
passive principle. As Aleida Assmann has pointed out, this difference is the
difference between memory and remembrance.[12]

The hero of the epic is a travelling knight who comes to visit a castle
in the respective passage of the text. The castle is a metaphor for the healthy
body of Alma, a clean and innocent soul, who is not spoiled by passion and

lust. After having described various body functions while looking around the house, the knight and - with him - the reader are taken up the stairs into the tower. There, there are three chambers in a row that are inhabited by three different men and that are assigned different functions. The first room, full of figments and immature ideas, is the room of a young man who seems to be slightly insane. It is dedicated to the future. The next room belongs to a man in his mature years, who represents wisdom and who cares about the present. The furnishings of the room document moments of sensible and responsible public behaviour, judging and decision making. The last room, however, leaves a rather dilapidated impression; the roughcast is falling from the leaning walls. The occupant is a half-blind old man whose physical infirmity is contrasted by his alert mind:

> And therein sate an old oldman, halfe blind,
> And all decrepit in his feeble corse,
> Yet liuely vigour rested in his mind,
> And recompenst him with a better scorse:
> Weake body well is chang'd for minds redoubled forse.[13]

This mental force is nourished by his memory - his library - which is an 'immortal shrine' in which the things are kept intact and unchanging. This man, Eumenestes, is so old that he is a witness of things from the beginnings of history.[14] He sits amidst his dusty collections of books and parchment scrolls, which are partially worm-eaten and full of canker holes.[15] He has a young assistant, who fetches him the needed volumes out of the library, even if they seem misplaced or lost entirely.[16] In Spenser's text, there is the notion of Aristotle's conception of the psyche and its various faculties. Similarly, scholasticists like St. Augustine have understood the mind to be divided into parts. In the eleventh book of his *Confessiones*, St. Augustine even describes the presence of the future as expectation, the presence of the present as appearance and the presence of the past as remembrance, thus anticipating the string of rooms in *The Fairie Queene*.

Spenser's metaphor of memory is very dynamic. It distinguishes an active and a passive principle. This difference is the difference between memory and remembrance. Eumenestes represents the infinite memory. Anamnestes embodies the active force that is necessary to find and dig information out of its merely latent presence. Memory becomes an archive from which remembrance selects, updates and takes material.[17]

Why should one take a closer look at Spenser's conception of *memoria*? By depicting memory not merely as a storeroom of the mind but rather connecting it with current events and history, of which Eumenestes is the chronicler; by depicting it as a library to which even visitors have access; by depicting it through a metaphor within a metaphor - the library/memory in

the chamber in the mind/in the castle tower/in the body of Alma/in the soul -
the boundaries between collective and individual possession are blurred. This
blurring also takes place on SNSs on the Web 2.0, as will be demonstrated in
my discussion below.

3.   Shortcomings of the Web 1.0

In his recent monograph *You Are Not a Gadget: A Manifesto*, the
Internet pioneer Jaron Lanier comments on the interpretation of the idea of
informational freedom which underlines that information should be free: 'I
say that information doesn't deserve to be free.'[18] He states:

> Information is alienated experience.
> You can think of culturally decodable information
> as a *potential form* of experience, very much as you can
> think of a brick resting on a ledge as storing potential
> energy. When the brick is prodded to fall, the energy is
> revealed. That is only possible because it was lifted into
> place at some point in the past.
> In the same way, stored information might cause
> experience to be revealed if it is prodded in the right way.
> …
> But if the bits [saved on a hard disk] can
> potentially mean something to someone, they can only do
> so if they are experienced. When that happens, a
> commonality of culture is enacted between the storer and
> the retriever of the bits. Experience is the only process that
> can *de-alienate* information.
> Information of the kind that purportedly wants to
> be free is nothing but a shadow of our own minds, and
> wants nothing on its own. It will not suffer if it doesn't get
> what it wants.[19]

This potential experience is graspable in Web 1.0 projects.
Information is stored in them. However, the triggering of experience happens
mostly outside the medium - in the head of the otherwise passive user - and is
not reflected therein. Thus, the information stored remains static. People with
the ability to programme for the Internet, to change and easily mash-up
information without the typical Web 2.0 tools would probably disagree here.
The father of the W3, Tim Berners-Lee, stated in an interview in 2006, that
the Web 2.0 did not exist at all. The Web was conceptualised as a medium in
which everybody was able to publish.[20] Thus, there is *a priori* an interaction,
an activation of information and a modification of it. However, the vast

majority of users do not have the ability to edit websites on the mark-up/source code level.

An example of the heaving of information to potential experience is 'Leipziger Erzählen,' a part of an educational project for elderly people - *Aktives Alter* -, that asks them to tell personal stories. The description states:

> Leipzig has an interesting as well as a dramatic history …
> which has been written officially. However, the own
> individual experience can be found in circles of writers
> only, or, if grandma or grandpa tell it. After that, it is gone
> for ever. Children and grandchildren demand: "That's so
> interesting. Write it down." Not many people dare to do it.
> Have courage! Have courage for your and for Leipzig's
> history![21]

Precisely this is done on the website. There are accounts, for instance, by people like Heinz Lohse, born in 1928, who tells about bombing raids on Leipzig in 1944. There is Inge Mothes, born in 1926, who describes a visit to a museum when she was 15 years old. She succeeds in presenting the very subjective point of view of a young girl in the first years of the war.

However much potential information on 'Leipziger Erzählen' might be stored, it will surely fail to be a medium for remembrance as it does not invite readers to comment on, link, quote or syndicate the stories. There might be people of the same age who share very similar or diverging experiences that could be added or confronted with the stories on the website in order to keep alive the memory or to revise it. There might be historians who could connect the information to other original sources or factual texts. However, all this is not intended. The information rests on the website like the stone on the window sill: There is potential experience. Alas! It is never going to be released.

The same seems to hold true for most similar projects. Looking for the 'online museums,' mentioned in Martin Pogačar's chapter about Mu-Blogging in this book, one will soon find many of them either looking rather dilapidated or even having been abandoned or closed in the very short mean time already. *The Museum of Online Museum - MoOM* provides a list of good examples. The museums that are still actively maintained are often parts of websites of 'off-line museums' or provide typical Web 1.0 functionality.

4.   Memory on the Web 2.0

Facebook is well known and does, therefore, not need to be introduced here. *GayRomeo* is mostly a dating website for gay, bi and transexual men. In Germany and some other parts of the world, the use of the network is almost natural for homosexual men: the frequency of use by the target group is probably comparable to the use of *Facebook* amongst American university students.[22] *Find a Grave*, by contrast, is something entirely different and, yet, some of the functions are parallel to the SNSs already mentioned. It is an international database of graves of famous as well as publicly mostly unknown people. More than 41 million graves are registered in the database. The records can be searched for names, dates of birth and death as well as for a given cemetery. Most often, people will use it to find graves of famous people, thus the search system bifurcates on the start page already into 'Find Famous Graves' and 'Find Graves.'

As described in the theoretical writings mentioned above, remembrance works via interaction of people. This is precisely the strength of SNSs. Halbwachs writes:

> Very often … images imposed on us by our milieu change the impression that we have kept of some distant fact, or of some person known long ago. …[T]hese images blend into our remembrances and seemingly lend them their own substance… . Just as we must introduce a small particle into a saturated medium to get crystallisation, so must we introduce a "seed" of memory into that body of testimony external to us in order for it to turn into a solid mass of remembrances.[23]

Images posted by others on *Facebook* or *GayRomeo* might become a seed of memory, especially if one was involved in the event whose document the picture is. The same is true for *Find a Grave* if one has been to a respective cemetery. An advantage of the SNS is that they allow immediate feedback. 'No memory can preserve the past. …[It] works by reconstructing, that is, it always relates its knowledge to an actual and contemporary situation.'[24] This adaptation is possible by a continuous discussion about the items that represent memory. Parts of this discussion are comments as text or as the infamous 'Like' and 'Poke' on *Facebook* or the footprints on *GayRomeo*, allowing a minimum feedback without too much interaction, giving just the necessary confirmation that a piece of information is correct, that the opinion on things is shared by others.

The British media scholar Joanne Garde-Hansen is more critical about the idea of memory: 'Facebook may not be liberating personal memory at all but enslaving it within a corporate collective in order to shore up abiding ideologies through its public sphere and commercial activities.'[25] However, as restricting as the system might be for the archiving of personal memory, the user becomes a *prosumer* - this ambiguous creature that is a producer and a consumer at the same time - and, thereby, creates at least a flavour within the corporate collective. Hansen admits that SNSs seem to retain collective memories:

> SNSs like Facebook serve to shore up the relationships between already existing, or once-existent friendships in very niche ways. In our fast-paced world of work and play, such sites appear to ensure that personal and collective memories are maintained and preserved. However, these memories are juxtaposed with the global and corporate-designed systems that project them.[26]

The problem, however, seems to lie in the influence of the archive as agent in the process. Relying on Derrida, Garde-Hansen argues that the technical structure of the *archiving* archive determines the structure of the *achievable* content.[27] She writes,

> SNS users do not simply attend a party, gig or meeting offline and then post their photos or thoughts as memorable record online. They actively engage with the archiving archive of the SNS, whose technical structure determines how those private memories come into public existence and allows the user to produce those digital memories in very specific ways that shore up the corporate memory of the SNS. How a user remembers and archives a rock concert in Facebook would be very different from how that same user remembers and archives it in Myspace.[28]

Garde-Hansen also comments on the replication of social norms on *Facebook*, on why there are no new friends made on SNSs, on the term *autistic social software*, the colour coding of these sites and the rejection of real history on them.[29] However, in terms of memory and remembrance, it seems to be noteworthy that the structure of them, as presented on SNSs, becomes 'formulaic.'[30] Also, a loss of narrative quality is discernable. 'One would like to say that Facebook's emphasis on memory, both personal and collective, allows for an escape from history and, therefore, linearity, order and narrative.'[31] The system is based on database logic, and the narrative trails are only projected while dynamically viewing timelines, wall-posts and the like. However, as memories are not merely recorded, but actively (re-)constructed,[32] Garde-Hansen's criticism loses some of the power it would have had by specifically addressing the writing of histories.

How can subjective evaluations of memory be retained within SNSs? One strategy is surely the disconnection from most other 'friends.'

What Joanne Garde-Hansen describes as a communication problem is actually one stronghold of personal-only memory:

> Sometimes users create mini-archives of photos that are added to and shared by multiple users on a specific theme, for example, an archive of bad hair cuts from the 1980s, and these stand as testament to a collective memory of a cultural moment. Yet, these moments of integration also reveal the differences inherent in any individual's life. Likewise, when reading a user's "Wall"... one is not able to understand the multiple contexts of the interwoven and often juxtaposed discussion unless one actually is the user or knows all aspects of their life extremely well. ...Hence, it is intensely personal rather than collective and connective.[33]

The disconnection from other people's lives may allow single users to retain a very personal view, a very subjective evaluation of memory. However, following Garde-Hansen's argument, it seems doubtful to surmise that it could be necessary to understand every aspect of a person's life to be able to intermingle with their entities of memory on SNSs. Rather a subgroup of their list of friends will be able to connect to the memory represented in the above mentioned mini-archives, while the majority does not share the common basis.

GayRomeo is an excellent example of the different layers of public and private memories, or - if you want - the disconnection from other people's lives that is represented in the inherent structure of the system. Users are able to save other users as contacts. They can decide whether a saved contact is able to see that he has been saved or not. Moreover, this contact can, if he allows it, be shown publicly as a link. If a user is saved as a contact, the saving user can add comments, that only he is able to see, to the profile of the other. By doing so, the public profile is augmented by a private narrative - usually consisting of notes - mnemonics - about real-life encounters, additional information that was collected during chats or even more private details.

Facebook provides a gradation of privacy with the help of lists that friends can be put into and the possibility to make information available to some of these lists only. Additionally, there are so-called official and community pages that offer levels of age restrictions (anyone, over 17, over 18, over 19, over 21 and alcohol-related) that seem to be relevant under certain jurisdictions. Groups restrict the accessibility on three different levels. There are open groups, accessible to everybody; closed groups, where only the group description is public and membership requests have to be approved; and secret groups that are accessible by invitation only.

On *Find a Grave*, the subjective part blends entirely into the publicly accessible files. Users add comments and pictures to the grave records, which are testimonies of individual connections to the respective grave - or the person that lies buried there. For the user who has added these materials, revisiting the website might be an act of individual remembrance. However, these materials are accessible to everybody. For other users, the reception of this data is surely an entirely different experience.

5.   Conclusions and Recommendations

Writing about political aspects of remembrance and memory, Aleida Assmann notes:

> While individual processes of remembrance take place spontaneously and follow general rules of psychological mechanisms, processes on a collective or institutional level have to be controlled by a purposeful policy of remembering and forgetting. As there is no self organisation of cultural memory, it needs to rely on media and politics.[34]

While subjective memory is retained on SNSs (Garde-Hansen), collective memory is an active process that has to be guided.[35] The mechanisms of the SNSs could serve as a possible option. Better would be an awareness of the users that the system influences their way of archiving and resulting from this more subversive usage that at times breaches the rules and the underlying functional principles of these systems in order to steer the system in the desired direction. This can also be achieved by active participation in the services offered by the system (having own groups, deciding on the visibility of information, creating own applications).[36]

The Web 1.0 services do not suffer from somebody taking control of the way they archive information but rather from no-body taking control over the archived information to discuss and update it.[37] The only way to keep these sites as possible memory is to open them, if not for direct comments and additions on the websites themselves then for comments and additions off-site using services like *digg*, tagging information to make it easier accessible for search engines, or to offer ways of using the information in other contexts - e.g. by providing a feed that can be aggregated somewhere else.

An example for this could be the 'blog' of Felix von Leitner, which is one of the most read German blogs. It does not allow leaving comments. However, there is a feed that readers can subscribe to. Content syndication and aggregation is possible. The discussion takes place somewhere else. The rating website *deutscheblogcharts.de* lists von Leitner's website as number five of the most referred-to German blogs (as of January 2010).

Joanne Garde-Hansen closes her analysis with the statement that SNSs 'are a symptom of a need: for identity, for memory, for stories and for connectedness. We are suffering from archive fever [...] and are in need of archives.'[38] However, if there is such an archive fever, why do websites like *Aktives Alter*, websites that are an insufficient medium for (re-)constructions of memory exist at all? Can they be understood to be merely some kind of occupational therapy? How safe are *our* memories on SNSs, and are there other ways of creating and maintaining archives on-line? There are many questions that remain yet to be addressed in this evolving field.

Notes

[1] Halbwachs also uses the term *sensory intuition* for recollections of a purely individual conscious state of mind that is not blended with any social thought. However, he makes clear that evoking such a recollection is actually a reconstruction thereof (cf. M. Halbwachs, *The Collective Memory*, Harper & Row, New York, 1980, pp. 34-35). Individual remembrance can only be understood as the intersection of various collective influences (cf. Ibid., pp. 44-48).

[2] Ibid., p. 23.

[3] Ibid., pp. 23-24.

[4] Cf. J. Assmann, 'Collective Memory and Cultural Identity', *New German Critique*, Vol. 65, 1995, p. 126.

[5] Ibid.

[6] Ibid.

[7] Ibid., pp. 126-127.

[8] Ibid., p. 129.

[9] Halbwachs, op. cit., p. 50.

[10] Ibid.

[11] Ibid., p. 51.

[12] A. Assmann, *Erinnerungsräume: Formen und Wandlungen des Kulturellen Gedächtnisses*, Beck, Munich, 1999, pp. 158-160.

[13] E. Spenser, *The Faerie Queene*, T. P. Roche and C. P. O'Donnell (eds), Penguin, London, 1978, II.IX.55.

[14] Ibid., st. 56.

[15] Ibid., st. 57.

[16] Ibid., st. 58.

[17] For a detailed discussion of the Internet as an archive versus a library, cf. Wolfgang   Ernst's   chapter   'Zeitkritik   der   Symbolischen

Kommunikationsmedien', in *Irritationen: Medieninduzierte Zeitaffekte*, Kadmos, Berlin, in preparation.
[18] J. Lanier, *You Are Not a Gadget: A Manifesto*, Alfred A. Knopf, New York, 2010, p. 28.
[19] Ibid., pp. 28-29, italics by me.
[20] Cf. . Berners-Lee, Interview, *developerWorks Interviews*, 25 Aug. 2006, 26 Jan. 2007,
<http://www-128.ibm.com/developerworks/ podcast/dwi/cmint082206.txt>.
[21] Trans. from *Aktives Alter - Neue Medien*, 2006, 9 Feb. 2010, <http://www.aktives-alter.de/portal1.html>.
[22] For more details on the impact of *GayRomeo* cf. Heiko Zimmermann, 'Erinnerung im Web 2.0: Das Internet als (persönliches) Gedächtnis', in *Vorträge aus dem Studium Universale 2004-2007*, E. Schenkel and N. Kroker (eds), Leipziger Universitätsreden, Vol. ns 106, 2009, pp. 131-149 and p. 136.
[23] Halbwachs, op. cit., p. 25.
[24] Assmann, op. cit, p. 130.
[25] J. Garde-Hansen, 'MyMemories?: Personal Digital Archive Fever and Facebook', in *Save As...: Digital Memories*, J. Garde-Hansen, A. Hoskins, A. Reading (eds.), Palgrave, London, p. 136.
[26] Ibid., pp. 136-137.
[27] Ibid., p. 137.
[28] Ibid., p. 137.
[29] Ibid., pp. 139-141.
[30] Ibid., p. 139.
[31] Ibid., p. 141.
[32] Cf. Ibid. and Assmann, op. cit., p. 130.
[33] Ibid., p. 143.
[34] A. Assmann, *Erinnerungsräume: Formen und Wandlungen des Kulturellen Gedächtnisses*, Beck, Munich, 1999, p. 15. The original German passage reads, 'Während im Individuum Erinnerungsprozesse weitgehend spontan ablaufen und den allgemeinen Gesetzen psychischer Mechanismen folgen, werden auf kollektiver und institutionaler Ebene diese Prozesse durch eine gezielte Erinnerungs- bzw. Vergessenspolitik gesteuert. Da es keine Selbstorganisation eines kulturellen Gedächtnisses gibt, ist es auf Medien und Politik angewiesen.'
[35] Ibid., p. 15.
[36] The recently introduced *Facebook Site Governance* is a piece of evidence of the influence users have on the corporate system.
[37] Insofar, the retreat to the personal website, as recommended by Steven Pemberton is no feasible solution to the problems posed. Surely, one gains

the total control over the data on this personal website. However, it does not work for purposes of remembrance or collaborative re-constructions of memory.
[38] Garde-Hansen, op. cit., p. 148. Cf. also J. Derrida, *Archive Fever: A Freudian Impression*, E. Prenowitz (trans), University of Chicago Press, Chicago, 1996.

Bibliography

Aktives Alter - Neue Medien. 2006, viewed on 9 February 2010, <http:// www.aktives-alter.de/portal1.html>.

Assmann, A., *Erinnerungsräume: Formen und Wandlungen des Kulturellen Gedächtnisses*. Beck, Munich, 1999.

Assmann, J., 'Collective Memory and Cultural Identity'. *New German Critique*, Vol. 65, 1995, pp. 125-133.

Berners-Lee, T., Interview. *developerWorks Interviews*, 25 Aug. 2006, viewed on 26 January 2007, <http://www-128.ibm.com/developerworks/ podcast/dwi/cmint082206.txt>.

Derrida, J., *Archive Fever: A Freudian Impression*. Eric Prenowitz (trans), University of Chicago Press, Chicago, 1996.

Ernst, W., *Irritationen: Medieninduzierte Zeitaffekte*. Kadmos, Berlin, in preparation.

Garde-Hansen, J., 'MyMemories?: Personal Digital Archive Fever and Facebook', in *Save As...: Digital Memories*. J. Garde-Hansen, A. Hoskins, A. Reading (eds), Palgrave, London, pp. 135-149.

Halbwachs, M., *The Collective Memory*. Harper & Row, New York, 1980.

Lanier, J., *You Are Not a Gadget: A Manifesto*. Alfred A. Knopf, New York, 2010.

Spenser, E., *The Faerie Queene*. T. P. Roche and C. P. O'Donnell (eds), Penguin, London, 1978.

Zimmermann, H., 'Erinnerung im Web 2.0: Das Internet als (Persönliches) Gedächtnis', in *Vorträge aus dem Studium Universale 2004-2007*. E. Schenkel and Kroker, N. (eds), Leipziger Universitätsreden, Vol. ns 106, 2009, pp. 131-149.

Dr. phil. **Heiko Zimmermann** studied Physics, English and Pedagogy at the University of Leipzig and the University of Leeds. He has worked at Leipzig, Bayreuth and the University of Trier, where he currently holds a lecturer position in English literature. Amongst his publications are scholarly papers on E. M. Forster, memory and remembrance on the Web 2.0 and hypertext theory as well as literary reviews, journalistic and literary texts. His recent monograph deals with reconfigurations of author- and readership in digital literature

Music Blogging: Saving Yugoslav Popular Music

Martin Pogačar

Abstract
Imagining, interpreting and appropriating the past in the digital age is a complex and manifold set of practices and processes that increasingly employ audio-visual components (sound, image, video) in addition to classical textual narrativisations. The interspersing of video-image-text-audio (v.i.t.a.) has become widely used in digital storytelling, particularly in terms of production, dissemination and consumption of digital content. Among others, the uses of digital technologies in narrating the past span official (museums) and unofficial (digital storytelling, blogging, websites) narrativisations, and problematise the role of national meta-narratives. This is particularly true in the newly established post-socialist states, which have experienced a thorough revision - sometimes an outright annihilation - of their socialist pasts; thus narrativisations of the past in digital media ecology feature prominently. One of the many means available to re-appropriate and reconfigure the past is the medium of music blogging, which employs v.i.t.a. to narrativise and preserve the disappearing facets of Yugoslav popular culture. In this chapter the author interrogates the potential of such blogging for preserving and archiving popular music from the former Yugoslavia. To that end the author analyses two blogs in terms of content management and its implications for the mediation of memories.

Key Words: Music blogs, digital media ecology, Socialist Federative Republic of Yugoslavia, history, memory, popular culture.

*****

1.   Introduction

Numerous online mediations of the past - spanning complex and elaborate websites (e.g. online museums, memorials, etc.) and the more grass-roots, DIY audio-visual statements such as, for instance, on YouTube, and posts and comments on forums and blogs - apply and utilise diverse sets of practices and strategies to re-present via media archaeology and reconfigure the past in both aesthetic and political terms. In other words, digital media ecology (DME) provides for extended places and tools for individual narratives of the past on a public level.[1] Concomitantly, history is increasingly becoming the result of the negotiation of contesting views via the remeshing and remixing of video, image, textual and audio sources. These practices are not at all entirely new, nor exclusively related to or emanating from the DME; they rely significantly on both offline media ecology and on 'old' practices and strategies of narrativisation and communication. Crucially relying on communication and central to combined, interpersonal interactions of creating the past is digital storytelling. Following the conceptualisation of digital storytelling promoted by Joe Lambert,[2] I propose to understand the notion in terms of any online activity that reconfigures, remediates, converges, remixes and remeshes video-image-text-audio (v.i.t.a.) sources of the past to narrate personal, collective, present or past experiences to be viewed, listened to, discussed, or simply ignored.[3] One of the most popular practices of digital storytelling and online communication in general is blogging.

This chapter discusses a particular type of blogging - music blogging - in relation to the re/narrativisation of the Yugoslav past through the remediation of Yugoslav popular music. More precisely, the role of music blogging in the scope of van Dijck's concept of 'mediated memories' is probed in relation to issues of preserving the Yugoslav musical past online,[4] and with that the preservation of an important portion of Yugoslav history and cultural heritage.[5]

I begin by examining the idea of the Internet as a popular archive, a ubiquitous and widely used tool for preserving immense amounts of data, and by discussing the view of music as a vehicle for preserving and transmitting the past. I then examine the issue of music in cyberspace, and more specifically music blogging as a practice to preserve the (musical) past, which significantly re-positions Yugoslav popular music as a media-historical source of Yugoslav popular culture and history. Significantly, the latter is closely related to and affected by the mobility of media objects that, in DME, can be very widely circulated massively among and between spaces, times, individuals, and machines.[6]

2.   The Internet: A Popular Archive of Collective Intelligence

The preservation of the past and related activities are an intrinsic characteristic of human existence and indeed a crucial social activity that enables and facilitates the preservation of a community over time and space. Throughout history, people have been trying to prevent their quotidian worlds from passing into the abyss of time and from their physical extinction by creating representations of important events, people, concepts, etc. As the present invariably becomes the past, such representations are retrospectively re-evaluated, endowed with meaning and interpretations to make sense in the future, in order to provide a transhistorical link in the continuity of a community. Records of the past can thus be found in monuments, paintings, literature, official documents, music, cinema, literature etc. It was not, however, until the age of modernity that Western societies began to preserve their present for their possible future. Late modernity brought the importance of the archive and archiving to a new level: 'Fail to archive, fail to remember.' This motto seems to have been put to use during the period of nation-building in the nineteenth-century and reflects the European Romantic quest for folk origins, which led to extensive transcriptions and documentations of ordinary everyday practices, folk songs, and stories in order to link a nation to an invented ancient past, and to constructions of 'tradition' to newly imagined nations. Nevertheless, ideological selection and censorship held sway upon what was to be preserved, not only due to the technologically limited recording equipment of the time and accompanying problems of storage, but also because of political motivations and the economies of collecting, storing and preserving. At the same time the ideological aspects of selection also crucially determined what was to be left out of the grand historical narratives and consigned to oblivion.[7] Along with 'little histories,' this often excluded significant portions of everyday life with all its trivial, yet fascinating and far from unimportant, minutiae.[8]

The development of the Internet over the last 25 years, and particularly the establishment of the World Wide Web and subsequently Web 2.0, is so far the closest and most potent realisation of the dream of preservation. Unlike the classical archive, with its limits imposed upon submission, storage, access and retrieval of data, the Internet offers relatively easy access, uploading, retrieval, and sharing of data. This data, however, often 'suffers' from issues of authenticity and veracity and, for example, Digital Rights Management,[9] at the symbolic level, but also at the more material or physical one, of problems of operating systems' compatibility over time, file formats, etc., at the more material or physical level. In terms of historical records and interpretations, online data continually evoke the question of the status, location, or authenticity of interpretive authority which is often taken for granted in official, national archives. In other words, the affluence of sources and information, and the re-use and re-application thereof, render the national (e.g. history or archive) as the ultimate definer of a veracity that is, at best, elusive. With the role of external referent once assumed by the State severely mitigated, the increasingly predominant user-generated interpretations, representations and mediations of history are, from the perspective of the nation-state, untrustworthy and unreliable. As well, such data are often difficult to keep track of and canonise. Hence, on the one hand, they largely elude control and censorship, and, on the other, they undermine the state-sponsored systems of knowledge dissemination and education.

A large amount of online content is intentionally published with an at least implicit archival agenda, as in many respects the Internet and the protocols that enable its operation facilitate unprecedented opportunities to save and preserve our digital lives. In terms of cost, availability, storage capacity, and ease of retrieval, the Internet, from the technophilic point of view, represents the ultimate tool for unhindered remembering and the ultimate means to never forget.[10] Social networking sites, webpages, blogs etc. all, in various ways, employ digital media technologies to provide social spaces for the individual or collective externalisation and presentation of everyday lives. Once content is uploaded it moves beyond the jurisdiction of the author and becomes, for better or worse, public property. This is not all that is out of the user's control, however.

Internet technology also contributes to the facilitation of the creation of another sort of involuntary archive that keeps records of user/visitor activity online, by logging IP addresses, search queries, credit card details, transaction tracks, 'items bought,' etc., thus creating a database of user behaviour, the geo-location of buyers, and other types of marketable information. All exist as fodder for the potential politicisation and securitisation of individual and collective, past and present.

Yet, in many respects, Internet-enabled archives, viewed as repositories of digital memories, can be seen, in their more idealistic incarnation, as an infrastructure of collective intelligence, which, according to Jill Walker Rettberg,

> doesn't lie in the individual videos on YouTube, or in each
> separate blog post we write, it's in the patterns we trace as
> we move through these media: the order in which we listen
> to songs, the books we buy after viewing a particular site,
> the links we make or the links we choose to follow.[11]

The content and data on past activities can thus be much more than mere tracks of individual conduct; as individuals tend to gather in groups, tracks are kept of group activity and consequently of individual and group histories of activities and actions on and offline. In this respect, the Internet offers various tools and a massive archive that can be used in reconstructing, re-evaluating, re/narrating, and re-envisioning the past. As important past-preserving and re-creating practices, online strategies of dealing with the past also have serious consequences for the wider social and cultural role of history and the potential of national histories within national contexts. The online, however, cannot be observed in isolation from the offline, as both environments are intrinsically interwoven and significantly reflect occurrences in the other. Online spaces of encounter feature as externalised, publicly available spaces, where personal, social, and communicative spaces converge, regardless of their temporal or spatial location. This emphasis will prove helpful in elaborating the arguments in the discussion below.

3.   Music as a Past-Preserving Machine

By definition, music is always elusive, in terms of its transitory, performative nature and even more so as a research object. Performed music emanates from live performance, radio broadcasts, or a playback device. It invades space, progresses over time, and cannot exist outside either. To hear or listen to music means to be permanently on the verge of losing its sound, melody, and lyrics|. Once a song is over, however, the listener is not entirely free from its grasp. One is left with one or a mixture of feelings of joy, melancholy, sadness, etc., which are as elusive to grasp as the music itself. Yet during the musical intake, music creates a space-time continuum of a distinctly different order than, for instance, that created by still or moving images. The duration of the sound, the melody and the lyrics in time and space, create specific soundscapes that are intrinsically related to the psychological constellation of the listening individual, her position in a historical, social, and cultural environment, and not least to the whim of a moment. The soundscape created by the interweaving of melody, rhythm, and lyrics is prone to being invested with individual feelings, visions, thought, and so on.

Here, Michel Chion's ideas about the role of popular song in cinema prove themselves useful. Chion writes about the specific characteristics of a pop song - it is delimited by the capacity of a circular single record to about three minutes; it has an overture, peak and ending; and most importantly, it is repetitive, in the sense that it can be played again and again - think of the round shape of the record, its circularity breeding repetition. It thus enables different words that fit the same melodic structure and melodies to be consumed ad infinitum and, what is more, this randomness facilitates different parts of the lyrics or in fact entirely new lyrics to be applied and re-applied in one's mind to this open musical structure.[12] The dramatic structure of the song is interspersed with a refrain, which breaks its temporal linearity and further establishes an impression of circular repetition. Thus, the song becomes a world of its own, a space into which an individual may invest mediatised images and personal renditions of realities, past and present. Importantly, this aids in creating an audio-visual landscape that significantly informs the way an individual perceives the song, the surrounding environment and the wider historical, social and cultural milieus. Consequently the song is inscribed into the memory of the listener. As Karin Bijsterveld and Jose van Dijck argue,

> sound and memory are inextricably intertwined with each other, not just through repetition of familiar tunes and commercially exploited nostalgia on oldies radio stations, but through the exchange of valued songs by means of pristine recordings and recording apparatuses, as well as through cultural practices such as collecting, archiving and listening.[13]

A remnant of the past, malleable and open to interpretation, the song transgresses emotional embeddedness on the individual level of the performer/listener to the level of a collectively shared social experience - think of the feeling you get when listening to a favourite song on the radio.

Moreover, as an experience that is both very private and communal, music captures, reflects and produces feelings: 'music's ability to elicit highly personal emotions and associations seems to help people to relive their past over and over again.'[14] For example, it is common, when listening to a treasured song related to one's past, to relive at least some of the feelings initially produced by its particular combination of sound and lyrics - or, for that matter, to redefine and reinterpret the feeling every time the song is heard. The collective aspect of music, the simultaneity of collective reception,[15] positions music in a way that inscribes the individual's experience into a broader social picture and concomitantly invests the individual's experience with her own rendition of the wider social and cultural *Zeitgeist* presumably residing in, or being transferred by, music. In this way, music also works as a social adhesive, a platform for shared experience amongst various populations, sub-cultures, or interest groups.

Relevant to the purposes of this paper is the capacity of music to capture a specific historical epoch and convey it to the present and the future. Also crucial for this paper is an investigation of the ways in which music is received, interpreted, and remediated today. Thus I am not examining specific production modes nor specific genres; this is not a history of Yugoslav popular music. The space-time, the past, or history captured within the songscape(s) interacts closely with one's set of very private experiences and feelings in the present, and is also in constant interaction with the realm of the anticipated community. Listening to a song can take us back to when we listened to a certain kind of music, it can remind us of what we were doing and/or feeling at the time. It can also serve to narrate a specific view or understanding of the past by virtue of transmitting both aural and visual images of a world no longer present, re-placing them into a world today. It is through this lens that I look at Yugoslav musical heritage.

The question arises as to whether music is capable of transmitting more than personal experiences. To put it in a different way; is it ever possible to gain through the music of a certain period access to that specific period? Due to the massive mediatisation of the quotidian, I think popular music can in fact re-present, if only fractionally, a scent of times passed, thus providing a glimpse into the socio-cultural environment of the late Yugoslavia. Moreover, music and audio recording can also be used in trying to control the inaccessible past.[16]

4.   Music in Cyberspace
When speaking about music in cyberspace the first thing that comes to mind is the massive availability of usually copyrighted and hence pirated material. Downloading mp3 format files and viewing audio-visual content has, over the past fifteen years, become a popular online pastime and has provoked a stifling reaction from the music industry trying to confine free file sharing by punishing the 'criminals.' Nevertheless, free music is still widely available on various more or less ephemeral sites that provide links to files hosted at numerous remote file-hosting sites. The more flexible policies, such as pay-per-song, or album, as promoted by iTunes, Amazon, and others, seem to provide a reasonable response to the changes in the digital media ecology and to the shifting power relations in the digital media economy. Instead of the rigidity immanent in the giants of music industry, this approach builds on generating income in small pieces from a wider crowd.

Nevertheless, sharing music outside of the financially sanctioned and copyright-acknowledging channels largely pervades digital media everyday practices and strategies. As fiercely as one might argue that this is an infringement of copyright and intellectual property, it can just as fiercely be argued that p2p file sharing in fact promotes obscure and marginal music, making it available to wider audiences. But this is not all that relevant for this discussion. For my purposes it is crucial to discuss the function of sharing music in the digital media ecology and the role of music circulation in DME to illuminate the practices and strategies of how music can be reconfigured to create a narrative about a Yugoslav past.

As discussed above, music emerges from a material object situated in space (an instrument, a playback device, a speaker system); it exists temporally for a certain period and, unless replayed, it is eventually lost to the flow of time. When played from a device it is actually read, yet it leaves no physical trace on the mind and body of the listener, despite its bi-sensorial characteristics. On the one hand, sound is a physical force capable of spreading through the air and 'make things move.' On the other, it also has the capacity to 'attack' the ears and mind through its content: its melody, rhythm and lyrics. The transience of sound and music was much more obvious before Edison's recording technology enabled its preservation (albeit initially for different purposes than we usually think of today) at an unprecedented scale, rendering the enjoyment and consumption of music considerably different.[17] However, as playback devices were rather expensive in the early days, the development of radio technology and its associated listening practices seemed to have developed enormously while still providing the setting where sound (music, news) could be consumed collectively, also to be collectively forgotten and remembered. It was perhaps radio that enabled the emergence of the special feeling one gets when hearing a song on the airwaves knowing that many remote others are probably also sharing this very same experience at this very same time.

> Look, its night already, and we're alone now
> Quietly, the radio's playing
> On the waves of the song, form me to you,
> From heart to hear
> Wades our joyful malady,
> Happiness, it's called
> Reminding lovers
> Of their desires.[18]

If, in the pre-recording music culture, listening was an ephemeral experience, in the analogue recording culture it became a repeatable one. Now, in the digital realm, a third, post-record, digital, music culture is emerging that relegates listening to music as a practice of listening to fragmented and recontextualised bits and pieces, of remixed samples.

In the good old days the object-, carrier-, and record-centred listening experience revolved around first buying an LP or cassette, and then playing it and listening to the recorded tracks consecutively, with optional skipping and audible forwarding/rewinding. The story changed somewhat with CDs, which introduced random, shuffle and repeat functions and the programming of track order, that were impossible with vinyl records. It could be argued that the need for the listener to physically engage with the machine to replay, rewind or skip a track kept her closer to the process of listening to music. In the digital realm of storing and replaying music, mp3 files require much less effort to set up a list that can then be endlessly replayed and/or updated, thus making music increasingly a soundtrack to our lives. Hence, the digital listener is, in a way, much more disengaged from the process of listening. Music becomes the medium of the everyday, one's silent companion: always there, without much to say. Keeping track of digital music becomes an act of devotion when we consider the sheer amount of music files compiled and stored in an ordinary hard disk. This is further intensified when downloading large amounts of music. This activity can turn into an obsession with compiling yet never really listening to most of the music. On the other hand, the means and chances of encountering new music are thus greatly improved.

Downloading, storing and sharing music is a case of mobility of media objects in the sense proposed by Lev Manovich who understands mobility not as 'the movement of individuals and groups accessing media from mobile devices, but to something else which so far has not been theoretically acknowledged: *the movement of media objects between people, devices and the web.*'[19] Mobility in this sense includes the downloading of music files, their potentially endless distribution, and the creation of unanticipated ad-hoc audiences, which becomes particularly relevant in view of the capacity of music aired on radio to entangle listeners into a chronologically uniform community where geographical location no longer constitutes a necessary condition. In this case it is through territoriality that the temporality of the community is likewise disintegrated. The ever-present media object, a music file, assumes existence beyond the limits of the here and now, becoming a transtemporal marker of another place and another time.

The interesting aspect of the mobility of music files lies in the motivation of the individuals engaged in enabling such mobility by uploading and/or downloading. One first interpretation might be that people refuse to pay money for physical sound carriers or digital tracks and albums. While this may be true to some extent, it is not, however, the whole story. This interpretation neglects the fact that uploaded music had to be bought at some point, and it completely ignores the uploader's motives in sharing the music. The use of the term 'sharing' hints at the direction where one can look for an answer. In this respect it is important to acknowledge the motive to find, digitise, and provide music for free to fellow music lovers despite the copyright issues and the potential to face criminal charges. The discussion below will provide some insight into this.

5.   Audio Blogging as a Past Preserving Practice

> I love it when you come here, but you should take a more active part in this blog as this is a heritage of a time and you should understand that any preserved sound may represent your part in preserving the memory of and truth about a country. Well, it had disintegrated but I think that it still lives as an idea and it will outlive all of us who come here, and one day, perhaps under a different name this will once again be the land of the South Slavs. Until then we will write about it and put up sounds from this former and pre-former Yugoslavia.
> The number of inhabitants of a large city visited this site or blog and thank you for this. We try (myself and my dear contributors) to provide you with more beautiful things.[20]

Music blogs (i.e., blog storage services) in general do not physically store any music files but rather provide links to remote file-hosting sites from where the music is then readily available for download. This strategy of remote file storage and particularly the structure of music blogs remains a constant feature in music blogging, regardless of the genres, periods, etc. that the blogs may cover. The main reason is clearly an attempt to avoid copyright breach, as in most cases the music is copyrighted. This is clearly discernible in many blog policies, for instance: 'The music that I post up on this site is NOT for commercial use. I'll spare you the legal jargon, but in essence, if you LIKE it, BUY it! - pw for most files: rideyourpony.' The blogger still provides links to full albums, but at the same time encourages visitors to buy. As ambiguous in terms of copyright compliance as this position may seem, this strategy clearly features as a cover when coupled with storing files on remote servers.

This is not really the central topic here, so first a few words on music blog structure. Much like any other blog, a music blog is usually introduced by a heading explaining in brief what the blog is about, declaring the 'blog policy' or providing a mission statement. Posts are ordered chronologically, with the newest at the top. A post usually contains a short description of the record, a track list, tags, and comments. Apart from that, a music blog usually gives the option to visitors to 'follow' it, and provides a selection of links to other music blogs. A visitors counter is a typical feature, as is the occasional inclusion of a feature such as 'whos.among.us' or something similar. The latter provides statistics on the number of users 'online in past the 24 hours,' 'what are they copying,' and 'where they come from,' which positions the locations of users on a map of the world. ('A map showing you where your visitors come from. Flashing pins are people that are online right now.') A music blog, much like any other blog, may also provide chronologically ordered menu of older posts (2009>November (13)).

Needless to say, in terms of content, the main focus is music, but music blogs differ in the ways content is presented. As personal as any blog can be or generally is, the modes of content presentation are innumerable.[21] There are two general genres that may be discerned amongst music blogging. A music blog can be a *focused genre-specific blog:* these blogs provide collections of music, an artist's more or less complete discography, occasional album reviews, track lists, the duration of songs, and occasionally a blogger's description and contextualisation of the particular music within her own socio-cultural milieu. A music blog can also be a *period-specific blog* focusing on music from a particular musical era, e.g. sixties or eighties music, or as in the cases discussed below, focusing on a specific historical period. This of course is a very general distinction as there are numerous combinations of these two types; one of the blogs discussed below, apart from being clearly a period-specific blog, also provides insight into the blogger's personal life, highly motivated by, and articulated through, music.

When it comes to specific music posted on music blogs, there is an aspect that should not be neglected: the origin of the recordings. In many cases the music in question is fairly old and not easily obtainable, unlike many other blogs, where music is simply ripped from CDs. This is the case of blogs that focus on the music produced during the existence of the Socialist Federative Republic of Yugoslavia. Much of Yugoslav music available via music blogs is, in fact, relatively old and in the offline world only available on vinyl. The Yugoslav music industry collapsed after the disintegration of the country. This means that it is all but impossible to buy any of this music in a shop, with the exception of second-hand shops or flea markets, as no re-issues have been made of vinyl records and very little has actually been digitally remastered and released on CDs. Thus, in many cases, these blogs provide links to music that has heretofore been all but lost. If it were not for these music bloggers, who go to second-hand record shops, flea markets, browse old collections of records in attics, etc. in search of rarities and oddities of a musical past, significant portions of Yugoslav popular music would only survive in fairly limited, private collections of those lucky few who have had the chance or the will to obtain these records. After physically obtaining the record in one way or another, the blogger digitises it, classifies the tracks, organises them within a folder (album>author>track name) and uploads zipped or .rar files to one of the many file-sharing sites (megaupload, drop.io, rapidshare ...). A link is posted on the blog that leads visitors to a remote storage site.

        The question that comes to mind is why someone would want to do this. This is a time- and money-consuming pastime: time is needed to find all these records, money to buy them, time to digitise them, and money again to spend that much time doing all this for free, while still making a living. Yet this is an activity that clearly thrives. It seems that there are people who believe that the musical past should not be forgotten and therefore they invest considerable time into making it available, generally to the post-Yugoslav public, but also worldwide.

        This is particularly interesting in view of the fact that all this music would otherwise be completely unavailable, forgotten, and in many cases gone forever. In the case of Yugoslav music thus preserved and shared, and in view of the country's history of demise and post-Yugoslav realities, music blogging is all the more an important socio-cultural practice that is, in effect, about the preservation of the past. Yugoslavia disintegrated in 1991 and the region plunged into wars out of which several new states emerged. In the processes of nationalisation and the gaining of independence, the former republics, now independent states, suffered a considerable memory loss. The newly formed countries tried to eradicate the once common past, and supplant it with newly established national(ist) narratives that, in essence, also meant breaking any links with the commonly shared Yugoslav popular culture. Past popular culture tends to find its way into the popular culture of the present, but in this case any such activities were actively discouraged. This is probably also why music blogs focusing on this music find a sufficiently large audience interested in these 'activists' striving to preserve what would normally be preserved in official records and institutions as well as in everyday media. These blogs attract an audience from across the former Yugoslavia, and yet, judging by the 'who's among us' feature on *Jugozvuk* (its counter turned over 600,000 visitors in two years), just as many visitors come from the rest of Europe and North America, with some from South America and Australia.

Thus, the bits and pieces of the Yugoslav past are preserved and distributed globally. Music blogging, both as a practice and as a result of a media archaeology and 'amateur' history, contributes significantly to creating a worldwide archive of Yugoslav popular music, even if it is largely limited to former Yugoslavs. The music blogging of Yugoslav popular music thus becomes a mediator of memories. What is more, as will be demonstrated further below, music on these blogs becomes a channel to express the blogger's personal views on music and other social and cultural issues of the past, present and future. In other words, music is no longer just music, but a powerful tool to recreate if but a fraction of a shattered past and to make it available for the future through digital preservation.

6.   The Two Cases of Music Yugoslav Popular Music

A.   *jugozvuk.blogspot.com*
In the section below I discuss two blogs whose aim is to preserve parts of Yugoslav musical heritage online; i.e., blogs that in their distinctly personalised ways mediate memories, both of the blogger and consequently of the visitor, out of first or second-hand nostalgia respectively, by enabling the mobility of media objects (mp3 files). I approach these blogs as cases of digital storytelling. First I look at *Jugozvuk* (jugozvuk.blogspot.com) managed by Aktivista, who, along with enviable quantities of music, also supplies other types of pop-historical material, such as newspapers and magazines' clippings, etc.

Aktivista begins by providing a mission statement,

> We're introducing You to the sounds of the old Yugoslavia, music, sports, theatre, politics, literature, propaganda, commercials and all that in the shape of sound. Everything that once made up Tito's Yugoslavia tells here before you its story. There are many stories about Yugoslavia and all of them are beautiful. It is also up to you to tell the stories and we'll publish them. YUGOSLAVIA is always a positive inspiration. Here on this weblog you can hear and watch the diverse sounds of former YUGOSLAVIA.[22]

With this statement, the blogger delimits the scope and aim of his endeavours while also positioning himself as a dedicated preserver and distributor of Yugoslav musical past.

> Here you can expect to find all sorts of SOUNDS and SOUND MEMORIALS of various events that adored this beautiful and strong country. It may sound silly to some, but it doesn't to me. This Yugoslavia meant a lot to me. I was born and raised there. Every single day I spent in this Yugoslavia. I listened to this and that and now it's time you've heard it as well.[23]

Aktivista passionately addresses the visitors with the hope of provoking enthusiastic responses by referring nostalgically to his personal experiences. To that end he also specifies the geographical coordinates of his endeavour: 'Most of all it's about music but of a special kind, music that goes nicely with a story or an event. There will be some live performances of certain great bands from all over the country "From Vardar River to Mount Triglav."' Furthermore, the scope of the endeavour is broadened by including 'silent sounds,' and rare treats.

> Here on this blog you can find a lot of sounds from YUGOSLAVIA, from theatre to music, from sport events to jokes and literature. Feel free to join the biggest collection of different sounds from the state that exists no more. If YOU do have some trash and trivia from that time please send me a message.

Aktivista attempts to make the blog an interactive platform by concluding the blog policy statement with an invitation for visitors to get in touch and to participate in its creation.

This regularly updated blog is divided into several sections, 'JUGOZVUK' (which will be the centre of discussion below), 'JUGOmemorabilia' (mainly featuring newspaper and magazine clips), 'JUGOZVUK forum,' 'Hronologija koncerata iz JUGOSLAVIJE' (featuring a rather extensive chronology of concerts of foreign performers in the period 1959-1992), 'Eks jugoslovenska muzika' (featuring links to music by once famous performers in the post-Yugoslav era),[24] and 'Izložbena galerija JUGOZVUKA,' which at present features several photographs but aims to be further developed into a 'a free gallery of JUGOZVUK dedicated to the all arts and performing in former YUGOSLAVIA.'[25] Yugoslavia's coat of arms and flag are situated in the blog's left-hand sidebar, along with a photograph of Yugoslavia's lifelong president Josip Broz Tito. Further down there is a section of links to other music blogs engaged in preserving and sharing music and music-related material from the former Yugoslavia, which effectively contributes to creating a wider, more or less closely knit, community of bloggers. The interlinking enables the exchange of music information, files etc., and not least an easy way for a casual visitor to find other sites of interest. A more general link selection further down the site includes links to 'friends' blogs and other sites related to Yugoslavia.

The blog also features a visitor counter that, at the time of writing, had registered 619,120 visitors, along with a widgeo.com widget that counts visitors 'today' (see above for figures). As well, *Jugozvuk* also features another counter (Live Traffic Feed by Feedjit) which provides a somewhat more detailed view of visitors' locations, time of access, where they left to from the blog, and where they surfed from, with a separate icon for each respective action. At the time of writing, there were 34 visitors from Serbia, 8 from Croatia, 7 from Bosnia and Herzegovina, 2 from Slovenia, 2 from Montenegro, 2 from Macedonia, about the same from Italy, Switzerland, the UK, and 8 from the USA. The Feed also records both the operating system of the accessing computer and the web browser used to visit the blog. Along with a map view of the user location 'today' (based on a Google Map) Feedjit tracks which particular sections of *Jugozvuk* have been accessed (in percentages) in a separate window, and also provides statistics concerning visitors' geographical locations (also in percentages).

This use of visitor tracking might suggest several things: it firmly grounds the fact that this site has a global reach and at the same time alludes to a not insignificant interest on the part of visitors located around the world in Yugoslav music. It should be emphasised, however, that, due to the linguistic specificity of music, the majority of these visitors are former Yugoslavs who have left either during the existence of Yugoslavia or at the aftermath of its demise, and who now use online environments, including this and similar blogs, as spaces for interpersonal interaction and tracing of their shared pasts.

Visitors to such sites more or less actively participate in a collaborative recreation of Yugoslav past. This is done on two levels: first, by listening to downloaded music individually or with friends, thus taking part in the soundscapes; and second, by participating online in reminiscing or discussing a particular song, artist or album. Not unimportantly, user counting serves the purpose of improving the rating of the site among visitors and fellow bloggers.

The central part of the blog, however, is devoted to its entries. In creating his narrative, i.e., in creating his digital story, Aktivista uses very informal language written in the first-person, which contains many grammatical and typographical errors and rather inconsistent use of upper case - although Yugoslavia is consistently in uppercase. In his posts he typically invokes details of the Yugoslav past in general, along with information about the posted music, and he regularly addresses visitors, inviting them to enjoy the music and reminisce about the good old times. He states in one of the posts: 'One great festival from former YUGOSLAVIA that took place in Belgrade, its capital city, in 1963. After all this fantastic music is not buried with YUGOSLAVIA, it lives on this blogs, forever I would like or until BLOGGER lives.'

An aspect that often comes to the fore in Aktivista's posts is explaining how he has acquired the records.

> I love such records and when I buy them I love to listen to them (I buy them at flea markets). This is a time long gone [Yugoslav period]. Such records are today unimaginable. Therefore I'll be putting them up until I am able to find them myself or download them from stealing sites.[26]

Aktivista admits to occasionally taking music from the 'stealing sites,' i.e., from bloggers who 'steal' the music from other blogs and invest no time into obtaining the records offline. This is established through inspecting the quality of the files (bit rate, artwork scan) and comparing it against their own work.

The time invested in finding music at flea markets, digitising it, and making it available online, is considerable. Apart from buying records at flea markets, Aktivista gratefully lists his donors, who help him by providing links to remote sharing sites of the material they have uploaded. As of August 2009, the donors are duly listed on the site, and some have also become blog editors. *Jugozvuk* is thus becoming a joint enterprise comprising several devoted preservers of Yugoslav musical heritage.

Music blogging clearly demands much time to be invested into digitising the music artefacts in high quality. Apart from that, there are issues of honesty and dignity involved in creating and maintaining such blogs, where genuine effort is rewarded by overt and public appreciation and doing it 'the easy way' is discouraged and condemned.

In a way, Aktivista and his donors perceive themselves to be 'messengers of the past,' bringing the beauty of the music into the present in order to save it from oblivion:

> Here we are back again at the BELGRADE SPRING [festival] but this time at the one from the long ago, from 1963. It seems that festivals then had a sort of inner beauty and shine and the music, of course, was extraordinarily, real festival music ... This festival is no more, YUGOSLAVIA is no more but what remains is this

extraordinary feel of a festival and a period when, it seems to me, we lived more carefree lives.[27]

In his storytelling, Aktivista fuses regret and nostalgia for the past and his posts are not only a means of preserving its music but also an expression of his memories, which he achieves through his posts: title, record's artwork, text, comment function, and the personal relationship that he establishes with the music he posts. The blog indeed offers very little personal information and the recounted memories do not extend beyond clichéd statements such as in those 'times we seemed to have lived more carefree.'[28] Nevertheless, bearing in mind the role of music in the lives of individuals and communities, it is the music itself that is the trigger of memories. Scarce as the posts may be in terms of content, they nevertheless provide an affective contextualisation of music and endow the very activities of following such blog, browsing through posts, and downloading music, with a particular aura of disinterring the past, on the part of both the visitor and, primarily, the blog manager. An equally intriguing aspect of music blogging, in this respect, is the act of discovering not only music that one once was a fan of but also of music one had no idea it was ever made, and consequently of sounds and images of the past one was not aware of.

B.   *nevaljaleploce.blogspot.com*
        This ability to discover more music is further expanded by interlinking with 'brotherly' music blogs, such as the next one that I will now discuss: *Nevaljaleploce* (ova ploca nista ne valja, ima rupu u sredini, meaning 'this record is in-valid, it's got a hole in the middle'), located at <http://nevaljaleploce.blogspot.com/>, and managed by Bassta! Pex a.k.a. Gramofonije Plocanovic. Cross-commenting between the two blogs, as well as others, suggests the existence and emergence of some sort of community between the music bloggers. Gramofonije takes a different approach compared to Aktivista and makes his blog a much more personal endeavour by also blogging about his private life, traveling, and his band. At the beginning he states,

> Vinyl and the likes - if someone finds anything disturbing or if I broke any law, please feel free to say so - we'll consider everything, but change nothing! I suggest you buy these records, if available [translation of text in Serbian]. If anyone is upset about anything, whether the content or copyright breach/whatever please get in touch. I recommend everyone and anyone and their families go out and buy these records, if available [original English text].[29]

In that part of the mission statement available in Serbian, Gramofonije ironically adapts the usual quotation used to provide some excuse for posting copyrighted material (e.g. 'let me know, I'll remove it') by saying, 'If someone finds anything disturbing or if I broke any law, please feel free to say so - we'll consider everything, but change nothing!' Thus he deliberately and consciously admits to not paying much attention to copyright issues and to going about his work on his blog regardless. In the English part of the statement this section does not exist and the tone is less ironic.

In terms of form, Gramofonije's blog is much more manageable and transparent compared to *Jugozvuk*. It offers access to posts in chronological order, which makes the blog easier to navigate and follow. In this respect the storytelling on this blog is much more straightforward, with textual narrative supported by music recordings that are clearly important for the author, who describes himself as a fan of certain groups and in that way establishes a much stronger, more personal relationship to the music he posts - the amount of music posted is considerably smaller than at *Jugozvuk*. For instance, he provides a longer description of the music of bands such as Piloti, Haustor and Paraf,[30] all 1980s punk / new wave music that significantly influenced the last decade of the cultural, social and political life in Yugoslavia.[31]

Gramofonije has posted more sporadically than Aktivista since 2007. In his very first post, he makes it his mission to post recordings that are as bizarre as possible, both in terms of music and artwork: 'Just checking if everything works as it should, and then I'm off to post some of our vinyls. I hope the selection will be significantly different from what is available on the Internet at present. The goal is: The more bizarre - the better! You shouldn't take this too literally - there'll also be valid records.'[32]

The interesting thing about this call for the bizarre is the way the 'bizarre' is selected and presented, and above all re-contextualised. Clearly the criteria are artwork and music, but when examined retrospectively, the application of the term 'bizarre' undergoes a process of recontextualisation. What is bizarre today was not necessarily so thirty years ago. For instance, it is fairly safe to claim that in the 1970s, when Miljuš published an EP and two singles, her demeanour was perceived to be rather lascivious as opposed to bizarre. Another consideration regarding this particular record as well as other albums filed under 'bizarre' is their status as music representative of a specific period, genre, era, or country. This raises another question related to representing the past via digitised music: as difficult as it is to assess the popularity of an artist in any given period, since charts may help only in a limited way, and decreasingly so in DME, it is just as difficult to assess the impact or influence of an artist's work from the past on the present. In other words, the availability of vinyl in various second-hand markets, and consequently the availability of digitised music online, is not a representation of past musical tastes and preferences. On the contrary, it is a multivariate result of what is available on the market, what 'attracts the eye' of the buyer and, in the last instance, what 'attracts the ear' of the one who downloads the music. Such blog-enabled preservation and dissemination of the musical past is prone to high personalisation and historical inadequacies in terms of figures related to the popularity of an artist, mostly via embedding the digital media objects into the personal and intimate spheres of individual experiences. Nevertheless, such newly created individual musical maps of the past succeed both in attracting visitors and preserving large portions of an otherwise doomed musical heritage.

Thus, in line with the above-mentioned personalisation, Gramofonije often provides more detailed information about the music, giving his personal opinion on the artists and songs, and intertwining it with bits from his personal life as a Yugoslav emigrant to Australia.

MLADIH - Kofa je busna
(1972)

When I was a kid this record ruled! If I'm not mistaken we would play it at least once a day, learn it by heart, all of the family would sing. The record disappeared, physically first, then from my memory. In May 2006 I visited an acquaintance of our descent, a guy who fairly PROLUPAO (among others he keeps stocks of bottled water "in case Iraq invades!") and at this occasion I bought many *our singles*, this one as well. I haven't heard this for nearly 30 years, but the minute I played it I remembered every single note and the feel. Yet, now I also understand some secretive sexual connotations, which escaped me then. And you?
<http://rapidshare.com/files/17548536/7_Mladih.rar.html>
Posted by Bassta! Pex, a.k.a. Gramofonije Plocanovic at 7:21 PM 14 comments[33]

The above post nicely illustrates how the record, acquired by chance, can serve as a kernel around which a personal narrative is built. Blogs are cases of digital storytelling precisely through the emergence of narrative bits via the interrelation of such kernels and the narratives developed around them. In this case one can observe the intertwining of memories of childhood, alluding to being an immigrant in search of connections to the parent country, and approaching records simultaneously as objects of the past and also immediately (re)integrated into the present. It is via this mechanism that blogged music becomes relevant to the preservation of musical heritage in general - as so many private memories are organically related to so much music. Another significant agent in this process, however, is the downloader: she simultaneously participates in a very private experience of downloading the music, which she may or may not know and relate to, giving it access to her own experiential reality, while at the same time participating in the story provided by the blogger.

This activity is in a way similar to listening to a song on the radio, but here it is more the case of 'discrete radio broadcasting' with the broadcaster and the recipient separated beyond the capacity of radio waves and temporal synchronicity. Nevertheless, the experience is very similar, particularly when taking into account the awareness on the part of the listener and the blogger that they are not alone in listening to the music from or about an audibly crafted past.

7.   Conclusion

Blogs like *Jugozvuk* and *Nevaljaleploce* make it possible to listen to large amounts of music that was once a part of everyday life and would, perhaps in different historical circumstances, remain more entangled in the everyday lives of people in post-Yugoslavia had the country not disintegrated in a bloodbath. Be that as it may, it is precisely due to enthusiasts such as Gramofonije and Aktivista that significant portions of the Yugoslav historical and musical past are saved from oblivion and the decay of vinyl, and preserved in a digital format for a digital future.

This last statement may seem a bit exaggerated as it quickly becomes obvious that there are certain problems with archiving music in this fashion. These are sometimes extremely large collections of music - Aktivista claims to have made 1,500 posts - and they are therefore quite difficult to navigate. Maintaining such a private archive is therefore extremely demanding. If this music is to be available globally and permanently, the archives need to be properly maintained and safe from the finitude of an archivist's life, the limitations of her resources, and so on. The problem with archiving is that the endeavours described, and many similar ones, are solely individual and personally motivated, and they are also funded by these enthusiasts themselves, apart from any compensation they may receive from ad-hosting. Consequently they are forced to use free or affordable, and thus expirable, remote file hosting web providers. Apart from the fact that music blogging is a sort of semi-legal activity, the sad reality is that many files are only available for a relatively short period of time, and may soon become extinct, unless continually updated or re-uploaded, which further adds to the issue of maintenance. For instance, some of the oldest posts on both blogs discussed are no longer available, and Aktivista noted in a comment that, as of January 2010, he will no longer be re-uploading the files as his archive has become too large and difficult to navigate. Re-uploading is the usual procedure in cases when the links have expired either as a result of the time-out restrictions of a particular remote storage provider, or because of no-visit expiration, and is mostly done upon request to the blogger. This means that large collections of already digitised music that is no longer available in shops will again be lost, as they have been in attics, before having been sold at flea markets. On the other hand, as with many pre-digital audio sources, its 'major impediment remain[s] the fact that most of our audiovisual memory is in one analogue format or another'[34] that has not yet been digitised. In effect this means that records are lying about in old suitcases, or neatly stored in private collections, and still unavailable to the public. It is hardly a question as to whether to make such activities part of larger institutional frameworks for the preservation of audio heritage by means of supporting such endeavours.

One question that arises is how to better exploit the digital storytelling capacity of blogs as a historical media resource. In most cases, including the two discussed, the attempt to create a narrative, albeit not in classical terms, is clearly discernible, particularly if we see blogging as related to writing a diary. It therefore can serve as an object for researching personal narrativisations of the past. The blogger's ambition to present her life, parts of it, or the music of her life, to perform and manage identity further, provides tools to examine music blogging as a historical source. Apart from that, music blogging, at least to some extent, contributes to community-building, from merely passive browsing and downloading to more active commenting and reciprocal linking among blogs, within which individual elements, and narrativisations of the past, emerge as grounded into wider, displaced and transtemporal, informal networks offering a casual visitor an impression of a wide network or community of people who are interested, impressed, and immersed by and into sharing and recreating a past.

Finally, what does the utilisation of such a medium mean for understanding or representing the Yugoslav past? First of all, it enables and facilitates recovering, disinterring, representing and re/narrating the past - or rather aspects of the past that usually escape the grip of historiography - via narrating fragments of personal histories, integrated within wider current socio-cultural environments of both bloggers and visitors. Furthermore, such mediations of memories, or rather digital media objects, function as tools and processes for the constant re-articulation of the past, and by that token a most ordinary everyday activity engaged in situating an individual within wider socio-cultural constellations that significantly rest on re-actualisations of the past. Unless digitised and made available in a digital media ecology, these aspects of the past would face a twofold extinction from both history and historiography as well as from everyday media, which would further exacerbate the consequences that the collapse of the state and the ensuing emigration had for the preservation of Yugoslav history.

Notes

[1] See A. Hoskins and B. O'Loughlin, *War and Media*, Polity Press, London, 2010, p. x.

[2] See Joe Lambert Center for Digital Storytelling (<www.storycenter.org>).

[3] J. D. Bolter and D. Grusin, *Remediation. Understanding New Media*, MIT Press, Cambridge, MA, 2001; H. Jenkins, *Convergence Culture: Where Old and New Media Collide*, New York University Press, New York, 2006.

[4] J. van Dijck, *Mediated Memories in the Digital Age*, Stanford University Press, Stanford, CA, 2006.

[5] The term 'Yugoslavia' refers here to the former Socialist Federative Republic of Yugoslavia (SFRY) which disintegrated in 1991.

[6] See L. Manovich, *Software Takes Command*, draft book, online version, 2008, <http://softwarestudies.com/softbook/manovich_softbook_11_20_2008.pdf>.

[7] See P. Connerton, *How Societies Remember*, Cambridge University Press, Cambridge, 1989.

[8] 'Little histories' refer to histories of subordinate nations, non-colonising forces, records of local events that barely reach significance on the national level.

[9] J. Sterne, 'The Preservation Paradox in Digital Audio', in *Sound Souvenirs, Audio Technologies, Memory and Cultural Practices*, K. Bijsterveld and J. van Dijck (eds), Amsterdam University Press, Amsterdam, 2009, p. 64.

[10] V. Meyer-Schönberger, *Delete. The Virtue of Forgetting in the Digital Age*, Princeton University Press, Princeton, NJ, 2009, p. 13.

[11] J. W. Rettberg, *Blogging*, Polity Press, Cambridge, 2009.

[12] M. Chion, *The Voice in Cinema*, Columbia University Press, New York, 1998.

[13] K. Bijsterveld and J. van Dijck, 'Introduction', in K. Bijsterveld and J. van Dijck, op. cit., p. 11.

[14] Ibid., p. 13.

[15] V. Burgin, *In/Different Spaces: Place and Memory in Visual Culture*, University of California Press, Berkeley, 1996, p. 158.

[16] Bijsterveld and van Dijck, op. cit., p. 20.

[17] See L. Gitelman, *Always Already New. Media, History and the Data of Culture*, MIT Press, Cambridge, MA, 2009.

[18] This is author's rough translation of excerpt from Arsen Dedić's and Janez Menart's lyrics for song 'Nježnost u mraku': Već je noć, gle, sad smo sami / Tiho radio svira, i nad pjesmom među nama / Od srca do srca / Brodi naša bolest laka / Kojoj sreća je ime / Koja zaljubljene sjeća / Onog što si žele. © PGP RTB, Beograd, 1979.

---

[19] Manovich, op. cit.
[20]   <http://jugozvuk.blogspot.com/2010/01/drugarice-i-drugovi-uskoro-prelayimo.html>.
[21] A note is in order here to explain that I am not examining blogs that *also* post music, along with other personal or professional content. Rather, the blogs in question are on a mission to post music, any other content is secondary.
[22] <jugozvuk.blogspot.com>.
[23] A more detailed blog policy can be found at the bottom of the front page: 'Here you can expect to find all sorts of SOUNDS and SOUND MEMORIALS of various events that adored this beautiful and strong country. It may sound silly to some, but it doesn't to me. This Yugoslavia meant a lot to me. I was born and raised there. Every single day I spent in this Yugoslavia. I listened to this and that and now it's time you've heard it as well.'
[24] <http://jugozvuk.blogspot.com/p/eks-jugoslovenska-muzika.html>.
[25] <http://jugozvuk.blogspot.com/p/izlozbena-galerija-jugozvuka.html>.
[26]   <http://jugozvuk.blogspot.com/2009/10/razni-izvodjaci-1976-mi-smo-mlada.html>.
[27]   <http://jugozvuk.blogspot.com/2010/02/razni-izvodjaci-beogradsko-prolece-1963.html>.
[28]   <http://jugozvuk.blogspot.com/2010/02/razni-izvodjaci-beogradsko-prolece-1963.html>.
[29] Viewed on 8th February 2010 <http://nevaljaleploce.blogspot.com/>.
[30] Viewed on 8th February 2010 <http://nevaljaleploce.blogspot.com/>.
[31] See M. Pogačar, 'Yu-Rock in the 1980s: Between Urban and Rural', *Nationalities Papers*, Vol. 36, No. 5, pp. 815-832.
[32] <http://nevaljaleploce.blogspot.com/2007_02_01_archive.html>.
[33]   <http://nevaljaleploce.blogspot.com/2007_02_01_archive.html>, italics added.
[34] D. Teruggi, 'Can We Save Our Audio-Visual Heritage?', viewed on 9th Fenruary 2010 <http://www.ariadne.ac.uk/issue39/teruggi/>.

Bibliography

Bolter, J. D. and Grusin, D., *Remediation. Understanding New Media*. MIT Press, Cambridge, MA, 2001.

Burgin, V., *In/Different Spaces: Place and Memory in Visual Culture*. University of California Press, Berkeley, 1996.

Center for Digital Storytelling, Joe Lambert, <www.storycenter.org>.

Chion, M., *The Voice in Cinema*. Columbia University Press, New York, 1998.

Connerton, P., *How Societies Remember*. Cambridge University Press, Cambridge, 1989.

Gitelman, L., *Always Already New. Media, History and the Data of Culture*. MIT Press, Cambridge, MA, 2009.

Hoskins, A. and O'Loughlin, B., *War and Media*. Polity Press, London, 2010.

Jenkins, H., *Convergence Culture: Where Old and New Media Collide*. New York University Press, New York, 2006.

<http://jugozvuk.blogspot.com/2010/02/razni-izvodjaci-beogradsko-prolece-1963.html>.

<http://jugozvuk.blogspot.com/p/eks-jugoslovenska-muzika.html>.

<http://jugozvuk.blogspot.com/p/izlozbena-galerija-jugozvuka.html>.

<http://jugozvuk.blogspot.com/2009/10/razni-izvodjaci-1976-mi-smo-mlada.html>.

<http://jugozvuk.blogspot.com/2010/01/drugarice-i-drugovi-uskoro-prelayimo.html>.

<http://jugozvuk.blogspot.com/2010/02/razni-izvodjaci-beogradsko-prolece-1963.html>.

Manovich, L., *Software Takes Command*. Draft book, online version, 2008. <http://softwarestudies.com/softbook/manovich_softbook_11_20_2008.pdf>.

Mayer-Schonberger, V., *Delete: The Virtue of Forgetting in the Digital Age*. Princeton University Press, Princeton, NJ, 2009.

<http://nevaljaleploce.blogspot.com/08/02/10>.

<http://nevaljaleploce.blogspot.com/2007_02_01_archive.html>.

Pogačar, M., 'Yu-Rock in the 1980s: Between Urban and Rural'. *Nationalities Papers*, Vol. 36, No. 5, pp. 815-832.

Rettberg, J. W., *Blogging*. Polity Press, Cambridge, 2009.

Teruggi, D., 'Can We Save Our Audio-visual Heritage?'. Viewed on 9 February 2010, <http://www.ariadne.ac.uk/issue39/teruggi/>.

Van Dijck, J., *Mediated Memories in the Digital Age*. Stanford University Press, Stanford, NJ, 2006.

Martin Pogačar, PhD, is a research assistant at the Scientific Research Centre of the Slovenian Academy of Sciences and Arts. He is currently interested in media and memory, post-socialism, popular culture.

Printed in the United States
by Baker & Taylor Publisher Services